# PROBING THE PAST

# Academic Introductions for Beginners

Volume One    **Wisdom for Thinkers: An Introduction to Christian Philosophy**

Volume Two    **Power in Service: An Introduction to Christian Political Thought**

Volume Three    **What Then *Is* Theology?: An Introduction to Christian Theology**

Volume Four    **Searching the Soul: An Introduction to Christian Psychology**

Volume Five    **Probing the Past: An Introduction to Christian History**

# PROBING THE PAST
## An Introduction to Christian History

WILLEM J. OUWENEEL

PAIDEIA
PRESS

PAIDEIA PRESS,
P.O. Box 500, Jordan Station,
Ontario, Canada L0R 1S0

©PAIDEIA PRESS 2014, 2020

All rights reserved. Permission to translate,
reproduce, or store in an electronic retrieval system
must be obtained through Paideia Press
at the above address.

Library & Archives Canada
ISBN 978-0-88815-293-0

Unless otherwise indicated, Scripture quotations
are from the Holy Bible, English Standard Version® (ESV®),
copyright © 2001 by Crossway, a publishing ministry of
Good News Publishers. Used by Permission. All rights reserved.

Scripture quotations or references marked as NKJV are taken from the New King James Version® Copyright © 1982 by Thomas Nelson, Inc. Used by permission. All rights reserved.

Scripture quotations or references marked as NIV are taken from the Holy Bible, New International Version®, NIV®. Copyright © 1973, 1978, 1984, 2011 by Biblica, Inc.™ Used by permission of Zondervan. All rights reserved worldwide. www.zondervan.com The "NIV" and "New International Version" are trademarks registered in the United States Patent and Trademark Office by Biblica, Inc.™

2$^{nd}$ printing cover design and layout by Steven R. Martins,
project manager, Paideia Press

Printed in the United States of America

*"A generation goes, and a generation comes,*
>    *but the earth remains forever....*
*What has been is what will be,*
>    *and what has been done is what will be done,*
>    *and there is nothing new under the sun.*
*Is there a thing of which it is said,*
>    *'See, this is new'?*
*It has been already*
>    *in the ages before us."* (Eccl. 1:4, 9-10)

*"Give ear, O my people, to my teaching;*
>    *incline your ears to the words of my mouth!*
*I will open my mouth in a parable;*
>    *I will utter dark sayings from of old,*
*things that we have heard and known,*
>    *that our fathers have told us.*
*We will not hide them from their children,*
>    *but tell to the coming generation the glorious deeds*
>    *of the LORD, and his might,*
>    *and the wonders that he has done."* (Ps. 78:1-4)

## About the Author

Willem J. Ouweneel (1944) earned his Ph.D. in biology at the University of Utrecht (The Netherlands, 1970), his Ph.D. in philosophy at the Free University in Amsterdam (The Netherlands, 1986), and his Ph.D. in theology at the University of the Orange Free State in Bloemfontein (Republic of South Africa, 1993). Among many other things, he has been professor of the Philosophy of Science for the Natural Sciences at the University for Christian Higher Education in Potchefstroom (Republic of South Africa, 1990-1998), and professor of Philosophy and Systematic Theology at the Evangelical Theological Faculty in Leuven (Belgium, 1995-2014. He is a prolific writer (mainly in Dutch, and has preached in more than thirty countries. Several times he was a candidate for Dutch Christian political parties.

# Table of Contents

| | |
|---|---:|
| **Foreword** | **xii** |
| **Chapter One – Introduction to this Introduction** | **1** |
| Terminology | 2 |
| Basic Elements | 6 |
| Historiography | 8 |
| Objectivity | 9 |
| Further Characteristics | 11 |
| Philosophical Aspects | 13 |
| Christian Historians | 16 |
| **Chapter Two – The Historical Modality** | **21** |
| Power and Justice | 21 |
| Historical Subjects and Objects | 22 |
| Historical Norms | 24 |
| Historicism | 26 |
| Two Levels | 27 |
| Some Other Philosophical Aspects | 29 |
| Learning From History? | 31 |
| The Driving Forces | 33 |
| Some Comments | 38 |
| **Chapter Three – The Meaning of History** | **43** |
| The Theodicy | 43 |
| God's Omnipotence | 45 |
| Omnipotence and Weakness | 46 |
| The Heidelberg Catechism | 47 |
| Danger of Determinism | 49 |
| Conflicting Views | 51 |

| | |
|---|---|
| Careful Weighing | 53 |
| The Best Possible World | 55 |
| Test of the Best | 57 |
| Chance | 59 |
| The Role of Satan | 60 |
| A Chess Match | 62 |

**Chapter Four – Patterns, Purposes, and Powers of History** — 65

| | |
|---|---|
| Toledoth | 65 |
| Cyclical Views | 67 |
| Linear Views | 69 |
| A Christian View: Linear and Cyclical | 71 |
| Teleology | 72 |
| The God of History | 74 |
| Driving Forces of History | 76 |
| Meta-history and Responsibility | 77 |
| History and Mythology | 80 |
| Fountains and Windows | 81 |

**Chapter Five – More About Biblical Historiography** — 85

| | |
|---|---|
| God's People in the Center | 85 |
| Four Beasts | 87 |
| Abr(ah)am | 89 |
| Cyrus | 91 |
| Xerxes | 93 |
| Copernicus | 95 |
| Versalius | 96 |
| The Reformation | 98 |
| Invisible Powers | 100 |
| Daniel 8 | 102 |
| A Final Remark on Angeology | 104 |

## Chapter Six – The Epochs of World History — 107
- Are We Living in the "Third Era"? — 107
- The *Dictum Elieae* — 108
- Joachim of Fiore — 110
- Are We Living in the "Fourth era"? — 113
- A Jewish View — 115
- The Four Middle Empires — 117
- Fourth and Fifth Empires — 118
- More on the *Translatio Imperii* — 120
- Are We Living in the "Fifth Era"? — 121
- Are We Living in the "Sixth Era"? — 122
- Early Millennialism — 124
- Are We Living in the "Seventh Era"? — 126
- Are We Living in the "Eighth Era"? — 127

## Chapter Seven – The Providence of God — 131
- The Hidden God — 131
- God's Providence — 134
- God's Ways — 135
- Counsel *versus* Ways — 137
- A Mystery — 139
- God's Breath — 141
- Two Ways of Divine Working — 143
- Further Biblical Examples — 145
- God Handling Sin — 147
- The Role of Satan — 150

## Chapter Eight – The Kingdom of God — 153
- God's Kingdom Under Man — 153
- The Kingdom of Satan — 156
- Satan versus Christ — 157
- The Announcement of God's Kingdom — 158
- The Kingdom: Spiritual Aspects — 160
- A Heavenly Kingdom on Earth — 161
- The Fullness of the Times — 163

| | |
|---|---|
| Yet Spiritual Too | 164 |
| The Kingdom: Political Aspect | 165 |
| Christian Rulers | 168 |
| Rulers of Light and Darkness | 169 |
| The Kingdom of God and the Roman Empire | 171 |

**Chapter Nine – A Christian View of Prehistory and Early History** ... 175

| | |
|---|---|
| Development of Awareness | 175 |
| Two Kinds of Prehistory | 178 |
| Development? | 179 |
| Does Prehistory Exist? | 180 |
| The Three Lines of History | 182 |
| Comments | 183 |
| Exceptions | 185 |
| Division | 186 |
| The National Angels | 187 |
| The Neolithic Revolution | 189 |
| Philosophical Aspects | 192 |
| Culture, Good and Bad | 194 |

**Chapter Ten – The Axial Age** ... 197

| | |
|---|---|
| Significance of the Axial Age | 197 |
| Synchronicity | 199 |
| Shem versus Japheth | 200 |
| The Eclipse of God | 203 |
| The Wonder of Simultaneity | 204 |
| Secularization in Greece | 206 |
| Architecture | 209 |
| Secularization in India: the Upanishads | 209 |
| Buddism | 211 |
| Emancipation | 213 |
| The Shekinah Again | 215 |

# Foreword

This book is Volume V of a series of Christian academic introductions to various academic disciplines. So far, volumes have been published on Christian philosophy (I), on Christian political thought (II), on Christian theology (III), and on Christian psychology (IV). The series is not intended to be one of scholarly books, with many learned footnotes and extensive bibliographies, but one of an accessible nature, suitable (I hope) for students in the last years of high school, or the first years of college or university, as well as for the general interested public.

For the present book, I had less of my own material available in Dutch than I had for the previous volumes, so that a great part of this book is entirely new. The main written sources on which I was able to draw were the volumes of my "meta-historical trilogy": (1) *De negende Koning: Het laatste van de hemelrijken: De triomf van Christus over de machten* (1996; now available in English under the title *The Ninth King*), (2) *De zevende koningin: Het eeuwig vrouwelijke en de raad van God* (1998), and especially (3) *De zesde kanteling: Christus en 5000 jaar denkgeschiedenis: Religie en metafysica in het jaar 2000* (2000). Besides this, I used an article of mine, entitled *The Year 2000 and the Epochs of World History*, published in the South African journal *Acta Theologica* (2000).

Understanding the present book requires some basic knowledge of fundamental philosophical concepts. Therefore, for a proper understanding of the present introduction to Christian biology, I highly recommend that the reader begin by reading the first volume of this series: *Wisdom for Thinkers: An Introduction to Christian Philosophy*. Apart from that, it would also be useful to read beforehand the third volume: *What Then Is Theology?: An Introduction to Christian Theology*.

Bible quotations in this book are usually from the English Standard Version. When other translations are used, this is indicated.

Willem J. Ouweneel
Zeist (The Netherlands)
Summer 2014

## Chapter One
# INTRODUCTION TO THIS INTRODUCTION

As in previous volumes, we must start this Introduction to Christian Historical Science with an introduction, where we get into questions such as (a) What is history? (b) What is the philosophy of history? (c) What is historical science? and (c) What is Christian historical science?

Right from the start, there are several semantic problems, even with the word "history" as such. History is:

(a) the whole of events in the human past [in humanity's past] (the history of city P is the range of events in the past of P);

(b) the record of these events (also called *historiography*) (historian X wrote the history of city P);

(c) the *historical science* that deals with these events (historian X teaches history at University Q).

Please note that, in this book, I use the term "historical science" (German: *Geschichtswissenschaft*; Dutch: *geschiedwetenschap*) in the limited sense, that is, without paleontology, archaeology, geology, cosmology etc. There is a certain ambiguity surrounding the term *history*, which in practical parlance is often the same as *historical science*. "I study history" means, "I am a practitioner of historical science." There is a similar ambiguity surrounding the term *historiography*, which can have both meaning (b) (the written history of P) and meaning (c) (historiography = historical science). A third type of ambiguity lies in the term *Christian Historical Science* in the subtitle of the present book. If I had just written "Christian History," this might have suggested that this book deals with the history of Christendom. In Christian Historical Science we are dealing with a Christian approach to history, not a historical approach to Christianity.

Many intellectuals are interested in history because the past helps us to understand the present; more concretely, history helps people to understand themselves. That is why so many people are interested in their family's history and in genealogy (I am too; I have identified about four thousand of my ancestors). In addition, many people want to know more about the history of their church, of their city, of their region, of their country. Being able to find their proper place (or to "situate" or "map" themselves) in history helps them to better understand why they are the type of people they are.

For the Christian, the study of history may specifically mean the study of so many human failures in the past, and so many wonders of God's mercy: "Then the Lord said to Moses, 'Go in to Pharaoh, for I have hardened his heart and the heart of his servants, that I may show these signs of mine among them, and that you may tell in the hearing of your son and of your grandson how I have dealt harshly with the Egyptians and what signs I have done among them, that you may know that I am the Lord'" (Exod. 10:1-2).

The singer Asaph said: "We will not hide them [i.e., God's great works in the past] from their children, but tell to the coming generation the glorious deeds of the Lord, and his might, and the wonders that he has done" (Ps. 78:4). And the prophet Joel said: "Hear this, you elders; give ear, all inhabitants of the land! Has such a thing happened in your days, or in the days of your fathers? Tell your children of it, and let your children tell their children, and their children to another generation" (Joel 1:2-3).

## Terminology

The English language makes a fine distinction between *historic* and *historical*. Historic refers to what is of special significance in history, for example: *Columbus's historic voyage to America*. It also refers to what is historically famous or interesting because of certain things that happened in the past; this is obvious from expressions like *a historic city*. Historical is a more neutral term, used for whatever existed in the past, whether significant or not. A *historical* novel is about events that happened in the past, such as Leo Tolstoy's *War and Peace* (1869, about the Napoleonic Inva-

## AN INTRODUCTION TO THIS INTRODUCTION

sion of Russia in 1812). A historic novel is one that exerted great influence after its publication, like *Uncle Tom's Cabin* (1852) by American abolitionist Harriet Beecher Stowe (1811-1896). Be prepared, though, to find that "historic" and "historical" are often used interchangeably. I will try not to mix them; so when I say that this or that happened in historical times, that is, long ago, this is different from saying that we live in historic times, that is, times that will turn out to have great epochal significance.

I find etymology extremely interesting but I am not sure that it is always very helpful. Thus, it is nice to know that the Greek word *historia* means "investigation," or the knowledge obtained through investigation. This shows that the meaning of history, "study of the past," is nearer to the original meaning of the term than "history" in the sense of "the whole of past events." In the term "natural history," that is, the investigation of nature, the original meaning of the term is still preserved. A Museum of Natural History, which can be found in many cities, does not necessarily display what *we* today call "history" (for instance, the alleged evolutionary history of the plant and animal kingdoms), but exhibits plant and animal specimens.

Another etymological point of interest is that the English language makes a distinction between "story" and "history," although the two come from the same word. We make a distinction between a "story-teller" and a historian writing a "history." In most European languages, though, there is no such difference: French, German and Dutch speak of the "stories" of the Bible, and use for this the same word as for "history" (French: *histoire*; German: *Geschichte*; Dutch: *geschiedenis*). The one who translates into English must always decide whether to translate the word as "story" or "history."

In the following chapters, I am not going to deal with cosmic history, geological history, or organic history. We will take the term "history" in the limited sense it usually has, namely, *human* history, or, as people often say, *cultural* history (German: *Kulturgeschichte*; Dutch: *cultuurgeschiedenis*). Historical science is the study of Man *and* his tools and devices, through which he surpasses any form of barbarism, or even animalism, by giving shape to his own life and to his environment.

## PROBING THE PAST

We speak especially of human, or cultural, history as soon as historic events begin to be recorded in inscriptions made on clay tablets or documents written on papyrus. Writing began at more or less the same time as the first ancient civilization. The time before written history we refer to as *prehistory* (see chapter 9). In a sense, this is a peculiar term because, from a paleontological or archeological point of view, this is "human history" just like history in the limited sense which I have just described. However, it is convenient, and common practice, to restrict the term "history" to human history from the point where it began to be recorded, or, cultural history. Before that time, we are dependent on paleontological and archeological investigations to find out anything about human history. Such knowledge is necessarily extremely limited.

Thus, in this book "history" will usually mean, "human history since the time that it began to be recorded." Or course, this differs from country to country. "History" in this limited sense began in Sumer and Egypt, but even today, some tribes, for instance in the Amazon jungles, are still living in "prehistorical" circumstances, as we put it. This is because such tribes are not familiar with writing, but only with oral traditions, and live under what we call "primitive" circumstances.

From an orthodox Christian point of view, the term "prehistory" raises all kinds of interesting questions. Could we say that the time between Adam and Noah was "prehistorical," in the sense that no writing existed as yet? Or was P. J. Wiseman *Ancient Records and the Structure of Genesis*, 1985, right when he suggested, on the basis of a literary analysis of the book of Genesis, that Adam, Noah and the patriarchs had actually written the first documents, which later became part of Genesis? And what about the first centuries after Noah's flood? Interestingly, as early as Genesis 5:1, we already find the Hebrew word *sefer*, which literally means "something written," that is, a written book.

The art of writing has turned out to be much older than liberal theologians thought for a long time. In the nineteenth century, the Bible was still ridiculed because it suggested that an arbitrary boy in the second half of the second millennium BC would have been able to write ("a young man of Succoth… wrote down for [Gideon]

## AN INTRODUCTION TO THIS INTRODUCTION

[the names of] the officials and elders of Succoth," Judges 8:14). Today we know that the art of writing underwent very little development; it was only the writing *materials* that improved (from clay tablets through papyrus to parchment). The oldest written language, Sumerian cuneiform writing on clay tablets, dates from 3500 BC. The subject matter studied by Sumerian schoolboys, as we find it on these tablets, is evidence of a highly developed mathematics and astronomy. I will come back to these questions in later chapters.

For the sake of completeness, let me also mention the term *proto-history*, which refers to a period between prehistory and history for any given culture. The period concerned is not yet historical because, within that culture, writing has not yet been developed. However, we can no longer say that it is prehistoric either, because that culture is described in the writings of neighboring civilizations. As far as Europe is concerned, a good example of this can be seen in the Celts (Greek *Keltoi*), who are mentioned by the Greeks already in the sixth century BC, and later by the Romans. The Celtic element forms one of the components of the present-day European population. One of these Celtic tribes was that of the Galli, a name that we still know from words like Gallia, Gaul and Galatia (found in the New Testament). (The term Gaelic seems to come from a different root.)

The Germanic tribes, who later acquired such predominance in Europe, and eventually in the whole world, were first mentioned in Roman sources, from the third century BC onward (according to others, the first century BC). They are discussed by such well-known authors as Julius Caesar, Pliny the Elder, and Tacitus. Later Latin writers (from the tenth century AD onward) also used the adjective *teutonicus* (from Germanic *thiud-*, "people"), which is familiar from words like Teutons, *deutsch* (the German term for German), *dutch* (the English term for the language and the people of the Netherlands), *duits* (Dutch for German) and *diets* (Dutch for the Middle Dutch language), and *tysk* (Scandinavian for German). The stem *thiud* is also found in the German name *Dietrich* and the Dutch name *Diederik* (English varieties: Derek, Derrick, Diderik).

Writing about the Germanic tribes was done basically in three stages:

(a) from Julius Caesar onward, Romans wrote about them in Latin (this is the period of Germanic *protohistory*);

(b) Germanic authors wrote about the Germanic world in Latin (this is the period of Germanic *history*); for instance, the *Historia Ecclesiastica Gentis Anglorum* ("The Ecclesiastical History of the English People") by Bede (c. 731), or the anonymous *Annales Regni Francorum* ("Annals of the Frankish Empire" (eighth or ninth century);

(c) finally, Germanic authors wrote about the Germanic world in some form of Germanic vernacular. Apart from some sporadic and very limited sources, Germanic literature started just before 1100 (English, German, Dutch; Frisian and Scandinavian literature began much later).

## Basic Elements

Historical science is the science that consists of at least the following elements, here summarized in a very short survey.

The first elementary question is: *What happened?* Through a study of historical sources, historians endeavor to establish as many relevant facts as possible with respect to a certain time period (long or short) and a certain region (varying from a village to a continent). One of his first criteria is to make sure that the facts are *reliable*; this presupposes a careful evaluation of the sources according to strict scientific standards. In fact this is the procedure already followed by the Gospel writer Luke: "Inasmuch as many have undertaken to compile a narrative of the things that have been accomplished among us, just as those who from the beginning were eyewitnesses and ministers of the word have delivered them to us, it seemed good to me also, having followed all things closely for some time past, to write an orderly account for you, most excellent Theophilus, that you may have certainty concerning the things you have been taught" (Luke 1:1-4).

Historical sources may consist of oral traditions, written texts (inscriptions on buildings and monuments, written or—in modern times—printed documents) and pictures (e.g., paintings). Of these sources, inscriptions and written documents, which may also include written reports of oral traditions, are the most im-

## AN INTRODUCTION TO THIS INTRODUCTION

portant. They may be governmental documents, private archives, historical works from the past (annals, chronicles, historiographies), etc. That is, they are either *part* of the past, or communications *concerning* the past. The historian has the problem that his material is always limited—he always wants to know so much more—and at the same time, it is too vast. He has to leave out many things, and limit himself to the relevant facts.

The next question therefore presents itself automatically: *What is relevant?* Although "relevant," a term that I have just used myself several times, is quite subjective, this is precisely what the historian has to find out: which were the most important facts that influenced, or even determined, the course of events in a certain situation in the past? Or, to put it another way: which "historical" events were of *historic* significance? That the king eats cauliflower today is not relevant. However, if it is poisoned, and he dies from it, this will definitely change the course of history to a greater or lesser extent.

Thus, history is never just a recording of the mere facts, apart from the question whether such things exist in the first place. As I have explained in my *Wisdom for Thinkers*, facts are always facts-for-people; they are always contextually delineated. As far as we can ascertain, the Greek historian Thucydides (c. 460–c. 395 BC) was the first, other than his somewhat older contemporary Herodotus (c. 484–425 BC), who attempted to limit himself to "the facts." However, both the choice and the representation of "relevant" facts means that the historian has to develop some ideas, not only about the *when, where* and *how* of history but also about the *why*: when did it happen, where did it happen, how did it happen, and especially why did it happen, or why did it happen in this particular way? What were the underlying patterns of cause and effect? Why did history—at a certain time and place—follow this course, and not one of many other possible courses? In other words, the historian is not only interested in facts but also, more particularly, in the *coherence* of the facts and the *causal relationships* between them.

**PROBING THE PAST**

## Historiography

The past is written down in the form of historiography, varying from the very primitive to the highly scientific (i.e., meeting the standards of historical science). also varying from [Various forms include]:

(a) *chronological* or year-to-year descriptions;

(b) *cultural* descriptions, which presenting a whole culture or civilization in a certain time period;

(c) *territorial* descriptions which present the history of a certain region, land or nation;

(d) *thematic* descriptions, e.g., the history of women, trade unions, churches, war, morals, the Renaissance, Revivals, etc.

There is also the history of theology, of philosophy, and, inevitably, the history of historical science. When, where and how did historical science originate? How did it develop? Who were the great figures in the history of historical science? What philosophical perspectives guided them? What are the differences in methodology and approaches between, say, eighteenth-century and twenty-first century historical science? What *paradigms* in historical science can we discern throughout the decades?

Historians also want to point out the significance of history for the present. Our present time can only be understood from the past. As the Dutch poet Willem Bilderdijk (1756-1831) wrote:

> Wat verschijne,
> Wat verdwijne,
> 't Hangt niet aan een los geval.
> In 't voorleden
> Ligt het heden
>  in het nu, wat worden zal.

> [What may appear,
> what may disappear,
> is not a matter of coincidence.
> In the past
> lies the present,
> in the present
> lies the future.]

## AN INTRODUCTION TO THIS INTRODUCTION

Our present conditions could not have been as they actually are if the past had been (very) different. And as far as the future is concerned, perhaps many futures are possible, but still their number is limited by the possibilities contained within our present circumstances. How and why did we get from the past to where we are now? How can the past help us understand the present?

There is also this question to consider: what can we *learn* from the past in view of the present? Opinions on this issue differ. On the one hand, the Irish philosopher Edmund Burke (1729–1797) once said: "Those who don't know history are doomed to repeat it." This statement suggests that it is not only possible, but necessary to learn from the past. But the German philosopher Georg W.F. Hegel (1770-1831) once said: "We learn from history that we do not learn from history." That is, even *if* we know our history, it does not seem to make much difference, because we continue to make the same mistakes over and over again anyway.

These considerations also involve a *moral* element, which the historian cannot avoid. We want to learn from the good and the wise in history what course we should follow ourselves, and from the bad and the foolish what course we should avoid. It is the historian who must help us to distinguish between good and bad, between wise and foolish, in history. He may try to remain as neutral as possible, but in many cases he cannot avoid taking sides. And when the distinction between good and evil is very black and white, his readers do not *expect* him to do otherwise.

## Objectivity?

Good historians are aware of the fact that there is no truly objective approach to the past. The least one can say is that historians necessarily look at the past from the perspective of their own time. A historical work often tells us as much about the time in which he lives himself as it does about the time with which the author is dealing. It is one of the greatest achievements of a historian if he, so to speak, can "leave" his own time for a while and get into the skin of the people living in the time he is investigating. He must understand their "language," their drives, their feelings, their motivations, their reasoning. He must also be able to "read" the objects they used: what do they "tell" us about the people that used them? The historian needs a lot of *empathy* with respect to the people and the circumstances he is describing and analyzing. (Cf. one of my previous volumes, *Searching the Soul*.)

This point has been emphasized by the German historian and philosopher Wilhelm Dilthey (1833-1911), who made a distinction between two German verbs: *erklären* (to explain) and *verstehen* (to understand). The first we find in the natural sciences, where phenomena are scientifically "explained" in various ways, for instance, by reducing new phenomena to phenomena already familiar to us. But in the humanities this is not enough; here we need to "understand" with all possible psychological and sociological means at our disposal. Dilthey has worked this out in volumes such as *Understanding the Human World* (2010a) and *Hermeneutics and the Study of History* (2010b).

In another respect, historical science is not objective either in the sense that history is always being written by the *victors*, or, as some would say, by the *survivors*. For instance, the history of the Greco-Persian wars was mainly written by Greek authors rather than by Persian authors. Thus, we inevitably look at these wars through Greek eyes. The history of Carthage was mainly written by the greatest enemies of the Carthaginians, i.e., the Romans. Thus, we see their history inevitably through Roman glasses, since the Carthaginians are not there anymore to tell us their side of the story. The history of European Paganism—the ruling religion in Europe before Christianity came to the fore—was mainly written by their greatest enemies, the early Christians. The history of the Christian movement of the Montanists in the late second century was mainly written by its greatest opponents, the Roman Catholics. The history of the Christian movement of the Anabaptists was mainly written by their greatest adversaries, established Protestantism. The history of the Native Americans (commonly referred to as "Indians") was mainly written by their greatest competitors, the early European settlers in North and South America. And so on.

But sometimes it is the other way around. After the American Civil War, both historians and novelists on the side of the losers (the Confederates) have exercised much more influence in deter-

## AN INTRODUCTION TO THIS INTRODUCTION

mining the picture of that war than did the side of the winners (the Unionists).

Sometimes losers become winners, after which they are strongly tempted to rewrite history. We call this *revisionism*. Some especially notorious examples are the ways in which Marxists and fascists have revised history. The worst types of subjective historiography are forms of *negationism*. These are forms in which great evils committed in the past are denied, such as genocides (e.g., denials of the Holocaust, or the Turkish denial of the Armenian genocide, 1915-18). In his novel *Nineteen Eighty-Four* (1949), English novelist George Orwell (1903-1950) describes a most outrageous example of historical revisionism.

## Further Characteristics

Biblical historiography seems to be the history of great men—and sometimes also of significant women (for example, the matri-archs, Deborah, Ruth, Athaliah, Esther)—in particular, from the patriarchs to the apostles. In common history, it seems to be the same. The Scottish historian and philosopher Thomas Carlyle (1795-1881) claimed that "the history of the world is but the biog-raphy of great men." These are the heroes, the geniuses, the great political or military figures, or the founders and conquerors of states or empires.

In the twentieth century, historical science has put much more emphasis on "forces" in history. These may involve whole classes, or social or religious movements. Thus, historians tend to put more emphasis on the significance of the common individual, or great masses of common individuals. What meaning would Israel's kings, or the early Christian leaders have had, if not for the nation and the church, respectively, that shaped them? What are great figures without the communities that mold them? As the English philosopher Herbert Spencer (1820-1903) said about the "great man": "Before he can remake his society, his society must make him."

Along the same lines, we see the rise of local historical science—which the Germans call *Heimatgeschichte*, and the Dutch *heemkunde*. Such a study, just like genealogy, is in most cases the study of inconspicuous people, who nevertheless formed and shaped their immediate environment. One example is the *British Association for Local History* (BALH), in which both professionals and lay people are involved.

Last but not least, every great historian was always a great story-teller. For instance, what made the American writer Barbara W. Tuchman (1912-1989) a great historian (for instance, in her books *The Guns of August* and *A Distant Mirror*)? There were several reasons, but one of them was that she was certainly a fine story-teller. The same thing is true, for instance, of the Dutch historian Johan Huizinga (1872-1945), especially in his *Herfsttij der Middeleeuwen* (1919), translated as *The Waning of the Middle Ages* (1924) and as *The Autumn of the Middle Ages* (1996). The story that the historian is telling us must be both fascinating and plausible. The historian is like an artist: he paints a portrait of a certain time, location or culture. It is *his* picture, which shows the hand of the master; the most superb portraits are highly artistic and intriguing. At the same time, the client usually demands that the portrait show a clear resemblance to the original; people should be able to *recognize* him immediately in the picture. This is the task of the historiographer: his picture must be both *beautiful* and *truthful* (truly representative).

Some historians are great investigators but not great story-tellers. Some people may not be professional historians but they write great historical works because they can tell a good story. To me, the British novelist and historian Tom Holland (b. 1968) is a great example of this (read his *Rubicon*, *Persian Fire*, *Millennium* [or, *The Forge of Christendom*], and *In the Shadow of the Sword*). Interestingly, Tom Holland is a novelist. The borderline between an exciting work of history and a thrilling historical novel is sometimes fuzzy. Nevertheless, the differences must be maintained. In a historical novel, many of the characters are imaginary, and even if some protagonists are real historical figures, their dialogues and the details of their circumstances are usually imaginary as well. The historian fashions a good story from the facts, while the novelist embellishes the facts with his own imagination to tell an even finer—albeit less reliable—story.

# AN INTRODUCTION TO THIS INTRODUCTION

## Philosophical Aspects

It was the French philosopher Voltaire (François-Marie Arouet, 1694-1778) who coined the term *philosophy of history* during the time of the Enlightenment. In 1765, he published in Amsterdam his book *La philosophie de l'histoire* ("The Philosophy of History"; German: *Geschichtsphilosophie*; Dutch: *geschiedfilosofie*). Of course, this is not to be confused with the *history of philosophy*. The philosophy of history is the discipline that studies the fundamental questions behind historical science, some of which have been dealt with already in the present chapter. These are questions such as: What is history? What is the evidence for certain historic events? How do we weigh historical evidence? What are objective criteria for the evaluation of historical sources? What are the paradigms from which historians work, and how are these paradigms related to certain cultural historical developments? These are the types of questions that are dealt with in what is called *critical*, analytical or formal philosophy of history.

Apart from the critical philosophy of history there is what we call the *speculative, substantial* or *material* philosophy of history, which deals with vital questions which are of the utmost importance for a Christian philosophy of history. To my mind, the most significant of these questions are the following:

(a) *Meaning*: Does history have a meaning? Or is history arbitrary, a matter of meaningless chance? For instance, in 1919 the German philosopher Theodor Lessing (1872-1933) published a book called *Geschichte as Sinngebung des Sinnlosen* ("History as Giving Meaning to the Meaningless"). That is, it lies in Man's nature to assign meaning to his own life and the lives of others, to the world and to history, although objectively such a meaning is lacking. Apparently, we cannot live without assigning such a meaning, which in fact is not there. It is very hard for Man to believe that his actions have no meaning at all; at the very least, they have the meaning of bringing him some personal happiness. Many people also have certain values and ideals that they would like to see realized in history, or at least in that small part of history which is within their own reach. But this does not necessarily mean that history has an *overall* meaning. However, Christians do believe that history has such an overall meaning for reasons that I will deal with in chapter 3.

(b) *Patterns*: Can we distinguish general patterns in the development of history? For instance, is history generally cyclical or linear? That is, does history revolve in cycles (like the rise and decline of subsequent empires), or does it follow a line, let's say from a starting point A to a final point Z? Or are both true, in the sense that history exhibits cycles which individually follow a linear course? Or do the subsequent cycles form a line from A to Z? Even if we believe that history has a goal (see [c] below) this may be viewed in a *cyclical* sense, that is, each cycle having a limited goal. Thus, distinct civilizations may have a goal, but civilizations rise and decline, after which civilization begins to blossom somewhere else, without some overall goal.

Division of history into epochs (think of the well-known distinction of Antiquity, Middle Ages and Modern Time) often betray a cyclical view of history, like the four "metal ages" that the Greek historian Herodotus (c. 484–ca. 425 BC) distinguished in the history of mankind: the Gold, Silver, Bronze, and Iron Ages (which have nothing to do with what modern archeologists call the Iron and Bronze Ages). Behind this was the ancient idea of an "eternal return," which we encounter in the culture of several ancient nations (Egypt, India, Greece). This idea of the *ewige Wiederkunft* ("eternal return" or "recurrence") was a central concept in the thinking of the German philosopher Friedrich Nietzsche (1844-1900).

(c) *Teleology*: Is there progress in history? Does history have a goal, which can be discerned within history itself as a kind of directive principle? In other words, does history exhibit design, purpose, teleology? Christians generally believe that the ultimate goal of history is the Kingdom of God. Such a view is in sharp contrast with views such as atheism, materialism, and naturalistic evolutionism, which cannot possibly recognize an overall goal of human history. A striking exception is Marxism, which believes in the utopia of a classless society in which everybody will be happy. Perhaps in this view, Marx's Jewish roots become manifest; his classless Paradise seems to be a secularized variety of the Messianic Kingdom as described by the Old Testament prophets.

## AN INTRODUCTION TO THIS INTRODUCTION

(d) *Driving forces*: Is history deterministic, that is, is it determined solely by underlying purely natural forces, or is it governed exclusively by the free will of its protagonists? Or is it a little of both? Besides purely natural forces and the human will, can we distinguish "meta-historical" forces—forces behind the scenes of history—that must, or may, be assumed to play a role? If Herodotus was the "father" of historical science as such, the church father Augustine (354-430) may be called the "father" of the *philosophy* of history because of his great work, *De Civitate Dei* ("The City of God," completed around AD 426). Augustine saw history as due to the activity of both God and Satan, with God in the end gaining the final victory in Jesus Christ. It was not a purely theological work, but rather a historical one, because Augustine tried to answer at least two historical questions. First, the Christian Church became more and more intertwined with the Roman Empire; what did they have to do with one another? Second, could the fact that Rome had been sacked by the Visigoths (410) be a punishment for having given up the traditional Roman gods for the God of the Christians? Augustine answered both questions by emphasizing that the Roman Empire might come under great pressure, but that the City of God would ultimately prevail anyhow.

I repeat, in a Christian-philosophical approach to historical science, the idea that the Kingdom of God will one day triumph over the kingdom of Satan (Matt. 12:25-26) is central. This is the great subject of that part of systematic theology which we call eschatology. (See my extensive Dutch works on this subject, *Het verbond en het koninkrijk van God*, 2011; and *De toekomst van God*, 2012.) History, which began at creation, is moving toward the end of ages, with Jesus Christ as its center, focus, instrument, perfecter and goal. History is at least as much the deeds of God as it is the actions of Man. In such a view, although history is certainly driven by *natural* (human) causes, it is propelled by *trans-historical* (angelic, divine) causes too. It is also the view that, in essence, "history" and "salvational history" coincide because the goal of history is the salvation of the universe.

Ancient Greek historians such as Herodotus (see above) and Plutarch (c. 46 AD–120 AD) wrote history in order to present moral examples to their readers, that is, to ennoble the world. How far does such a purpose influence historiography as such? Is it inevitable that historians look at history through their ideological or religious glasses? Think of the War of Independence, otherwise known as the Eighty Years' War (1568-1648), in which the Dutch population broke away from the Spanish regime. More leftist historians thought (and still think) that the socio-economic circumstances were the main cause of the rebellion. On the contrary, Protestant historians view the war especially as a rebellion of a largely Protestant population against a Catholic regime, while Catholic historians have their own version to tell.

Of course, there might be truth in all three approaches, but we would like to understand the *main* causes, as far as our subjective view of the facts allows it. I remember a museum in the formerly communist DDR (German Democratic Republic), where the (German) Reformation of the sixteenth century was explained *entirely* in terms of the class struggle, that is, in socio-economic terms, while all the religious elements were left out or downplayed. In this presentation, the Protestant theologian and leader of the Peasants' Revolt, Thomas Müntzer (c. 1489-1525), was the great hero because he pleaded for a new egalitarian society, whereas Martin Luther was rejected because he was against this Revolt. The exposition was entirely in line with the book by Marx's friend and fellow-thinker, Friedrich Engels (1820-1895), *The Peasant War in Germany* (1850).

## Christian Historians

Now I would like to introduce nine of the most outstanding Christian historians, or theological historiographers, of modern times. They belong to seven different nationalities and seven different denominations. (I am limiting myself to those who have passed away *and* whose writings are available in the English language.) I ask your forgiveness in advance if I have left out some names that you consider to be very important! I will list these historians in chronological order.

1. First and foremost, there is the German historian *Leopold Ranke* (1795-1886), ennobled in 1865, after which time he was

## AN INTRODUCTION TO THIS INTRODUCTION

known as Leopold von Ranke. He is perhaps the most important founder of modern historical science. In this modern approach, his emphasis on source study (investigation of "primary" sources, especially archives and historical documents) was most characteristic. He uttered interesting objections against the Enlightenment idea of "progress" by underlining the uniqueness of historical events: "After Plato, there can be no more Plato." Though a Lutheran, he became well known for his fair presentation of the Roman Catholic Church in the sixteenth century. To him, Christian morality was superior; viewing history from a Christian standpoint was natural for Ranke. His greatest work in English language is probably *The Secret of World History* (1981).

2. The Dutch statesman *Guillaume Groen van Prinsterer* (1801-1876) is perhaps the greatest Dutch Christian historian, who viewed history from a Reformed point of view, in opposition to the revolutionary standpoints that were fashionable in his time. His principle was: "The gospel instead of the revolution." He was the father of the Anti-Revolutionary Party in the Netherlands, founded three years after his death. ("Anti" here does not mean "contra" but "instead of," as in "the gospel instead of the revolution.") Groen van Prinsterer elaborated this principle in his famous work *Ongeloof en revolutie* (1847; English translation: *Lectures on Unbelief and Revolution*, 1989). Another important work of his was his *Handboek der geschiedenis van het vaderland* ("Handbook of the History of the [Dutch] Fatherland," 1846). His influence on Protestant thinking has been enormous; it is difficult to imagine the great Dutch theologian and politician Abraham Kuyper (1837-1920) and the great Dutch philosopher Herman Dooyeweerd (1894-1977; see my volume *Wisdom for Thinkers*) without the influence of Groen van Prinsterer.

3. The Swiss historian *Jacob Burckhardt* (1818-1897), who was interested in both art history and cultural history, was one of the most outstanding historians of the nineteenth century. He was of great importance as the historian of the Age of Constantine in the fourth century AD, at the boundary between Antiquity and the Age of Christendom; see his work *Die Zeit Constantins des Grossen* (1853; English translation: *The Age of Constantine the Great*, 1964). His negative picture of the Emperor Constantine has been bom-

barded with criticism. Another important work by Burckhardt is *Die Kultur der Renaissance in Italien* (1860; English translation: *The Civilization of the Renaissance in Italy*, 2010), which could almost be called the opposite of the previous work. It is the description of the rise of the freedom of spirit in Europe that would ultimately lead to its secularization. Burckhardt has been criticized for his alleged anti-Semitism and ethnocentrism ("Caucasian superiority"), and his rejection of democracy.

4. The Russian religious philosopher *Nikolai Alexandrovich Berdyaev* (1874-1948) has been called a Christian existentialist (like Karl Jaspers, Gabriel Marcel, Miguel de Unamuno, Lev Shestov, and with forerunners such as Søren Kierkegaard and Fyodor Dostoevsky). In 1922, he was forced to find refuge in the West. For our purposes, his book *The Meaning of History* (1923; English translation 1936) is of especial importance. It must be viewed against the background of his Russian national consciousness, and his great desire for a (Russian) religious philosophy of history. After two World Wars and the Russian Revolution (1917), we notice in Berdyaev a much stronger sense of the apocalypse than we find in many Western Christian philosophers of history. Berdyaev emphasized that ancient India and Greece did not perceive history as a linear movement with an end-purpose. Only from the Bible we learn that the world has a teleology.

5. The American theologian and existentialist *Reinhold Niebuhr* (1892-1971), who was a professor at Union Theological Seminary in New York City, has been called a scholar for whom theology involved in the first place a Christian interpretation of history, with special emphasis on social and ethical aspects. For him, the meaning of history is only reached "beyond history," in the Kingdom of God, though he did not view this in an orthodox-eschatological way, but more as an ongoing and continual tension between time and eternity. Many of his works could be mentioned here, but I will limit myself to the following: *Beyond Tragedy: Essays on the Christian Interpretation of History* (1937); *The Nature and Destiny of Man: A Christian Interpretation* (1943); *Faith and History* (1949); and *The Self and the Dramas of History* (1955).

6. The English historian *Herbert Butterfield* (1900-1979) was a Professor of History at the University of Cambridge. A devout

## AN INTRODUCTION TO THIS INTRODUCTION

Methodist, he was highly interested in developing a Christian perspective on history. This becomes clear in two important books of his, both written in 1949: *Christianity and History* and *The Origins of Modern Science*. A famous quote from the first book is this: "Hold to Christ, and for the rest be totally uncommitted." As the American theologian Carl T. McIntire (1906-2002) put in: "the cardinal points of his [i.e., Butterfield's] historical approach are Christian: the features and limits of historical study, the high view of persons, insistence on human freedom and responsibility, imaginative sympathy, the exercise of charity, the perception of rationality in the universe, elasticity of mind."

7. The French historian *Henri-Irénée Marrou* (1904-1977), a Roman Catholic, was a specialist in early Christendom, in the church father Augustine in particular, and in the philosophy of history. He has been called a "Christian humanist." In this connection, the following works must be mentioned: *De la connaissance historique* (1954; English translation: *The Meaning of History*, 1966), *Théologie de l'histoire* (1968; English translation: *Time and Timeliness*, 1969) and *Crise de notre temps et réflexion chrétienne* (1930-1975) (1978). Marrou had an international reputation, and drew many disciples to himself. He also played a great role in the Roman Catholic Church, both before and after the Second Vatican Council.

8. The American theologian and philosopher *Arthur W. Munk* (1909-1992) deserves a place here because of his book *History and God: Clues to His Purpose* (1952). In this work, Munk reviews all the major philosophies of history, and concludes that history points to the presence and activity of God, which is "far greater than men had ever before dreamed." Also relevant is his work *A Synoptic Approach to the Riddle of Existence: A World View for a World Civilization* (1977).

9. Dutch historian *Meijer C. Smit* (1911-1981) taught history and philosophy at the Free University in Amsterdam in the footsteps of Reformed philosophers Herman Dooyeweerd (1894-1977) and Dirk H.Th. Vollenhoven (1892-1978). To date, Smit has been the most significant philosopher of history to come out of this school. His publications in the English language include: *The Divine Mystery in History* (1955); *Toward a Christian Conception of History* (2002); and *Writings on God and History* (1987). One of his central theses

## PROBING THE PAST

was that historical science should be open to the active presence of God shimmering just beneath the surface of historical events. This idea is directly related to Smit's interesting distinction between the "first" and the "second history"; on this, see chapter 2.

## Chapter Two
# THE HISTORICAL MODALITY

In the first volume of the present series, *Wisdom for Thinkers*, I introduced a number of terms that I will now take for granted here because I assume you have read that book. In it, I spoke about sixteen *modal aspects* (or *modalities*) of cosmic reality, one of them being the historical or formative aspect. I have argued why I think it comes in between the logical and the lingual modality. The historical aspect is one of the nine *spiritive* aspects (to be distinguished from the *natural* aspects, which include everything from the mathematical to the sensitive modalities).

### Power and Justice

In the earlier book, I described the kernel of the historical modality as "formative power." This refers to both the human power that we observe in history as the driving force that guides its course, and the human power that we observe in technology. We have seen that not every historical event is *historic*: historic events are those in which the formative power of humans can be most clearly seen, that is, whose effects upon the course of history are most obvious.

Power (the kernel of the historical aspect) and justice (the kernel of the juridical aspect) are two parallel ideas in history. Power has to do with what people *can* (are able to) do, while justice has to do with what they *may* (are allowed to, have a right to) do. People are not allowed to do everything they have the power to do. Nor are they capable of doing everything they have the right to do. As the French Christian thinker Blaise Pascal (1623-1662) put it in his famous *Pensées* ("Thoughts"): "Justice without power is inefficient, and power without justice is tyrannical. Justice without power is gainsaid, because the wicked always exist, power without justice is condemned. Justice and power must be brought together so that whatever is just may be powerful, and whatever is powerful may be just."

The Australian-Welsh lawyer James Richard Atkin (1867-1944) once said that "power corrupts and absolute power corrupts absolutely." History is full of men (and some women as well) who have proven how true this is. Power must be *checked* by justice. As the British politician William Pitt the Elder (1708-1778, after whom Pittsburgh was named) once said in the House of Lords (London, 1770): "Unlimited power is apt to corrupt the minds of those who possess it; and this I know, my lords, that where laws end, there tyranny begins." The historical modality is one of the *normative* aspects, as opposed to the natural aspects, where natural laws reign. That is, the use of historical power is subjected to *norms*, and not only ethical norms but principles of justice, as laid down in fair and righteous laws possessed by every civilized country.

There never was a nation in the world with such perfect laws as Israel. "What great nation is there," asks Moses, "that has statutes and rules so righteous as all this law that I set before you today?" (Deut. 4:8). The Levites praised God and said: "You came down on Mount Sinai and spoke with them from heaven and gave them right rules and true laws, good statutes and commandments" (Neh. 9:13). Even the power of the greatest kings in Israel was checked by the law of God: "And when he sits on the throne of his kingdom, he shall write for himself in a book a copy of this law, approved by the Levitical priests. And it shall be with him, and he shall read in it all the days of his life, that he may learn to fear the LORD his God by keeping all the words of this law and these statutes, and doing them, that his heart may not be lifted up above his brothers, and that he may not turn aside from the commandment, either to the right hand or to the left, so that he may continue long in his kingdom, he and his children, in Israel" (Deut. 17:18-20).

## Historical Subjects and Objects

In previous volumes we have seen that all things (inanimate things, plants, animals, humans), all events and all states of affairs function in each of the sixteen modalities of cosmic reality. Thus,

## THE HISTORICAL MODALITY

all entities and all events also have a historical aspect, although most things are not *qualified* (or *typified*) by this but by some other aspect. One might suggest that those entities, events and states of affairs that *are* characterized by this modality are *historic* things etc. (notice again the difference between historical and historic). Museums of history are full of objects that have played such historic roles. Think, for instance, of the Rosetta Stone, now in the British Museum, which was discovered in 1799 and which helped Western people understand Egyptian hieroglyphs for the very first time. Or think of the Tel Dan stele, now housed in the Israel Museum, which contains the expression *bytdwd* ("house of David"). This discovery marked the first time that the name David had ever been found outside the Bible. It helped skeptics understand that David was really a historical figure (although, of course, not everybody was convinced).

Other top "historical objects" are the Dead Sea Scrolls, the cities of Pompeii and Herculaneum, the cave of Altamira with its prehistoric paintings, the tomb of Tutankhamun, the megalithic temples of Malta, and the terracotta army of Xi'an in China. And far more recently, one could think of many technological inventions that have drastically changed the life of modern Man: the first steam engine, the first weaving and spinning machines, the first Leyden jar (a device to store static electricity), the first automobile, the first telegraph, etc. These are all historical *objects* of historic significance.

Please, remember again that the term "modal aspects" as such never refers to the phenomena themselves but always to *aspects* of these phenomena. In this connection, we sometimes speak of the modal and entitary dimensions of cosmic reality, and these two are, so to speak, perpendicular with respect to one another. To put it in ontological terms, aspects are ways indicating how entities are: they are arithmetical, biotic, historical, etc. To put it in epistemological terms, aspects are also ways we can view entities: they can be viewed from arithmetical, spatial, biotic, or historical angles, etc. Some entities may be *qualified* by the historical aspect, that is, the historical modality most appropriately describes their actual nature. But remember that these entities always function in all other modal aspects also.

Functioning in *all* modal aspects means that entities function in them either as *subjects* (that is, as being subjected to the laws or norms that appertain to these aspects) or as *objects*. Man is the only historical *subject* within our cosmic reality, that is, the only being that, in obedience or disobedience to historical norms, can affect the course of history in a conscious and purposeful way. Historically qualified animals, plants, inanimate things, events, and states of affairs always function as historical *objects*, that is, they function in whatever way humans use them in affecting the course of history.

Let me give some examples. The Rosetta Stone is a historical (in this case even a historic) *object*, but the French philologist Jean-François Champollion (1790-1832), who used it to decipher the hieroglyphs, acted as a historic *subject*. The first steam engine is a historic *object*, but the Scottish engineer James Watt (1736-1819) who developed it acted as a historic *subject*. It is historic subjects that steer history with the help of historic objects.

Historic objects always deserve the greatest interest of the historian. For instance, describing the Renaissance implies first and foremost a description of great paintings, sculptures, musical compositions, and literary works. But, of course, history can never forget the historic *subjects* who made these great objects of visual, musical and literary art. The historian is interested not only in their personal life stories, but in their education, their cultural environment, their sponsors, and the question of who induced them to bring forth these great works, etc.

## Historical Norms

Every modality is characterized by certain laws or norms attached to it. Thus, there are also historical norms, like the norm of *historical continuity*, that is, the gradual, uninterrupted progress of cultural development. This implies following a middle path between traditionalism and reactionism on the one hand, and revolutionism on the other. To put it very simply, traditionalism and reactionism cling to the good things of the past but also to things that are now outdated, and therefore should be given up. Revolutionism is the opposite of this: it wants to overthrow the bad things in a society or culture, but along with it, the good

## THE HISTORICAL MODALITY

things are automatically destroyed as well. Therefore, both reactionism and revolutionism involve disobedience to God-given norms. Clinging to wrong things and destroying good things are both serious trespasses against the historical norms that are valid for cosmic reality.

The fact that such historical norms exist is illustrated by the fact that Man can disobey them; disobeying historical norms leads to "unhistorical" or "ahistorical" behavior. Striking examples of this are sects or denominations that, in a self-assured way, really believe that authentic church history started with them. After the New Testament period, the "lights" soon went out, and this situation of darkness lasted for centuries, until the pioneers or founders of the movement in question arose, who put the lampstand once again in its proper place. Such people have no true sense of (church) history, or of the historical developments that led to the origin of the sects concerned. In the strict sense of the word, relativ*ism* is wrong; but not being able to relativize one's own group enough to view it in the proper historical light is just as wrong.

This ahistorical self-confidence usually leads to two ways of thinking. On the one hand, there is the tendency to carry the history of one's own movement, as it were, all the way back to the beginning of church history. This is done in an effort to make clear that one stands on the foundation of the apostles, and that one represents the tiny minority in church history that has allegedly remained faithful to God's Word. On the other hand, a far-reaching disinterest for church history can be noted, with the exception of the thin line that leads to one's own movement. For the rest, church history is hardly deemed to be of interest because it was allegedly largely governed by the powers of darkness. These are the consequences of a lack of historical consciousness.

Church history is just one example. A similar lack of interest can be noted in school systems that focus too much on the history of one particular country—as if, from a South African point of view, world history started only in 1652, or, from an American point of view, only in 1776. In the Netherlands, I notice the tendency to lay too much emphasis on the twentieth century as being of special importance for understanding our own time, with a serious disregard for older history.

PROBING THE PAST

## Historicism

In the book I have mentioned above, *Wisdom for Thinkers*, I tried to demonstrate that each and every modality has been absolutized at some time in the history of thought. "Absolutizing" here means making it absolute, making it the one and only thing to which all other things can be reduced. We sometimes speak of functionalism, that is, the absolutization of one specific modal function. In the past, such functionalisms have been invented for virtually every modality: materialism, spiritualism, rationalism, socialism, economism, etc. Thus, *historicism* is a feature of several philosophical schools, particularly in the nineteenth century, that see all culture as nothing but products of historical development, thus absolutizing the formative or historical aspect.

Historicists consider "history" to be everything; all other aspects of cosmic reality are subservient to it. A great example of this is the aphorism of the German historicist Georg W.F. Hegel, who said, "Philosophy is the history of philosophy." That is, you will begin to understand philosophy when you begin to understand its history. Everything can be explained from history. Thought, social life, economics, the arts, justice, morality, and religion are nothing but the products of historical development. Understand history, and you will understand Man, and all aspects of human life. This view involves a strong relativism: all aspects of culture are not only products of history, but they will also undergo further changes as history itself develops. There cannot be any absolute values—whether they be social, juridical, moral, or pistical—because values are subject to continual historical development.

By the way, Hegel, whom I have just mentioned and who formed the climax of the movement known as "German Idealism," was probably the quintessential historicist of the nineteenth century. He saw history as the unfolding of "spirit" or "mind." His pupil and later materialist counterpart, the German philosopher Karl Marx (1818-1883), applied Hegel's historicism consistently in his own Marxist theories, but in a strictly materialist way. It is because of his strictly historicist approach that Marx approved so highly of the evolutionary theory, made public in 1859 by the English naturalist Charles Darwin (1809-1882), because he took it as a

## THE HISTORICAL MODALITY

natural-scientific buttressing of his own strongly historical views.

From a historicist perspective, history does not *have* an ultimate goal, but history *as such* is the goal, purpose, teleology. History is not subject to norms, history *as such* is the norm. History does not *have* a meaning, but history *as such* is meaning. This is historicism *par excellence*: "everything is history"—which is just as absurd as Pythagoras' statement that "everything is number," the materialist idea that "everything is matter," spiritualism's belief that "everything is spirit (or, mind)," etc.

No philosophy has broken with this historicist view in a more radical way than the Christian philosophy of the Dutch thinkers Herman Dooyeweerd (1894-1977) and Dirk H.Th. Vollenhoven (1892-1978). This philosophy had the great merit of pointing out that "the historical" is only one out of many modal aspects of cosmic reality, none of which should ever be absolutized. On the contrary, they must be viewed in their mutual coherence, and in their common orientation toward the Creator. Where this is recognized, it can no longer be claimed that history is identical with its own meaning and purpose. Meaning and purpose cannot be found in any of the modalities of cosmic reality but only in the transcendent reality, in which all the immanent modal aspects find their unity, integrity and fullness.

## Two Levels

Please study my books *Wisdom for Thinkers* and *What Then Is Theology?* again to understand very precisely that the immanent, historical reality and the transcendent, "supra-historical" reality are *not* dualistically opposed to each other. I briefly describe this distinction here, and add two other relations which have been proposed by various thinkers:

(a) In the Dooyeweerdian view that I represent here and in the books mentioned above, the immanent historical and the transcendent supra-historical cannot form any kind of dualism whatsoever because the historical *is identical* with the (transcendent) supra-historical in its (immanent) diversity and variability, and the supra-historical *is identical* with the (immanent) historical in its (transcendent) unity and fullness. See also my volume

## PROBING THE PAST

*Searching the Soul,* where I defend the related view that the human functions *are* the (transcendent) human heart in its (immanent) diversity and variability, and that the human heart is the totality of the (immanent) human functions in their (transcendent) unity and fullness.

(b) The distinction between immanent and transcendent, or between history and supra-history, or between diversity and unity, is related to the distinction that was made by Swiss theologian Karl Barth (1886-1968) between *Historie* and *Geschichte*. These German words cannot be rendered satisfactorily by equivalent words in English; both are commonly translated as "history." *Historie* is that which is part of common historiography; it contains everything that falls within the horizon of the historian—say, the "bare facts" (I would add, on the immanent level). But *Geschichte* contains these same facts on the level of meaning and purpose (I would add, on the transcendent level). I believe one could put it this way: the former is the level of historical science as such; the latter is the level of the philosophy of history—in our case: a Christian philosophy of history.

In modern theology, there has been much discussion about the alleged distinction between the *historische* Jesus and the *geschichtliche* Christ, the former being the Jesus of history, the latter being the Christ of faith. Much of this distinction was spoilt by the dualism that some would interpose between the two, such as the assertion that Jesus' resurrection never took place in a *historisch* sense, but that it did take place in a *geschichtlich* sense; this was the opinion of the German theologian Rudolf Bultmann (1884-1976), among others. In our Christian philosophical approach, such a dualism cannot possibly exist; *Geschichte* is *Historie* on the transcendent level, while *Historie* is *Geschichte* on the immanent level. There are no events within *Geschichte* that do not have their counterpart in *Historie*. Thus, it makes no sense to accept the resurrection in a *geschichtlich* sense but to deny it in the *historisch* sense, as Barth himself rightly argued against Bultmann.

(c) Another distinction, which reminds us both of the immanent–transcendent distinction and the *Historie–Geschichte* distinction, is the one between "first" and "second history" made by the Dutch historian Meijer C. Smit (see chapter 1). As Smit explains,

## THE HISTORICAL MODALITY

human relationships are characterized, among many other things, by righteousness or unrighteousness, and by love or hatred. It is impossible to describe human history without recognizing such basic principles to be operative in human history. However, righteousness or unrighteousness, and love or hatred are not *products* of the historical process, as historicists would claim; they are pre-given divine and absolute norms. Matters such as juridical and moral norms, their origin as found in God, and their orientation toward God cannot be explained in terms of the "first history"; they belong to the "second history." However, as a good Dooyeweerdian, Smit emphasizes that there is no room for any dualism here. To him, history is basically one. By speaking of the "first" and "second history," he wished only to make a philosophical distinction between things that in reality have been given to us as one.

## Some Other Philosophical Aspects

If a certain culture at a certain time were in perfect rest, there would not be much to describe. History is a process of continual *changes*. This fact leads us to an interesting theological question, namely, will the new heavens and the new earth (Isa. 65:17; 66:22; 2 Pet. 3:13; Rev. 21:1) experience such a state of absolute rest, or will they be the scene of "events"? Will it ever be possible to write a history of the new heavens and the new earth, or will nothing be going on there that is worth describing? Will they be an eternal *state* of rest? We need not concern ourselves with this question any further here. I mention it only to show how difficult it is for our thoroughly historical minds to imagine such a state of perfect rest without occurrence. In our world, there is *occurrence* all the time, and this is what historical science is all about.

As for the "old" earth, if Zechariah 1:11 says that "all the earth remains at rest" and that the nations are "at ease" (v. 15), everybody will realize that this must not be understood in an absolute sense. Many things were going on among the nations, Israel included, and this was precisely why the book of Zechariah had to be written in the first place. The sense of the expression is that there was relative peace within and among the nations, whereas Israel was in turmoil.

## PROBING THE PAST

Historians always have a lot of work to do because, in an absolute sense, nations, societies and cultures are *never* at ease; they are changing continually. This is why the past is so interesting. It is, almost by definition, so very different from the present, and yet the present has come forth from the past and is a continuation of it. This necessarily implies that many things have changed, but also that many things have remained more or less the same, otherwise we could not even recognize historical development. We can speak about Australia as it was in the Stone Age, as it was in the time of the first British settlers, and as it is today. It has changed very much throughout the centuries, and yet it is still the same Australia, even though the name Australia was given to the continent only in the seventeenth century.

It is like the baby and the old man; they are the same person, but what a difference between them! Just as we would like to know the biotic and spiritual changes that have led from the baby to the old man, we would like to know, for instance, what developments led from seventeenth-century Australia to present-day Australia, or from eighteenth century America to present-day America. But also, what development created the world of seventeenth century Australia or eighteenth century America? These questions lead to a study of changes, of dynamic developments, of growth, blossoming and declining, appearing and disappearing.

Like in all sciences, the matter of subjectivity and objectivity plays a great role in historical science, perhaps a greater one than in some other sciences; at any rate a greater one in the humanities than in the natural sciences. The question of whether light is made up of particles or waves—or both—is (or has been) a hot debate among physicists, which might affect their careers. But the issue of particles or waves is one that hardly touches them *personally*. How different this is in the science of history (and in all humanities for that matter). Of course, the historian must try to be as objective as he can. He is not allowed to distort the facts, to leave out facts that do not fit into his picture of things, to smuggle imaginary "facts" into his reconstruction of the past, or purposely to place the wrong emphases on the various facts.

However, at the same time, in other respects he is quite subjective. If he is a Maori, he can hardly help taking sides when

## THE HISTORICAL MODALITY

describing the history of New Zealand. The same is true when describing, for instance, the American Civil War, especially if the historian is an American who takes his Northern or Southern heritage very seriously. Probably, his readers *want* him to takes sides, in particular when they share his perspective. They want to hear from him who was right and who was wrong; but, they also want his account to be fair enough to say also what faults the right people sometimes committed, and what virtues the wrong people sometimes displayed. Therefore, one could almost say that it is indispensible to have two histories of the American Civil War, one from a Confederate standpoint, and another from a Unionist standpoint. Although one could also presume that, after a century and a half, today a more objective view of this War should be possible, perhaps if it is written by a foreigner.

Foreigners writing "our" national history are especially interesting, because they have a perspective that we who are an integral part of this national history might be lacking. I am thinking in particular of the British historian Jonathan Israel (b. 1946), who is a great writer on, among other things, Dutch history (e.g., *The Dutch Republic: Its Rise, Greatness and Fall, 1477–1806*, published in 1995). It is quite refreshing to read about my own history as seen through the eyes of an "outsider" (although this is not entirely true, since during the seventeenth and eighteenth centuries there were no less than four wars between the Dutch and the English!).

In South Africa, there have already been both British and Afrikaner accounts of the Great Trek (1830-50) and the Anglo-Boer Wars (1880-81, 1899-1902). Since the fall of *apartheid* in 1992, there is now room for a Black view of these wars as well, a view which differs from both the British and the Afrikaner perspective—just as we now possess African-American perspectives on the American Civil War, which are often so refreshingly different from the perspectives we were used to.

## Learning from History?

I have already quoted Hegel's pessimistic statement that we learn from history that people do not learn anything from history. At any rate, we keep making the same mistakes over and over again.

## PROBING THE PAST

*Can* we learn from history? Or does our human nature discourage this? Usually historians have made at least some effort to present history in such a way that we can discern good human actions, that are worthy of imitation, and bad actions, that are examples of conduct to be avoided. In general, this is what readers want. We cannot think of the Second World War without desiring for ourselves a clear picture of which ones were the "good guys" (the Allied Forces, "of course") and which ones were the "bad guys" (Germany, Italy, and Japan, "of course"). Or, even more obviously, we would not appreciate a historian who undertook to present us with an "objective" description of the history of the Holocaust (the massacre of the six millions Jews during the Second World War). On the contrary, we want to *hear* in his account his disgust with respect to the atrocities of that massacre, and his sympathy with the victims.

Of course, this makes great demands on the historian. There is a false kind of objectivity which can be assumed by the historian that is not appreciated by readers, as I just said. But there is also a disgusting form of subjectivity, such as communist or fascist "re-writing" of history, or revisionism by any other dictatorial regime, or negationism (see chapter 1). The study of these forms of objectivity and subjectivity, and many other things, is called the history of historical science. It tries to answer, for instance, the question as to how historians from *different* epochs described the history of an epoch in a yet more distant past. For instance, how did historians of the seventeenth, the nineteenth or the twentieth century write about the Renaissance? As I said, historical works tell us something about a certain epoch, but they always tell us something about the historian and his own epoch as well.

Take, for instance, the terms "Middle Ages" and "medieval." They have their origin in the work of German historian Christoph Cellarius (1638-1707), who was the first to divide European history into three parts: Ancient, Medieval, and Modern. In fact, the term "Medieval" (from Latin *medium aevum*, the "age in between") actually has negative connotations. Apparently, what really mattered for Cellarius and many of his contemporaries were Antiquity and the Modern Age. The Middle Ages were a less significant "in between," ["space filler"?] a period that implied that

## THE HISTORICAL MODALITY

there had been a deterioration with respect to Antiquity. In the nineteenth century, the Middle Ages were often described as the "Dark Ages," a term that had already been introduced by the Italian Renaissance scholar Petrarch (1304-1374). The idea was that, after the glorious light of Antiquity had waned, the lamps went out in Europe, only to be lit again in the fifteenth and sixteenth century. However, one could hardly call the Middle Ages a "transitory" period because it lasted for a thousand years (from c. 500 to c. 1500)!

No historian in our time would speak about the Middle Ages in this derogatory fashion; the term "Middle Ages" could hardly have been invented in the twentieth century. It was typical for the Renaissance and the beginning of the modern age to sneer at the past. We, who are at a far greater remove from the Middle Ages, feel much more positive about this grand millennium in European history. However, it is too late to change a term which has become so familiar to us.

The past is finished; it is over, and can no longer be changed. It is fixed. But what does change constantly is our *picture* of the past. As I said, every epoch has its own picture of a certain part of the past, and, of course, even within one and the same epoch, different pictures of a certain part of the past can be painted, depending on one's philosophical or paradigmatic perspective. Yet, this fact should not lead to relativism, as if any one picture is as good as any other. No, the historian must be convinced that he presents the best picture that is possible under the given circumstances. He must *believe* in his picture, even if he knows that posterity will nuance it. Or, to put it in more general terms, historians—or philosophers of history—develop standards according to which one picture of the past is "better" (more scientific, more responsible, accounting better for the indisputable facts) than another.

### The Driving Forces

In several previous volumes in this series, I have underlined the fact that all science is rooted in the special philosophy (German: *Fachphilosophy*; Dutch: *vakfilosofie*) of that particular science. In its turn, this special philosophy—in the present case the philosophy of

## PROBING THE PAST

history (*Geschichtsphilosophie, geschiedfilosofie*)— is rooted in a more general ontology and epistemology. (If this is not immediately clear, please consult my *Wisdom for Thinkers*.) Moreover, we have seen that general philosophy is always necessarily rooted in pre-scientific and pre-philosophical *worldviews*. Within the cultural sciences, or humanities, these worldviews play a far more obvious role than in the natural sciences. Whether light is a particle or a wave phenomenon is a matter that is hardly influenced by worldviews. But our view of history is! For one thing, history is the work of humans, and therefore every view of history presupposes a certain *anthropology*, a certain philosophical view of Man. Such an anthropology always presupposes a certain pre-scientific view of Man, which is part of the scholar's worldview, his pre-scientific beliefs.

As I said, history is a dynamic event. Dynamics involve forces that are operative, and changes that are caused by these forces. There are no effects without causes. The vital question is, however, *what* forces are driving history. The answer to this question does *not* itself belong to historical science as such. That is, no historical investigation as such can ever answer this question. However, it can indicate certain things, for instance, certain socio-economic factors, strong and powerful people, new discoveries that affected mankind, etc. But these factors remain more or less at the surface. Below the surface, there are other factors working, and the question of their exact nature depends more on one's worldview, including one's view of Man, than on strictly historical investigations; let us think once more about Karl Barth's distinction between *Historie* and *Geschichte*, and Meijer Smit's distinction between "first" and "second history."

Let me try to give a very brief survey of such driving factors, mainly belonging to *Historie*, or "first history," which I arrange according to the various idionomies (basic structures) of Man's existence (to understand what that means, see in detail my volume called *Searching the Soul*). Earlier in this chapter, I warned against a phenomenon called "functionalism." This is the tendency to absolutize one of the sixteen modal aspects at the expense of the others. In the following survey of driving forces in history, we may observe the tendency of some historians to reduce the historical to one of the other modalities, or at least to forge a strong link between the historical and one or more of the other modalities.

## THE HISTORICAL MODALITY

**I. Forces *outside* of Man**

These are the forces of Man's natural environment from which culture is supposed to develop. Views emphasizing the environment assert that, in the end, human history is determined by nothing but climate, the soil, the sources of food and water, the traffic possibilities, the economical relationships, and the like.

**II. Forces from *within* Man**

These are the forces within Man's own being that allegedly determine his historical vicissitudes (i.e., history must be understood from the starting point of *anthropology*), in particular the following factors:

*A. The biotic idionomy,* for example:

1. *Racial differences.* We can think, for instance, of the view of Hitler's national-socialism, with its racist emphasis on ethnicity or, to use its own terminology, *Blut und Boden* ("blood and soil," i.e., the right ancestry and the right homeland). It exalts the relationship that a nation has to its *Heimat*, "homeland"—land here taken literally: the land that is cultivated. It is the glorification of the countryside with its rural living. Quite a different example is the focus on ethnic and racial aspects in the writings of those American historians who think and work from a civil rights perspective.

*B. The perceptive idionomy,* for instance:

2. *Man's instinct for self-preservation*: Society originates from the agreements people make to arrive at an equilibrium in which, although each of them has this same urge, they can still maintain themselves as well as society as a whole; thus, for instance, English philosopher Thomas Hobbes (1588-1679). Central to his thinking was the social contract theory, claiming that individuals consent to surrender some of their freedoms and submit to a central authority in order to ensure that their remaining freedoms are guaranteed. It is calculated self-preservation of individuals, thus defending themselves against each other.

3. *Man's hunger*: The entire human history is nothing but a re-

flection of the economical relationships within a society between the haves and the have-nots; thus, especially German philosopher and economist Karl Marx (1818-1883). Also compare the "hierarchy of needs," constructed by American psychologist Abraham Maslow (1908-1970), according to which the first needs to be fulfilled are breathing, food, water, sleep, and the like. Man will only concentrate on his higher needs (safety, love and/or belonging, esteem, self-actualization) after the lower needs have been met.

C. *The sensitive idionomy*, for instance:

4. *The libido*: In the end, history is driven by nothing but Man's sexual drives; thus, especially Austrian psychologist Sigmund Freud (1856-1939). According to him, it is not necessarily sex as such that drives history, for the libido (the sex drive) can also change its object, a process that he called sublimation. Through this process, the sex drive is transformed into socially acceptable actions. To Freud, this was a sign of maturity, even of civilization, allowing people to function normally in culturally acceptable ways. In his view, sublimation was a conspicuous feature of cultural history. The German-American historian Peter Gay (b. 1923) is an admirer of Freud, and has been called a leading champion of *Psychohistory*. This is the study of the emotional motivations of historical events, especially in the light of (Freudian) psychotherapy and the modern social sciences.

5. *The "will to power"*: This term is central to the thought of the German philosopher Friedrich Nietzsche (1844-1900); in fact, the phrase was coined in his book *Thus Spoke Zarathustra*. It is a "Dionysian" affirmation of the eternal cycle of life and death, rising and declining, lust and grief, an elementary power that keeps the "wheel of being" rolling. Nietzsche saw this as the main driving force in the human world: it is responsible for ambition, achievement, self-realization, the striving for the highest possible positions in the world.

6. *Self-interest, ethnocentrism*: Explanations of history must be based on the conflicts between individuals (self-interest), or between the groups to which they belong (ethnocentrism). We can think of theories such as the utilitarianism of the British philosophers Jeremy Bentham (1748-1832) and John Stuart Mill (1806-

## THE HISTORICAL MODALITY

1873), or the "enlightened self-interest" of the liberalism of British philosopher John Locke (1632-1704), or the "class conflict" of Karl Marx (whom I have just mentioned).

D. *The spiritive idionomy*, as it appears in the following :
   7. *The logical modality*: History is driven by rational insights, or by the rational choices that people make. It is useful to compare, for instance, the positivism of the French philosopher Auguste Comte (1798-1859) with his idea that mankind moves through three stages: the theological stage, in which Man is led by divine powers); the metaphysical stage in which Man is led by impersonal forces; and the positive stage, in which Man is led by positive science, that is, by his ratio. More recent historians have been focusing on intellectual aspects of history, such as the significance of new ideas (in the "history of ideas"); cf. the English historian Herbert Butterfield (see chapter 1), the German-American historian George Mosse (1918-1999), and the German historian Ernst Nolte (b. 1923).

   8. *The social modality*: It is typical of socialism to seek the essence of history in the social relationships among human beings, which are viewed as more important than the interests of individuals. Some examples of historians who have strongly emphasized social factors in history are Lucien Febvre (1878-1956), Marc Bloch (1886-1944), and Emmanuel Le Roy Ladurie (b. 1929) of France; Fritz Fischer (1908-1999) and Hans-Ulrich Wehler (b. 1931) of Germany; and Lawrence Stone (1919-1999) of Great Britain. We should also consider what is called *historical sociology*, the study of how societies—for instance, states—develop in history.

   9. *The economical modality*: History is driven by (socio-) economical "production relationships" (see the discussion of Karl Marx, above). From more recent times I mention the American economic historian Robert Fogel (1926-2013). He is a leading champion of *cliometrics*, or New Economic History, that is, the systematic application of economic theory and econometric techniques as tools in the study of history. (The term *cliometrics* comes from Clio, the muse of history in Greek mythology.)

   10. *The aesthetic modality*: History is basically driven by Man's striving for harmony. We encounter this idea in the thought

of the German poet, philosopher and historian Friedrich Schiller (1759-1805). I also think of those who view history as a work of art, such as the German historian Gerhard Ritter (1888-1967); the Canadian historian Donald Creighton (1902-1979); the British historian Hugh Trevor-Roper (1914-2003); the American historian Gertrude Himmelfarb (b. 1922); and the Hungarian-American historian John Lukacs (b. 1924).

11. T *he juridical modality*, especially in the political sense, which can be found, for example, in the works of the German historian Karl Dietrich Bracher (b. 1922). As we have already seen, power must be checked by justice. Therefore, Bracher focuses especially on democracy, its preservation and its perils, on human rights and on constitutional values, especially against the backdrop of the undemocratic phases in German history of the twentieth century.

12. T *he moral modality*: History is driven by Man's desire to realize a moral order that is beyond himself. We encounter this view in the movement known as German idealism, in such notable figures as: Immanuel Kant (1724-1804); Johann G. Fichte (1762-1814); Friedrich W.J. Schelling (1775-1854); and especially Georg W.F. Hegel (1770-1831).

13. T *he pistical modality*: History is governed by immanent and transcendent religious forces, which elevate mankind above barbarism, and which form the driving forces in every civilization. From a specifically Christian perspective, this means that history is driven by (a) powers in the invisible world, both positive (God, Christ, good angels) and negative (Satan, evil angels, demons), and (b) the orientation of the human heart, whether it be *anastatic* (directed towards God) or *apostatic* (directed away from God to the idols).

## Some Comments

Of course, none of these various views says it all, although, in a functionalist way, they may try to convince us otherwise. Even if we take a Christian approach, emphasizing factors such as God and Satan, the Spirit and the flesh, the other factors also play a role.

## THE HISTORICAL MODALITY

Here, we are reminded of an important distinction that I have dealt with in several of the previous volumes, namely, the distinction between *structure* and *direction*. Factors such as the Spirit and the flesh, or the new nature of the regenerated person and the old, sinful nature, have to do with the *direction* of the human heart. Factors such as the forces mentioned above (in section II on forces from within Man), which are connected with the various idionomies of Man's immanent, corporeal existence, have to do with *structure*. This is that other dimension, which is "perpendicular" to that of direction. Whether we are driven by God or by Satan, by the Spirit or by the flesh, we are dealing with environmental factors (see section I) and personal factors (see section II, especially the remarks on race, hunger, preservation of self, libido, social relationships, economical and aesthetic factors, justice, morals, immanent religious factors, etc.).

A responsible view of history, such as the Christian approach endeavors to be, takes both the horizontal structure and the vertical direction into account. In doing so, by the way, we will find that in some of the personal factors the direction of the human heart becomes easier to see than in some others. In Man's urge for self-preservation, and in factors such as the libido, the "will to power," self-interest, and ethnocentrism, the danger of sin is clearly lurking.

The various theories discussed in the previous section all run the danger of absolutizing certain aspects of cosmic reality while neglecting all the others, an attitude that I have called functionalism. Good examples of this are found in the sensitivism of Freud, the rationalism of Comte and so many others, socialism, the economism of Marx, and aestheticism. (For the precise nature of these "-isms," consult again my *Wisdom for Thinkers*.) There is also a kind of "pisticism" (absolutizing the pistical modality), which takes the (vertical) religious factors (God, Satan, Spirit, sin) into account, but not the (horizontal) biotic, perceptive, sensitive and spiritive factors. Nevertheless, the latter clearly play a role in all human functioning, and have to be accounted for in any Christian philosophy of history.

Likewise, those views which place particular emphasis on the spiritive factors easily run the risk of neglecting the biotic,

## PROBING THE PAST

perceptive, and sensitive factors. Man is not only a spiritive being but also a natural one. For instance, views accentuating the spiritive may give much prominence to human *freedom* without seeing that, if so many non-spiritive (biotic, perceptive, sensitive) factors exert such a great influence in human history, we must ask the question of how much room is actually left for that highly exalted freedom. This has always been one of the central questions in philosophical thinking: how free is Man really?

Even the greatest dictators in history, who have exerted great strength in steering its course, were bound to their environment, their cultural and social circumstances, and especially the historical moment. If Napoleon Bonaparte had not been around right after the French Revolution (1798), and if Adolf Hitler had not lived right after the First World War (1914-18) in a humiliated Germany, they would probably never have become dictators. Such people live in the right situation, one that brings them to power, and at the same time, they have the opportunity to drastically change that situation, but in all cases it is only within the historically given boundaries.

There is another aspect to this: no people seem to be freer than dictators, who have so much power over the people and can do as they like (cf. Dan. 5:19, "Whom he [i.e., Nebuchadnezzar] would, he killed, and whom he would, he kept alive; whom he would, he raised up, and whom he would, he humbled"). In reality, dictators are usually strikingly similar to each other: sooner or later, almost all of them become obsessed either with the arrogance of power (pride, boasting, abuse of power, sadism), or with money (financial gain, greed), or with sex (because of so many women being available to them), and usually with all three. In this sense, one may wonder exactly how "free" dictators are, seeing that they always seem to fall victim to the very same vices.

Behind this is the ancient theological and philosophical problem of whether human freedom really exists at all. Christians do believe in true freedom, but it can be found only "in Christ," through the power of the Holy Spirit, which places a check on our vices (John 8:36; Rom. 8:2; 2 Cor. 3:17; Gal. 5:1). The person who thinks he is "free" from God, easily becomes a victim of his own lower instincts and drives, that is, of profligacy and dissipation (Gal. 5:13-24; 1 Pet. 2:16).

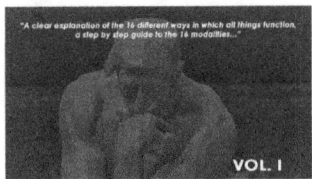

## WISDOM FOR THINKERS
*An Introduction to
Christian Philosophy*

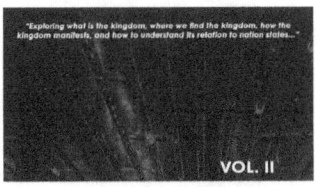

## POWER IN SERVICE
*An Introduction to
Christian Political Thought*

## WHAT THEN *IS* THEOLOGY?
*An Introduction to
Christian Theology*

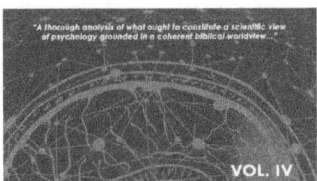

## SEARCHING THE SOUL
*An Introduction to
Christian Psychology*

# Chapter Three
# THE MEANING OF HISTORY

In the previous chapter, I have distinguished four key questions that must be dealt with in any philosophy of history, and are also a challenge to any Christian approach. These questions are:
   (a) the *meaning* or *arbitrariness* of history;
   (b) *patterns* in history, such as cyclical or linear, or a combination of them;
   (c) *teleology* (design, purpose, goal) in history;
   (d) the *driving forces* of history: natural or supernatural; determinism or free choices.

Let us consider these four questions from a Christian philosophical viewpoint. In this chapter, we will deal with the first of these four fundamental subjects, that is, the meaning of history from a Christian point of view, *versus* the arbitrariness of history from various secular points of view.

## The Theodicy

The Christian who believes in God and the Bible, and has some knowledge of the counsels and the ways of God is *a priori* convinced that history has a meaning. He is convinced of this in spite of the many seeming examples of "meaninglessness" in his personal life and in general history. The clearest and most painful examples of this are the numerous cases of seemingly meaningless suffering. Human history could almost be described as one long series of sufferings, such as wars, conquests, violence, rivalry, earth quakes, floods, volcanic eruptions, epidemics and other diseases, poverty, famines and natural disasters. Not only any theological apologetics but also any Christian philosophy of history has to account for the presence, the meaning and the purpose of suffering in human history.

## PROBING THE PAST

It is not sufficient to say that suffering is caused by Man's fall into sin. In a very general sense there is truth in this statement, of course; without the fall there would have been no suffering. However, we have to realize that not all suffering is a direct consequence of sinful actions by humans, for there is also suffering caused by diseases, famines and natural disasters. Although we might claim that the latter are also consequences of Man's fall, this does not explain why certain good people often have to suffer so much more than some bad people. This is the deep existential question with which Asaph wrestles in Psalm 73. If we as Christians believe that God is behind everything that happens in this world, it seems to be impossible to avoid the conclusion that in some way or another, God is responsible for the bad things that strike not only the wicked but also the good.

In the light of this problem, we understand why a Christian philosophy of history always involves a *theodicy* (from Greek *theos*, "god," and *dike*, "justice," thus: "justification of God"). A *theodicy* is a theory designed to "justify God," that is, to account for the fact that God is both almighty and full of love, and yet allows evil and suffering. Can an omnipotent (i.e., almighty) God who allows evil also be called a loving God? And can a loving God, who apparently does nothing to stop evil, be called an almighty God?

Some of the most famous theodicies came from great Christian thinkers such as the church father Augustine (354-430), the Italian philosopher Thomas Aquinas (1225-1274), the French bishop and theologian Jacques-Bénigne Bossuet (1627-1704, *Discours de l'histoire universelle*), the German philosopher Gottfried W. Leibniz (1646-1716), and the French-Dutch philosopher Pierre Bayle (1647-1706). Leibniz pointed out that what *we* perceive as "meaningless" evils are in fact part of a larger plan of God, of which we cannot get an overall view. They are not only meaningful but necessary in order to reach God's goal. The very influential Italian philosopher of history, Giambattista Vico (1668-1744), was of great importance here, because he made historiography subservient to theological notions such as the providence and goodness of God.

## God's Omnipotence

What is the relationship between God's power and the evil in this world? Traditionally, theology distinguishes between God's *prescriptive* will with respect to what people ought to do (cf. Matt. 7:21; 12:50; John 4:34; 7:17; Rom. 12:2), and God's *descriptive* will, which specifies what God himself does and will do (cf. Ps. 115:3; Dan. 4:17, 25, 32, 35; Rom. 9:18-19; Eph. 1:5, 9, 11; Rev. 4:11). We find this distinction in many passages. God wishes Abraham to sacrifice his son (prescriptive will: command to Man), and makes sure that in the end this does not happen (descriptive will; Gen. 22:2, 12). God wants Pharaoh to let the Israelites go (prescriptive will; Exod. 4:22), but hardens his heart, so that he does not do it (descriptive will; Exod. 9:12, 16). He does not desire Man to condemn the innocent (prescriptive will: Exod. 23:7; Deut. 19:10; 27:25; Prov. 6:17; Isa. 59:7; Jer. 7:6; 22:3, 17), but according to his counsel he delivered Jesus into the hands of sinners (descriptive will: Acts 2:23; 3:18; 4:28; cf. Matt. 17:22-23; 20:18-19). God wants all people to be saved (Ezek. 18:23, 32; 33:11; Luke 13:34; 1 Tim. 2:4; 2 Pet. 3:9), yet he has mercy on whomever he wills, he hardens whomever he wills (Rom. 9:18), and he "has made... the wicked for the day of trouble" (Prov. 16:4).

In order to explain this paradox, theology describes the prescriptive will of God as the desiring or resistible will of God (which expresses itself in commands, exhortations, chastisement, discipline), and his descriptive will as the absolute or irresistible will of God. The former clearly deals with the *ways* of God in history, and the latter with the *counsels* of God (see the detailed discussion of this distinction in chapter 7). In other words: the prescriptive will of God guarantees Man's responsibility and freedom of choice, that is, his exalted position as the image and likeness of God (Gen. 1:26-27). If Man were unable to resist this form of God's will, he would be nothing more than a robot, a machine. However, the descriptive will of God, the will of his counsels (cf. Eph. 1:11b, God "who works all things according to the counsel of his will"), is irresistible; eventually it will be carried out, whatever Man may try to undertake against it.

Christian thought has always wondered how God's omnipotence relates to his love. As I said, it has been claimed that, if God is really omnipotent, he cannot be absolute love (cf. 1 John 4:8, 16), for if he were love, his omnipotence would not allow the suffering of innocent human beings. Conversely, if God really is love, in view of the enormous amount of suffering of innocent people in the world, he cannot possibly be really omnipotent. Anyone who closely observes human history sees only suffering upon suffering. Either God is omnipotent, but then he cannot be love, or he is love, but then he cannot be omnipotent. It seems we cannot have both. People who reason like this do not see that terms such as love and omnipotence are only *approximations* of God's being, which surpass all human conceptualization and definition. Therefore, God's love and omnipotence can stand alongside each other, without necessarily contradicting each other.

## Omnipotence and Weakness

As soon as we recognize what I have just stated, we learn to speak of God's omnipotence and love without trying to bring them together into one logical scheme. In my view, it is only in this way that we can arrive at a theodicy that is truly in harmony with Scripture. Only in this way will we be able to recognize God's omnipotence in history ("Our God... does all that he pleases," Ps. 115:3) as well as his love ("I have loved you with an everlasting love; therefore I have continued my faithfulness to you," Jer. 31:3). The fact that God will ultimately fulfill his counsel of grace and mercy will be the definitive demonstration of both his omnipotence—no power can stop him from accomplishing his counsels—and his love, because God's counsels aim at the full blessing of mankind.

The cross of Jesus Christ seemed to be the opposite of divine omnipotence, for Jesus "was crucified in weakness" (2 Cor. 13:4). It is through this very weakness that God will ultimately accomplish the counsels that will prove his omnipotence. This is the power of the Lamb image because no mammal seems more defenseless than the Lamb, as we see, for example, in the description of the Suffering Servant, who is "like a lamb that is led to the slaughter" (Isa. 53:7). But it is this very Lamb that will gain the victory: his adversaries "will make war on the Lamb, and the Lamb will conquer them, for he is Lord of lords and King of kings" (Rev. 17:14).

In history, this has always been the pathway for God's people as well. If the serpent's seed bruises the heel of the woman's seed, this is true for all the Abels of history that have been killed by the Cains: "... all the righteous blood shed on earth, from the blood of righteous Abel to the blood of Zechariah" (Matt. 23:35). But in the end, the Abels will triumph together with the King of kings (see the continuation of Rev. 17:14 NIV, "... and with him will be his called, chosen and faithful followers"). "The God of peace will soon crush Satan under your feet" (Rom. 16:20).

God's faithful have usually been the underdogs of history, with the exception of a few truly faithful kings and presidents. This is one of the mysteries of history: the people of the *omnipotent* God have usually been the weak and the small. "It was not because you were more in number than any other people that the Lord set his love on you and chose you, for you were the fewest of all peoples" (Deut. 7:7). But: "The least one shall become a clan, and the smallest one a mighty nation; I am the Lord; in its time I will hasten it" (Isa. 60:22). Here, number is also a metaphor for power and strength: "the kingdom and the dominion and the greatness of the kingdoms under the whole heaven shall be given to the people of the saints of the Most High; their kingdom shall be an everlasting kingdom, and all dominions shall serve and obey them" (Dan. 7:27 note).

## The Heidelberg Catechism

From its outset, Reformed thinking strongly underlined the sovereign will of God in history. Thus, the Heidelberg Catechism (Sunday 10) speaks of the "almighty and ever present power of God by which he upholds, as with his hand, heaven and earth and all creatures, and so rules them that leaf and blade, rain and *drought*, fruitful and *lean years*, food and drink, health and *sickness*, prosperity and *poverty*—all things, in fact, come to us not by chance but from his fatherly hand" (italics added). Here, only two options are mentioned: things come by chance, or from God. Of course, in principle more options are conceivable. A third option is that lean years, sickness, and poverty are often the result of Man's own negligence. Abuse of the land leads to meager harvests; abuse of the body (lack of sufficient movement, rest, and relaxation) leads to all kinds of diseases; laziness leads to poverty (Prov. 20:4; 24:30-31). (Of course, we should not reverse these statements, as not all diseases or poverty come from abuse or laziness.)

A fourth option, which is not mentioned in the Heidelberg Catechism either, is that trouble comes from Satan. Think of the woman in Jesus' time who was bent over and could not straighten herself (Luke 13:10-17). Scripture tells us that she had "a disabling spirit" and that Satan had "bound" her. It was not God's "fatherly hand" that had given her this disease but Satan (although God allowed it, of course). It was not God's "fatherly hand" that had made Job sick but Satan: "And the LORD said to Satan, 'Behold, he is in your hand; only spare his life'. So Satan went out from the presence of the LORD and struck Job with loathsome sores from the sole of his foot to the crown of his head" (Job 2:6-7). Scripture also speaks of "mute" and "deaf spirits," that is, demonic angels of Satan that make people mute or deaf (Luke 11:14; Matt. 9:32-33; Mark 9:25). Peter said that Jesus healed "all who were oppressed by the devil" (Acts 10:38), that is, sickness can be an oppression by Satan. Also note the connection elsewhere: "their diseases left them and the evil spirits came out of them" (Acts 19:12). And whatever the "thorn" was which was given to the Apostle Paul "in the flesh" (there are dozens of explanations for it), at any rate he described it as "a messenger of Satan to harass me" (2 Cor. 12:7). Paul delivered the apostate "man to Satan for the destruction of the flesh" (1 Cor. 5:5).

According to the Heidelberg Catechism, transcendent causes in history are simple: all things that "happen" to us come from God. In my view, a more complete view of transcendent causes in history also includes the wise or foolish decisions that people make in their own hearts, and that often have dramatic historical consequences, as well as the activities of Satan and his angels. Of course, all such things occur with the "permission" of God; but that is not the same as saying that all things "come" to us from

God's fatherly hand. And please note, not only the good things but also the bad things (drought, lean years, sickness, and poverty) allegedly come directly from God. If everything comes from God, that also includes the bad things. Thus, American theologian and philosopher Gordon Clark (1902-1985) states very clearly in his book *Religion, Reason, and Revelation* (1961) that if a man gets drunk and shoots his family it was God's will that he did this (not just by God's permission). He explicitly added that God decrees not only moral deeds but also immoral ones.

## Danger of Determinism

In my opinion, this is a deterministic, almost fatalistic view. Theological determinism in its strictest form claims that all events that happen have been pre-ordained to happen by an omnipotent and omniscient God ("predestination"). It does not matter whether we believe that God has decreed everything before the foundation of the world, or that he decrees certain things throughout human history. In either case, everything that happens is God's personal work. He not only (passively) *allows* it, he (actively) *does* it.

Imagine the consequences of such a view! Would deterministic Christians also say that the Holocaust came to the Jews "from God's fatherly hand"? Was it God's *active work*? It is already difficult enough to say that God *allowed* the murder of six million Jews. But how can we ever assert that it was God himself who killed them? How could such atrocious outrages be harmonized with God's goodness and love? Moreover, what possible "divine goal" could have been served by the Holocaust? It is true that without the Holocaust there would probably have been no revival of the Jewish identity or of the Jewish state. But could an omnipotent God not have reached this goal without sacrificing six million innocent victims? (They were indeed innocent; it was mainly the very pious Eastern European Jews who were murdered, not the far more secularized Jews of North America.) Moreover, what remains of the responsibility of the Nazis if everything they did had been planned by God, perhaps even before the foundation of the world?

In my view (for a fuller discussion, see my dogmatic work *Het plan van God*, 2008), criminals are fully and solely responsible for their own actions. These actions do *not* belong to the counsels of God; we do not even have to design a theodicy, that is, to find some meaning of evil actions in the ways of God in order to "justify" him. Clark is wrong: it is outrageous to assert that God has ever decreed immoral deeds. This is a confusion of God's counsels and God's ways (see chapter 7 for more details). Even in his *ways* God does not perform or decree immoral deeds. It is only Satan and his angels, or sinful humans, who decide on and commit immorality. Clark's position is a typical consequence of Scholastic rationalism within theology, that is, an overheated logic that leads to absurdities. God may *allow* immoral deeds in his *ways*, if they help to attain a higher goal, but he never *decrees* immoral deeds in his *counsel*.

In the Bible we see several cases where believers knew how to distinguish between God's actions and Satan's. The Apostle Paul dared to say that "Satan hindered us" (1 Thess. 2:18)—not God (as, e.g., in Acts 16:7). We might add to this that God *allowed* this hindrance of Paul, so long as we maintain that Satan was the primary agent. Evil deeds do not result from the will of God but they are the consequences of the freedom that God bestowed on his creatures, both spiritual powers and humans. Such deeds belong to the deep dark elements of history, which God makes possible because of human freedom, and at the same time, he *wages war* against the powers of evil in his *ways* in order to ultimately realize in his omnipotence his glorious *counsel*.

The difference between God's counsel and God's ways is of the greatest importance. His counsels are fixed and unassailable from the foundation of the world, but the ways through which God may realize his counsels can vary, depending on what the heavenly and earthly powers (angels, demons, humans) may do. It was God's *counsel* that Israel, who had been freed from Egypt, would one day enter the Promised Land. It belonged to God's *ways* that, because of their own sins, it took them forty years to reach this goal. Angels and humans have no influence whatsoever on God's counsel. But they do interact with God's ways through which he realizes his counsel.

Or, to take an example of a different kind, let us consider this verse: "God is our refuge and strength, a very present help in

## THE MEANING OF HISTORY

trouble" (Ps. 46:1). This means that it is not always God who *sends* us troubles in order to then be with us *in* these troubles. Troubles may come from various sources, but wherever they come from, we can count on God. God does not (always) *send* the waters and the fire, but when believers have to pass through them, he will be with them *in* the waters and the fire (Isa. 43:2). Let us look at an example involving water. It was not God who caused the storm on the lake but his adversary, who threatened his people in the boat. (If it was God who did it, how can the Gospel say that Jesus *rebuked* the wind and the waves?) But as it happened, Jesus was with the disciples in the boat so that they could not perish (Mark 4:37-41). Now let us turn to fire. It was not God who prepared the fiery furnace in Babylon; but when his followers were thrown into it, the Son of God was with them in the fire (Dan. 3:25 KJV). God does not always *send* the water and the fire, nor does he always *prevent* them; but he has promised to be with his people *in* the water and the fire. "Even though I walk through the valley of the shadow of death, I will fear no evil, for *you are with me*" (Ps. 23:4, italics added).

## Conflicting Views

God's sovereignty does not necessarily imply that he has ordained every event that occurs at any time or place whatsoever in history, because this would annul the freedom and responsibility of Man. Rather, I am convinced God has sovereignly chosen to create people who can make their own decisions. Of course, there *are* many events that are directly brought about by God; we find a clear-cut example of this in the story of Jonah, where God hurled a great wind upon the sea, God appointed a fish, a plant, a worm, and a wind (Jonah 1:4,17; \4:6-8). And of course, people can only make decisions within the boundaries that God has set around them. But at least we can never make him responsible for any evil.

Much evil is committed by people in accordance with to their own free decisions. At the same time, God can use these evil actions in his ways to realize his counsel anyway. As Augustine put it, not all things are directly *caused* by God—but nothing happens *apart from* God. Let us compare this saying of Jesus: "Not one [sparrow] will fall to the ground apart from your Father" (Matt. 10:29). Translating "outside your Father's will" (NIV note; Belgic Confession, Art. 13: "... nor a sparrow, can fall to the ground, without the will of our Father") may be confusing, or even simply wrong. God did not necessarily *cause* the sparrow's fall but he *knew* about it, or, to say it a bit more strongly, he *allowed* it. At best we could perhaps put it this way: God did not *want* the sparrow to fall, and yet it did not happen apart from his *will*. Because of his love and holiness, God can never want evil. Because of his omnipotence, nothing can happen beyond his control. This is not necessarily an inner contradiction as long as we realize that any statement about God's will is only an approximation. That is, we leave the two statements intact, alongside each other, without playing the one off against the other.

A perfectly good God can never want evil to happen as such; no evil can ever be a part of his *counsel*. But it is certainly conceivable for evil to be allowed as part of God's *ways*. As the Apostle Paul puts it, "We know that for those who love God all things work together for good" (Rom. 8:28). Thus, it is conceivable that a greater good (a "better world") could be reached by tolerating evil in a certain measure and for a certain time. In other words, it might very well be the case that, without allowing some amount of evil in God's *ways*, a realization of his *counsel* would not be possible. It is also conceivable that that which seems evil to us is in fact part of a greater whole that is good. Or it is conceivable that in some peculiar way it might conflict with God's nature to annul a certain evil at a certain time, which might be too early, because this might prevent a greater good from coming.

To mention one example of this kind of reasoning (which I consider to be a fair approach to this extremely complicated subject), the church father Ambrose (337-397) spoke of the fall of Adam as "fortunate" in that his sin brought more good to humanity than if he had remained innocent. The church father Augustine (354-430) wrote: "God judged it better to bring good out of evil than not to permit any evil to exist." In Catholic liturgy, this thought reappeared in the words: *O felix culpa quae talem et tantum meruit habere redemptorem* ("O happy guilt that merited to have such, and so great, a Redeemer"). Thomas Aquinas (1225-1274) quoted this

# THE MEANING OF HISTORY

when explaining that God allowed evils to happen in order to bring a greater good out of them.

## Careful Weighing

We have to argue very carefully here because we can easily go astray in this minefield. On the one hand, Hyper-Calvinism actually denies the responsibility of Man, making God the cause of everything that happens, and thus also making him in effect responsible for the fall of Man. This is wrong. Accepting Man's freedom and responsibility does not threaten God's sovereignty at all for the simple reason that it was God himself who sovereignly decided to grant Man a certain freedom. I repeat, evil can be part of God's *ways* but it is never part of God's *counsel*. Evil comes from celestial powers (demons, angels of Satan) or from human beings. On the other hand, Arminianism (including what today is called Open Theism) actually denies God's counsel, for instance, by reducing divine predestination to God's foreknowledge, or even by limiting God's foreknowledge as such.

In opposition to both views, I claim that the concept of God's predestination is fully warranted in the sense that the evil decisions of demons and humans can change God's *ways* but never God's *counsels*. At the same time, God's love is fully maintained in that a God who truly loves Man grants him a certain freedom so that he can voluntarily return God's love. God's love is also maintained in that his counsels of love are carried out no matter what sinful Man may undertake.

A verse such as the following is often misunderstood: "Does disaster come to a city, unless the Lord has done it?" (Amos 3:6) is often misunderstood. Actually, the text says *the* city (KJV); the prophet is speaking here about a specific disaster that is coming over a specific city. The verse does not make the universal statement that all disasters, always and everywhere, are directly caused by God. Many disasters (such as famines, floods, volcanic eruptions, fires, and earthquakes) are consequences of certain natural laws, while others are the product of human failure, negligence, and sometimes the evil intentions of people. Therefore, I repeat, it is *not* true that all suffering comes directly from God.

## PROBING THE PAST

God's omnipotence becomes obvious not so much in the fact that he *causes* all suffering but in the fact that he *checks* and *combats* it, in his ways and at his time. Every time Jesus healed the sick, freed the possessed or raised the dead, he gave a foretaste of the full salvation that will arrive one day: "If I cast out devils by the Spirit of God, then the kingdom of God is come unto you" (Matt. 12:28).

Apart from Christian views such as Hyper-Calvinism or Arminianism, non-Christians have also thought about the relationship between evil and the alleged Deity. Many of them have used the tremendous amount of evil in history as an argument against God. How can a supposedly omnipotent and loving God not only allow evil, but allow *so much evil*? Such critics make this argument especially by speaking of evil perpetrated against the "innocent." It is "poor Man" who suffers, and especially "poor children," while God (so they say) sits idly by, looking on. How can a God who is supposed to be both omnipotent and full of love allow innocent children to undergo so much undeserved evil?

When we consider this from a superficial point of view, we can have some sympathy for such a criticism. Yet, the argument I have just mentioned is quite inconsistent because, on the one hand, non-Christians love to emphasize the freedom and autonomy of Man against the (alleged) Deity. They love to run their own affairs without any interference from "beyond." On the other hand, they are immediately ready to blame the (alleged) Deity for all human suffering, in spite of the fact that, in the majority of the cases of suffering, human responsibility (negligence, violence) plays a role. That does not work. One cannot have both: postulating Man's autonomy as well as blaming God for human suffering.

It is not God but *people* who bring wars, violence, pain, grief, accidents and even diseases on other people, or on themselves. It is Man who brings floods on himself by not taking care of dams and dikes, or by taking insufficient care of them. It is Man who must take the blame for the fact that an earthquake of a certain strength causes only limited damage in California, while in a Third World country a similar earthquake causes tremendous damage. It is Man who, through economic or agricultural mismanagement as well as the selfish refusal to help the poor, makes himself co-responsible for famines. And so on. There is food enough in the world to feed all its inhabitants. The fact that this food does not reach all inhabitants is not bad luck, nor is it God's fault, nor is it even the devil's work—it is Man's fault.

Only a rigorous theological determinism can attribute all disasters, without any distinction, to God, using the argument that everything that happens has been determined by God in his eternal counsel. This kind of theology falls victim to its own overheated logic, in which only certain parts of Scripture are brought forward, while others are discarded.

## The Best Possible World

God is a perfectly good and wise God. There is no necessity within him that dictates why he should create the world. But *if* he decides to do it, even if it is a world that contains rational, moral beings, it must necessarily be the best possible world that he can produce, or at least it must possess the *potential* to become the best possible world. An omnipotent and omniscient, perfectly good and wise God cannot do with less. Indeed, it is possible to argue plausibly that a morally perfect world supposes a specific type of historical process that leads to its attainment. This is a world in which people are morally perfectly free but never do evil. The long historical road *to* this perfect world is one on which people were morally perfectly free but were able to choose evil, and unfortunately did so, right at the beginning (Gen. 3).

It can also be argued plausibly that the process through which this morally perfect world comes must contain sufficient evil to teach Man how to distinguish between good and evil, to avoid evil and strive for the good. It is far more difficult to see how a morally perfect world could ever be reached *without* this evil. This means that Christians believe that no world satisfies the conditions for attaining a better world better than our present world. The all-good and all-wise God is the best—and only—guarantee that the present world in Christ will ultimately pass into the perfect world.

In this connection, it is important to point to the tree of the knowledge of good and evil in the Garden of Eden (Gen. 2:9, 17; cf. 3:5, 22). Before the fall, Adam could not be called "good, just

## PROBING THE PAST

and holy" (*contra* Belgic Confession, Art. 14) because in that case he would have had knowledge of good and evil even before he ate from the tree of the knowledge of good and evil. He was *innocent*, which is something very different—innocent like a new-born baby. Before the fall, Man did not know evil, but at the same time he did not know the "good, just and holy" either; finite beings can know good only in contrast with evil, and vice versa. Therefore, we cannot even say that before the fall Man already had a conscience (from *scientia*, "knowledge"). It was not his conscience that was the measuring-rod for his obedience, but simply submitting himself to the clear commandment of God. It was only the eating of the forbidden fruit that *gave* Man a conscience (cf. Gen. 3:8), that is, knowledge of good and evil. This was not in an absolute sense—for only the infinite God knows good and evil in a perfect way—but he did know now the relative difference between the two.

What is more, he who had been innocent before had now become evil. He had come to learn evil, but this evil now thoroughly characterized his new condition. In contrast with this evil, he now also knew the good—but this had become an unreachable ideal for him. *This could be called the essence of history*: Man's way back to the good, which is ultimately on a level much higher than the level of innocence he had lost. In the end, Man will *learn* what true holiness is because he has been so familiar with unholiness, both in his own life and in the lives of others. He will *learn* what true goodness is because he has been so familiar with wickedness. He will *learn* what true righteousness is because he has been so familiar with unrighteousness. In the Garden of Eden, Man could not possibly know what happiness (or, if you like, bliss) was—he can and will learn true bliss only through a lot of misery. For finite Man, there is apparently no other way.

The infinite God does not need such a learning process, but we do. Only because we know what darkness is do we learn to know and appreciate the light. Only because we know what hatred is do we learn to know and appreciate love. Only because we know what death is do we learn to know and appreciate life. Only through darkness, hatred and death will we ultimately come to the light, love and life of the Kingdom of God (cf. chapter 8). We could not possibly know what light, love and life are without hav-

# THE MEANING OF HISTORY

ing been familiar with darkness, hatred and death: "... so that they may turn from darkness to light and from the power of Satan to God" (Acts 26:18). "He has delivered us from the domain of darkness and transferred us to the kingdom of his beloved Son" (Col. 1:13). God "called you out of darkness into his marvelous light" (1 Pet. 2:9).

The *atheist* can simply deny all meaning and purpose within the cosmos—but he cannot truly *live* with such a view. Every person lives *as if* what he says and does is, to a certain extent, meaningful, even if this meaning would not reach any further than his egocentric self-interest. The *Hyper-Calvinist* denies the free will of Man—he chose this view using his own free will for it does not follow from the Scriptural data—and in a sense he holds a cheap view, in which Man has no freedom at all, and everything is firmly enclosed in God's eternal counsel. The traditional *Arminian* and the *open theist* also hold an easy view; here, everything depends on the free choices that free people make, and God cannot be blamed for anything. In my opinion, I myself have chosen the most difficult standpoint of all, in that I wish to maintain both God's absolute sovereignty and Man's freedom and responsibility, even though the two seem to be in conflict with each other.

## Test of the Best

What is the best possible world to which God is on the way throughout history? How can we determine what is "the best," the very best, which in this history of the world comes to light? It is a principle with God that, in order to prove that a certain matter is truly the best, it has to undergo the heaviest trials. We see this in history in a striking—and touching—manner in the path God travels with Israel from its very beginning, in which he made use of all the well known "elements" of Antiquity, i.e., the trial through the *earth* (one of the torturing methods was the burying alive of Jews); through *fire* (from the fiery furnace in Babylon [Dan. 3] to the incinerators in the Nazis' destruction camps); through *air* (the gas chambers); and through *water* (already in Egypt the male infants were drowned; Exod. 1).

It happened the same way with Job, who was one of the most

striking "types" of Israel in the Old Testament. The *earth* dwellers robbed his herds (Job 1:14-15, 17). The *"fire* of God" burnt his sheep and shepherds (1:16). A heavy tempest (*air*) destroyed the house where his children were, and killed them (1:18-19). And Job's friend Eliphaz could say of him: "Snares are all around you, and sudden terror overwhelms you, or darkness, so that you cannot see, and a flood of *water* covers you" (Job 22:10-11). Nowhere more clearly than in Job do we see that the trial of the *best* ("blameless and upright, one who feared God and turned away from evil," 1:1, 8; 2:3) is necessarily the *heaviest* trial. This is the kernel of all anti-Semitism: the hatred and envy towards the very best of God. If the true Israel is the best that world history has ever known, then the trial of Israel is the heaviest that world history has ever seen. God triumphs over Satan in the fact that the best that he has produced can survive under the worst circumstances—albeit, of course, through the grace of God.

This is revealed in the highest [clearest] manner in Christ, who has strikingly been called the true Self of Israel. In the midst of Israel he was the best that that nation had ever seen. Therefore, his trial was really the heaviest. The *water* of all God's breakers and waves went over him (Ps. 42:7; cf. 69:2). The *fire* of God's wrath burnt in his bones (102:3). Over him raged the storm (*air*) of God's judgment (cf. 83:14-16). And he descended to the lower parts of the *earth* (Eph. 4:9). His sufferings as *atoning* sufferings, blotting out Man's sins under the judging hand of God, have been unique. However, at the same time, in all his sufferings that men caused him to undergo, he made himself perfectly one with the true remnant of Israel. This applies to Psalms 69 and 102 but, also for psalms of suffering such as Psalms 22, 41-44, 88, and others. He is with his people in the *water* and in the *fire* (Isa. 43:2), he is with them in the *storm* (Mark 4:35-51), and with them he is "crushed to the ground" (*earth*) (Ps. 143:3; cf. 17:11).

An *atheist* is not able to discover any meaning or purpose in a history such as that of Job, Israel, Christ, or the many "righteous Abels" (cf. Matt. 23:35), just as he does not see any meaning or purpose in world history as a whole. What struck Job was just "bad luck." And if you can pass through this world without too much misery, you are "lucky."

A *Hyper-Calvinist* does not know how to handle the liberties

## THE MEANING OF HISTORY

Job takes and the objections he puts forward when reasoning with God; this approach conflicts so strongly with the resignation and acquiescence that fits the Hyper-Calvinist view of history. How could Job have protested if his vicissitudes had already been determined before the foundation of the world? In 1990, Anson Laytner published his book *Arguing with God: A Jewish Tradition*, in which he gave many more biblical examples of faithful servants of God who nonetheless protested against him, such as Abraham (Gen. 18), Moses (Exod. 33), Elijah (1 Kings 19), and Jeremiah (Jer. 20). These men never doubted God's *counsel*, but they certainly challenged his *ways* openly and audaciously. Such men could never have been Hyper-Calvinists, whose attitude of resignation and acquiescence is much closer to that of the priest Eli, who said: "It is the LORD. Let him do what seems good to him" (1 Sam. 3:18)—whereas the judgment of God to which he referred was not simply God's counsel but largely Eli's own fault.

## Chance

Other philosophical approaches are faced with the opposite problem of having to believe that all Job's vicissitudes were only and entirely dependent on his own choices, *or* on coincidence or bad luck. Here again, history can only be understood as a fine balance between God's absolute sovereignty and Man's freedom and responsibility. However, the question may come up whether all events in history are determined by just these three factors: God's acting, Satan's acting, and Man's acting. Is there nothing in between, such as the role of chance, hazard, accidence, coincidence, or arbitrariness?

Many orthodox Christians would hasten to respond that nothing happens by chance in human history. Nevertheless, the Bible speaks several times of chance, or similar concepts. For instance, Ruth *"happened* to come to the part of the field belonging to Boaz" (Ruth 2:3, lit. "her chance chanced upon," ASV note). "If a bird's nest *chance* to be before thee in the way in any tree..." (Deut. 22:6 KJV); "it happened to us *by coincidence"* (1 Sam. 6:9); "time and *chance* happen to them all" (Eccl. 9:11). Jesus also used the term: "By *chance* a priest was going down that road" (Luke 10:31).

Several of these examples clearly show that "chance" is a relative idea. Let us first take the example of Ruth, in whose story it is quite obvious that God was leading her way all the time. When she came home from the field of Boaz, her mother-in-law Naomi did not say that Ruth had been lucky, but that the kindness of the Lord had apparently not forsaken the living or the dead (Ruth 2:20). What at first had looked like chance turned out to be nothing but the kindness of the Lord.

Even though Jesus himself used the words "by chance" (Greek *kata synkyrian*) in the parable of the good Samaritan, apparently this was simply a way of telling us how things looked in the eyes of Man. Seen from God's viewpoint, everything happened under his guidance (without affecting the priest's and the Levite's responsibility). God had something better in store for the man who had fallen among the robbers.

The statement of Solomon, which says that "time and chance happen to them all" (Eccl. 9:11), must be seen in the light of the fact that the author purposely limits his deliberations to things that are "under the sun" (see also Eccl. 9:9, 13). This is like the viewpoint of the modern naturalist, who can believe only the things that belong to his empirical world. Within this limited horizon, "time and chance" seem indeed to rule almightily. But later in the Book, Solomon widens his horizon, and brings in God, his judgment and his commandments (11:9; 12:1, 13-14). When we examine the matter from this transcendent perspective, there can no longer be any room for chance and coincidence.

## The Role of Satan

Do God's absolute sovereignty and Man's freedom and responsibility make up the whole story? What can we add here with respect to Satan's role (a problem I already briefly touched upon before)? In the Hyper-Calvinist view, where all things have been predestined by God, the devil too, even though he has his own will, cannot do anything else than that to which God has destined him. In reality, God has allowed to Satan, just as he did to Man, a certain amount of room for maneuvering. Thus, Satan can play his own active role in world history. God has even sov-

## THE MEANING OF HISTORY

ereignly allowed him to actively hinder him (God) from time to time. A striking example of this can be found in Daniel 10. As a response to Daniel's prayer, God sent him an angel, but in the spiritual world this celestial messenger was delayed by the powers of darkness for no less than three weeks. Apparently, this is *possible*: an evil power tries with all its strength to frustrate God's will, and manages to do so for three weeks. Indeed, in the end he has to give in, but nevertheless he has had the opportunity to show his strength.

There is not the slightest ground for the claim that all Satan's obstructions, or even some of them, have been predestined by God, either before the foundation of the world, or during the course of history. A striking example of this is the parable of the darnel (Matt. 13:24-30). When the servants asked the master of the house how the darnel got among the weeds, the master answered: "An enemy has done this" (Matt. 13:28). In the explanation of the parable, Jesus makes clear that this enemy is the devil (v. 39). In no way can the parable be explained as if the answer would have to be: "The master of the house has allowed the enemy to do this." Even less can the parable be interpreted as saying: "Actually, the master of the house decided it himself, and he used his enemy to carry it out."

If everything that the devil does had been predestined by God, there would be no question of any spiritual battle whatsoever. However, both in the Bible and in our practical experience this battle is very real. People, but especially the spiritual powers of darkness, have their own range of action assigned to them to obstruct the work of God. The believer who can distinguish between "spirits" (cf. 1 Cor. 12:10) knows where and when this is the case. Luke writes: "They went through the region of Phrygia and Galatia, having been forbidden by the Holy Spirit to speak the word in Asia. And when they had come up to Mysia, they attempted to go into Bithynia, but the Spirit of Jesus did not allow them" (Acts 16:6-7). But in another case, Paul says decidedly: "We wanted to come to you—I, Paul, again and again—but Satan hindered us" (1 Thess. 2:18). Imagine if we had to believe that it does not matter at all whether we are hindered by the Holy Spirit or by Satan—because God has supposedly predetermined everything anyway... No, being hindered by the Holy Spirit is always for a *good* purpose—the Lord wanted to lead Paul to Europe—but being hindered by Satan is always for a *bad* purpose, Satan obstructing the work of the gospel.

Satan can explicitly take his own initiatives, but always insofar as God allows him. A well-known case is Job 1-2, where Satan robs Job of everything, even including his health; but he cannot do more than God permits. Thus, we understand the discrepancy between 2 Samuel 24:1 ("the anger of *the LORD* was kindled against Israel, and he incited David against them, saying, 'Go, number Israel and Judah'") and 1 Chronicles 21:1 ("Then Satan *stood* against Israel and incited David to number Israel"). Satan is the seducer here, but only insofar as God allows him.

Thus it is in 2 Corinthians 12:7, where Paul is harassed by "a messenger of Satan," although the Lord apparently allows it (v. 8-9). The angel of Satan did the harassing with a *bad* purpose, namely, to obstruct Paul's ministry; but God allowed it with a *good* purpose, namely, to keep Paul "from becoming conceited." If Christians would think in a less deterministic manner, and more in terms of God's *ways* (not only his *counsels*), they would take more account of the power that Satan possesses, and of the spiritual battle in which they as believers are involved: the battle between the Kingdom of God and the kingdom of Satan (see chapter 8).

## A Chess Match

God is like a chess grandmaster, Man is his very moderate opponent, and history is like a great game of chess (the simile comes from American theologian Greg Boyd [b. 1957].) God has sovereignly decided to play this game, and to respond to Man's awkward and foolish moves, which are an insult to his genius. Time and again, he has to adapt the game to the moves of his mediocre, clumsy opponent, which may lead to disappointment and irritation on his side. But he is so tremendously superior that, in whatever manner, the grandmaster's victory is certain from the very start of the game.

The grandmaster does not demonstrate his greatness by "determining" the moves of his opponent, as theological determinism would have it with respect to God. In other words, God, the grandmaster, is not busy playing a match whose moves have already been fixed on forehand. No, he wins by optimally anticipating Man's moves, and by always responding to them in an adequate and sovereign way. His sovereignty does not rule out the free choices of his opponent, but shows itself in the way it supremely overrules the opponent's moves, and reaches its own planned goal.

God's ultimate victory is just as certain as his counsel. But the ways of history though which the victory is gained and his counsel realized are *un*certain because they depend on God's opponents. He has sovereignly chosen to make the match dependent not only on his own perfect expertise but also on the moves of his opponents. It is certainly true that the opponents determine to a certain extent the moves of the grandmaster. But that has no influence on the ultimate outcome of the game. This outcome remains established in God's *counsel*; his moves are the *ways* in which he realizes his counsel. As sure as it is that the wicked—humans and spiritual powers—can heavily obstruct God's ways, so sure is it that they will finally succumb to him.

History is not a kind of script or libretto, written before the foundation of the world, and rigidly followed throughout history; it is rather like an enormous fight in the battlefield. In a theatre play or an opera, battles taking place on the stage are carefully orchestrated. Both parties make the prescribed moves, and utter the prescribed statements. But it is not like that on a real battlefield, or, more generally, in history. There, not a single move has been prescribed by some playwright. All moves are open. The only thing that is fixed is the outcome of the battle, not the moves needed to reach that outcome.

# Chapter Four
# PATTERNS, PURPOSE AND POWERS OF HISTORY

Let us begin with a simple question: does the word "history" occur in the Bible? The ESV has it in 2 Chronicles 9:29 ("history of Nathan"), where other translations have "records," "book," or "account"; literally it is simply "words."

## Toledoth

A far more interesting passage is Genesis 2:4, which says: "These are the generations of the heavens and the earth when they were created." The NKJV reads "history" instead, and gives "generations" in the footnote. The NKJV also reads "history" in Genesis 37:2: "This is the history of Jacob." In both verses of Genesis, the Hebrew word is *toledoth*, which also occurs in 5:1; 6:9; 10:1; 11:10, 27; 25:12, 19; 36:1, 9. Apart from 5:1 ("this is the book of the generations of Adam"), the formula is repeated ten times as follows: "These are the *toledoth* of..."

The word *toledoth* comes from the Hebrew verb *y-l-d*, "to bring forth, to give birth to, to generate, to father" (*yēled* = "child"). Thus, the verb can be used both for men and women who are becoming parents. *Toledoth* in Genesis usually is best understood as "generations" in the sense of "those that have been generated (brought forth, fathered)." Thus, "the *toledoth* of Noah" (6:9) can be understood as: "the account of Noah's family line" (cf. 11:10 NKJV), or shorter, "the account (record, history) of Noah (and his family)." Genesis 2:4 is a little different because here the meaning does not seem to be "that which is brought forth by the heavens and the earth," but rather the reverse "the account of how the heavens and the earth themselves were brought forth." The word "history" fits here quite well, but also in most other places in Genesis; that is, the Book of Genesis contains the history of (the beginnings of) heaven and earth, but also the history of Noah and his sons, of Terah, of Ishmael and Isaac, of Esau and Jacob.

Genesis is a book of histories (origins, generations). These are not just histories of individuals but of family lines. It is the book of the histories of whole generations, of whole nations (Israel, but also Edom, Midian and other Arab desert people), even of the heavens and the earth, all in the process of being formed. The Septuagint, the ancient Greek translation of the Jewish Bible, gave the book its well-known name: *Genesis*, which means "birth, becoming, formation, creation, generation." There is hardly any important element in the Bible whose birth and origin we cannot find in the Book of Genesis. Even the New Testament Church is already there, albeit only—provided you are an adherent of typology—in the form of types (for example, Eve, Rebekah, Leah, and Asenath).

If we keep the stem *y-l-d* in mind, then we can take "history" in the sense of a continual becoming, a permanent rise of new things, and a continual further development of older things. At the same time, the perpetually recurring phrase "These are the *toledoth* of..." points to repetition. *L'histoire se répète* ("History repeats itself"), as the French saying goes (see previous chapter). History in Genesis is a linear process, from the beginning of the world to the beginning of Israel as a nation. But it is also a cyclical process in that every time we encounter new *toledoth* a new family line begins. Seen from a linear perspective, everything in history is fundamentally new. Seen from a cyclical perspective, history infinitely repeats itself. As King Solomon said: "There is nothing new under the sun" (Eccl. 1:9b). The reason is simply that people remain basically the same; time and again they commit the same sins, and endeavor to do the same good things. All empires and all dictators look very much alike.

Yet, no two phases of history are ever identical; in that sense it is equally true that everything is always perfectly new in history. And in the succession of all these new things, historians try to discover patterns that may give us a deeper insight into the progress of history. At any rate, such patterns are clearly visible in biblical history. Notice how, at the end of the Babylonian Exile, God announces "new things," wholly new developments in the history of Israel that they had never seen before: "Behold, the former things have come to pass, and new things I now declare" (Isa. 42:9). "Remember not the former things, nor consider the things of old. Behold, I am doing a new thing" (43:18-19). "From this time forth I announce to you new things, hidden things that you have not known" (48:6b).

## Cyclical Views

In the previous chapter, I have distinguished four key questions that must be dealt with in any philosophy of history. They are questions about:
    (a) the *meaning* or *arbitrariness* of history;
    (b) *patterns* in history, such as cyclical or linear, or a combination of them;
    (c) *teleology* (design, purpose, goal) in history;
    (d) the *powers*, that is, the *driving forces* of history: natural or supernatural; determinism or free choice.

In the previous chapter, we have dealt with the meaning of history from a Christian point of view, versus the arbitrariness of history as seen from various secular points of view. In this chapter, we will deal with the other three key questions I have mentioned.

The second question listed above is this: what are the possible *patterns* in history, such as cyclical or linear patterns, or a combination of them? Some historians and philosophers of history, such as the German philosopher Arthur Schopenhauer (1788-1860) or the English historian Herbert Fisher (1865-1940), did not believe that the course of history exhibits any pattern at all. However, they form a minority. Usually, historians do believe that the course of history follows a certain pattern. They differ sharply, though, in their opinions about the nature as well as the extent of that pattern. With regard to the latter point, some historians claim that we should not pursue historiography any further than describing the vicissitudes of the various nations and states. Others believe they can distinguish larger units in history. In that case, people speak of cultures, or civilizations, which include a number of nations or states.

## PROBING THE PAST

Apart from this, we need to answer an even more essential question; in fact, I believe it is one of the most essential in historiography. That is the question as to how the various cultures are interrelated in space and time. One possibility is the linear approach, chosen by the church father Augustine (354-430); that is the line from creation to the new heavens and the new earth. However, a cyclical one is also conceivable. In Antiquity, such an approach was defended by the Greek historian Herodotus (c. 485-425 BC), the Greek philosopher Plato (429-347 BC), the Greco-Roman philosophical school of the Stoics, the Roman philosopher Cicero (106-43 BC), and in more recent times, historians such as the German Oswald Spengler (1880-1936) and the English Arnold Toynbee (1889-1975).

In the Books of Daniel and Revelation, with their succession of four world empires (Babylonian, Medo-Persian, Greco-Macedonian, and Roman), each rising, flourishing, and declining, the authors seemingly follow a cyclical approach, but that only appears to be the case. In the succession of these empires, from gold through silver and bronze to iron, the linear pattern becomes clearly obvious, especially in the fact that this succession works its way to a definite climax, namely, the coming of the Son of Man and the establishment of his everlasting Kingdom.

Cyclical views of history focus especially on the rise and fall of great empires or civilizations, without bothering too much about the far more difficult—and fascinating—question as to a possible "linear" view, from the beginning to the end of history (the "last day"; John 6:39 etc.). The Italian historian and philosopher Niccolò Machiavelli (1469-1527) set the tone with his *Discorsi sopra la prima deca di Tito Livio* ("Discourses on the First Ten Books of Titus Livy," completed 1519), in which he analyzed the decline of the Roman Empire. This theme was picked up and developed further by the English historian Edward Gibbon (1737-1794) in his famous work *The History of the Decline and Fall of the Roman Empire* (completed 1789). This work was placed on the Roman Catholic *Index of Prohibited Books* because of his savage attack on Christianity.

In more recent times, we find similar cyclical approaches—views in which history is seen as a succession of rises and declines—in the works of historians and philosophers of history,

## PATTERNS, PURPOSE AND POWERS OF HISTORY

such as the Russian Nikolay Danilevsky (1822-1885, especially in his *Rossiia i Europa* ("Russia and Europe," 1869); the German Oswald Spengler (1880-1936), especially in his *Der Untergang des Abendlandes* ("The Decline of the West", 1918-1922); and more recently the British-American historian Paul M. Kennedy (b. 1945), especially in *The Rise and Fall of the Great Powers* (1987).

## Linear Views

Besides these cyclical approaches, the period of the Enlightenment, with its optimistic idea of progress, afterwards coupled with historicism (see chapter 2), produced a number of linear views of history but, unlike the traditional Christian views, they were strictly secular. Great examples were secular philosophers such as:

(a) The Germans: Immanuel Kant (1724-1804) with his *Idee zu einer allgemeinen Geschichte in weltbürgerlicher Absicht* ("Idea for a Universal History with a Cosmopolitan Purpose," 1784); Georg W.F. Hegel (1770-1831) with his *Phänomenologie des Geistes* ("Phenomenology of Spirit," 1809); and the German Karl Marx (1818-1883) with his *Das Kapital* ("Capital," 1867).

(b) The French: Nicolas de Condorcet (1743-1794) with his *Esquisse d'un tableau historique des progrès de l'esprit humain* ("Sketch for a Historical Picture of the Progress of the Human Spirit," 1795), and Auguste Come (1798-1857) with his *Discours sur l'esprit positif* ("A General View of Positivism," 1844).

Some of them (Comte, Hegel, Marx) believed that they could discern a "law" in history, which they believed could be used to point out the *overall* goal toward which history was heading from the beginning to a fixed end. The "law" of Comte (theological phase – metaphysical phase – positive phase) I have mentioned already. The "law" of Hegel was a *dialectical* one, which means in this case a development through contrasts. In his view, every *thesis* calls forth an *antithesis*, both of which eventually merge into a *synthesis*, which then itself becomes a "thesis" which serves as the start of a new developmental stage. Marx adopted this scheme, not (like Hegel) in a spiritualist way, but in a strictly materialist way.

The French Catholic theologian and paleontologist Pierre

## PROBING THE PAST

Teilhard de Chardin (1881-1955), in his *Le Phénomène humaine* ("The Phenomenon of Man," 1955), saw the world as constantly developing towards higher levels of material complexity and consciousness until it would reach Point Omega, which for him coincided with Christ. This was his specific version of a (liberal) Christian view of history.

Very different was the approach of the American political economist Francis Fukuyama (b. 1952), who in his book *The End of History* and the *Last Man* (1992) argued that the universal acceptance of Western liberal democracies and free market capitalism in his time might indicate that mankind was approaching the end point of its socio-cultural evolution, after which there was no longer anything to "develop."

Speaking of evolution, the most famous linear approach to history was the biological one developed by the English naturalist Charles R. Darwin (1809-1882). In his book *The Origin of Species* (1859), he presented his theory of (amoeba-to-Man) evolution in terms of natural selection. In 1871 he published *The Descent of Man*, in which he applied his theory to Man's alleged evolution from ape-like animals. The great importance of the *Origin* was that it was supposed to provide a natural scientific basis for the historicism which, at that moment, seemed to dominate all philosophical schools. Karl Marx and other philosophers of history saw in Darwin's book a powerful support for their own historical views.

At the same time, one could argue that Darwin's approach was not linear at all. The amoeba was no starting point, and Man is no ending point. Evolution is without any direction, without any goal or purpose. After Man, many more evolutionary stages might follow. They cannot be predicted because evolution is basically nothing but what the Book of Ecclesiastes suggests: a matter of "time and chance." Given enough time—life is supposed to be almost four billion years old—plus the random processes of nature, "all things are possible for one who believes" in evolution (cf. Mark 9:23).

Evolutionism was in perfect harmony with the historicism, naturalism, positivism, atheism, scientism, and cultural optimism of the nineteenth century. In this intellectual environment,

## PATTERNS, PURPOSE AND POWERS OF HISTORY

history was viewed the same way people viewed evolution: without any direction, without any goal or purpose, a matter of "time and chance."

## A Christian View: Linear and Cyclical

Of course, when we think of the Christian view of history, the linear aspect is the first thing that comes to the fore. As in the Jewish view, history begins with the creation of the world and ends with the Messianic Kingdom, and subsequently the new heavens and the new earth. In between, the key events in Jewish history (with, in my view, global consequences and significance) are the following:

(a) The Exodus from Egypt, the giving of the Law on Mount Sinai, and the entrance into the Promised Land (fifteenth or thirteenth century BC, depending on the chronology one prefers).

(b) The kingship of David and his descendents, and the building of the First Temple by David's son, King Solomon (tenth century BC).

(c) The Babylonian Exile, the return from captivity, and the building of the Second Temple under David's descendent Zerubbabel (sixth century BC).

(d) The destruction of the Second Temple; Israel's Diaspora; and rise of Judaism (first century AD).

(e) The Holocaust; the foundation of the State of Israel (twentieth century); and preparations for the Third Temple.

(f) The next stage, which is still in the future, is the coming of the Messiah.

*The* key events in Christian history are the birth, life, death, resurrection, ascension and glorification of Jesus Christ; the outpouring of the Holy Spirit; and the founding of the Christian Church (all occurring in the first century AD). The next stage, which is still in the future, is the second coming of the Messiah, Jesus Christ. The centrality of Christ in the Christian view of history has been wonderfully described by theologians such as the German Oscar Cullmann (1902-1999) in his *Christus und die Zeit* (English translation: Christ and Time, 1964), and the Dutch Hendrikus Berkhof (1914-1995) in his *Christus de zin der geschiedenis* (English translation: Christ the Meaning of History, 2004), and also by the Russian Christian existentialist philosopher Nikolai Berdyaev in his important work *The Meaning of History* (repr. 2006).

Both orthodox Jews and orthodox Christians look forward to the coming (for Christians, the coming again) of the Messiah, the anointed King of Israel, the Savior and Restorer of the world, and the Founder of the Messianic kingdom of majesty and glory, peace and righteousness (for more details, see chapter 8 below).

Besides this obviously linear aspect of the Christian view of history, there is also a certain cyclical aspect. We find this in the manner in which the history of Israel, and later of the Christian Church, is linked with the great world empires (for a more in-depth discussion, see chapter 6 below). These were:

1. The (Neo-)Assyrian Empire (934-609 BC); subsequently the four empires described in Daniel 2 and 7:
2. The (Neo-)Babylonian Empire (626-539 BC);
3. The Medo-Persian (or Achaemenid) Empire ([705?]-539-330 BC);
4. The Greco-Macedonian Empire (or Alexandrian Empire, after Alexander's death in 323 BC, followed by the Macedonian kingdom (flourished 359-158 BC with Alexander's decisive battle occurring in 330 BC), the Seleucid dynasty (323-64 BC) in Syria and the Ptolemaic kingdom (305-30 BC) in Egypt;
5. The Roman Empire: the pagan phase (30 BC- 312 AD);
6. The Roman Empire: the Christian phase (312-476 in the West and 330-1453 in the East);
7. The Messianic Kingdom.

## Teleology

We now come to the third question listed at the beginning of this chapter: is there a *teleology* to be discovered in history? In other words, does history exhibit design, and does it have an end-purpose, a goal? Many materialist, positivist, naturalist, atheist, and scientistic philosophers have answered these questions firmly in the negative. Among the thinkers who have made a contribution to the philosophy of history, I mention the following negativists: the German nihilist philosopher Friedrich Nietzsche (1844-1900), and some French philosophers of similar orientation: Louis Althusser (1918-1990), Michel Foucault (1926-1984) and Gilles Deleuze (1925-1995).

From a superficial standpoint, it may seem strange that the typical positive Enlightenment idea of *progress* in history can be combined with the idea that there is no design, no teleology in history. However, such a combination can certainly be made plausible because progress does not necessarily have a purpose. I point again to evolutionism as *the* example of this. Neo-Darwinian evolution is governed by random processes; all "design" in living nature is haphazard and accidental. The many steps that led from the amoeba to Man may be called progress, but from the evolutionary perspective there was no plan behind it. Some have argued that evolution is the necessary outcome of the character of natural laws but that is very different from a plan or design. This might mean that even the term "progress" could be rejected—unless one wishes to call the development of higher levels of order, complexity and information content "progress." That is a purely semantic question.

Of course, the question concerning a possible teleology in history is closely linked with the previous one concerning a possible pattern in history, whether that be cyclical or linear. That is, if history is to be viewed in a cyclical way, this can only involve limited goals, namely, the flourishing of distinct empires or civilizations. If history is to be viewed in a linear way, the goal of history can be very different:

(a) *Purely secular*: We can think of the realm of "the positive," that is the realm of pure science, which Auguste Comte discerned at the end of history, or the communist society that Karl Marx (stimulated by Darwin's evolutionism), had in mind as the culmination of history, or the worldwide liberal democracies and the worldwide free capitalist market that Francis Fukuyama considered to be the end of history.

(b) *Semi-secular*: One example is the Realm of the Spirit that Georg W.F. Hegel had in mind as the culmination of history.

(c) *Liberal Christian*: For instance, the Omega Point that Pierre Teilhard de Chardin saw as the end of history. Or we could think of the world of peace and justice—described in the vaguest terms—that certain liberal theologians expect, the contours of which are allegedly appearing already now. In this view, nothing is located in the near or distant future that in principle could not be realized already today: the liberation of non-white races, of the poor and needy (Gustavo Gutiérrez), of women, of homosexuals, etc. We may also remember the view of Reinhold Niebuhr, which I briefly described in chapter 1.

(d) *Traditional Christian*: Eschatology finds its culmination in the second coming of Jesus Christ, to be followed by the new heavens and the new earth.

(e) *Evangelical Christian*: Eschatology finds its culmination in the second coming of Jesus Christ, and the "millennial" Messianic kingdom of peace and justice, to be followed by the new heavens and the new earth.

## The God of History

In the Bible, God is explicitly the God of history. The prophet Isaiah gives us some striking examples of this: "Remember not the former things, nor consider the things of old. Behold, I am doing a new thing; now it springs forth, do you not perceive it?" (Isa. 43:18-19). I have already quoted the saying "History repeats itself," but God sees that differently. He says, as it were: "Do not look at how I did things in earlier times (such as the exodus from Egypt); I do not repeat myself; I can redeem you in totally new ways that you have never thought of before." As the prophet Jeremiah said: "Therefore, behold, the days are coming, declares the LORD, when they shall no longer say, 'As the LORD lives who brought up the people of Israel out of the land of Egypt,' but 'As the LORD lives who brought up and led the offspring of the house of Israel out of the north country and out of all the countries where he had driven them.' Then they shall dwell in their own land" (Jer. 23:7-8).

"[R]emember the former things of old; for I am God, and there is no other; I am God, and there is none like me, declaring the end from the beginning and from ancient times things not yet done, saying, 'My counsel shall stand, and I will accomplish all my purpose,' calling a bird of prey from the east, the man of my counsel from a far country. I have spoken, and I will bring it to pass; I have purposed, and I will do it" (Isa. 46:9-11). Here again, the "former things" are God's redemptive deeds performed in the past, including the exodus, which demonstrate his uniqueness (cf. 41:22; 42:9; 48:3). In this case, God proves his uniqueness and creativity in that, this time, he will accomplish redemption through a "bird of prey from the east." In this post-exilic situation, the reference is clearly to the Persian King Cyrus, here as an obvious type of the Messiah, *the* true "Man of God's counsel" (see the following chapter). Cyrus was a "bird of prey" because he would bring judgment on Babylon (539 BC).

Note in this passage how at the same time, God is the one who predicts ("declaring the end from the beginning"), decides and executes history ("I have spoken, and I will bring it to pass; I have purposed, and I will do it"). God *knows* what is going to happen because he himself is the one who *makes* it happen. The remnant of Judah did not have to be concerned, since God himself would make sure that its redemption would be accomplished.

Listen also to this *maskil* of Asaph: "Give ear, O my people, to my teaching; incline your ears to the words of my mouth! I will open my mouth in a parable; I will utter dark sayings from of old, things that we have heard and known, that our fathers have told us. We will not hide them from their children, but tell to the coming generation the glorious deeds of the LORD, and his might, and the wonders that he has done" (Ps. 78:1-4). In verse 1, we find a very special meaning of the word *torah* (normally rendered "law" but literally meaning "teaching, instruction"), namely, the lessons from history that God wants to teach his people. The "dark sayings" (NIV: "hidden things")—at other places the same word is rendered "riddles"—are the often obscure and mysterious ways in which God used to deal with his people, which Asaph is now going to explain, and which the Israelites have to pass on to their children and grandchildren.

Believers need divine "keys" to history in order to understand it from a divine perspective. In New Testament language this means that they need the guidance of the Holy Spirit to understand both past history and coming "history." This is what Jesus taught his disciples about past history: "The Helper, the Holy

Spirit, whom the Father will send in my name, he will teach you all things and bring to your remembrance all that I have said to you" (John 14:26). And about coming history, he said: "When the Spirit of truth comes, he will guide you into all the truth, for he will not speak on his own authority, but whatever he hears he will speak, and he will declare to you the things that are to come" (16:13).

## Driving Forces of History

We finally come to the fourth question asked at the beginning of this chapter. What are the *driving forces* of history? Besides natural forces, both outside and within Man, can we also distinguish supernatural forces driving history? Is history deterministic, or is it governed by the free choices of responsible people?

Some would argue that we are now entering the domain of the greatest subjectivity, but that is inherent in a religious approach to history. Those who limit themselves to the "solid facts," such as those of a biological, psychoanalytical, social, economic, political, artistic, demographic, or technological nature, may count upon the benevolence of the modern historian. Those who, in addition to this, prefer an interpretation expressed in terms of a worldview (idealism, materialism, [neo-]positivism, historicism, pragmatism, existentialism, postmodernism, etc.), have already left the domain of strict historiography and entered that of the philosophy of history. However, those who go even further and seek their explanatory approach in *transcendent* factors, particularly in spiritual powers behind the scenes of history, will have to deal nowadays with the pity or even the abhorrence of the average modern historian.

The view that the course of history is governed by divine and angelic powers is surely the most ancient view in historiography, as I explained extensively in my book *The Ninth King*. Yet, no modern self-respecting historian will dare admit to endorsing it. Moreover, the average Christian historian does his job like any other historian, that is, for all intents and purposes, like an agnostic in the sense of someone who ignores God's presence in history. At best, he may in his free time venture to express the conviction that, in one way or another, "God's hand is working" in history. He says this with extreme caution, hardly daring to express himself in a more concrete way. This is a task he leaves to the philosopher of history. He would be even more wary of including angels and demons in his view.] Above all, he does not wish to be placed on one level with a Homer (eighth century BC?) or a Hesiod (c. 700 BC?) or, to a lesser extent, with a Herodotus (fifth century BC), who time and again saw the earthly struggles of their heroes and nations being influenced behind the scenes by the immoral, quarreling, intriguing gods of Mount Olympus.

It is obvious that the Christian historian cannot view history in such a way. However, is it possible today for him or her to view history in a way similar to how the church father Augustine did? Does the modern Christian still have any knowledge of the Kingdom of God with its heavenly angels and earthly believers, which, until the last day, will be entangled in a continuous struggle with the realm of Satan and his demons as well as his unbelieving followers (cf. Matt. 12:25-28)? Even though it may not be possible in this way to interpret every single historical event off the cuff, does the Christian still have at least some idea of the fact that, in the most basic sense, history is precisely a matter of this struggle?

With the brief remarks that I offer here, I claim no more and no less than to throw some light on this struggle. In other words, my thought on this subject stands unashamedly in the tradition of the oldest interpretation of history, i.e. the Augustinian one. This is the approach that sees behind history a *meta-history*, that is literally, a "history behind history." The earthly events are a consequence of, and a reflection of, meta-historical events behind the scenes of world history. These are the scenes that divide the immanent ("inner-worldly") realm from the transcendent ("outer-worldly") realm.

## Meta-history and Responsibility

"Meta-history" is described as that which lies behind history, and actually determines and governs it. In my opinion, a study of meta-history involves to a large extent a penetration into the invisible realm of the "divine" powers. This higher realm remains hidden

## PROBING THE PAST

to most people. We will learn to discover this realm only in the light of God's written revelation. Only *from* the "outer-worldly" can there can be light shed *on* the "outer-worldly" (*and* the inner-worldly as well). A truly Christian view of history and culture can be developed only in the light that divine revelation throws sheds on the cultures of the Middle East and the West, from ancient Egypt to the eschatological world power. The real "soul" of a culture, and of the history of culture, is beyond scholarly (causal-analytical) research, and lies at the "level" on which only God's revelation can throw light.

In this study, I use Scripture as the most important source of knowledge. I do so grounded firmly in the idea that Scripture does indeed involve divine *revelation* concerning the spiritual world behind history. This means that Scriptural communications about spiritual powers are based neither upon subjective human imagination and reflection, nor on adoptions from the heathen nations which surrounded Israel, but on disclosures made on God's behalf. Of course, I do not deny here that Scripture describes examples of human imagination and reflection. Neither do I deny the value of exegesis, which is necessary in order to find out, for instance, to what extent we are dealing in a certain passage of Scripture, with a literal or a symbolical description of spiritual realities, what the literary genre of that passage is, etc. However, these distinctions do not diminish in any way the transcendent reality content of the descriptions given.

According to the Bible, history is governed by "forces" that belong to an "invisible realm." Of course, we think here primarily of the dominion or providence of YHWH (for a fuller discussion, see chapter 7). It is the God of Jacob who leads, carries, guides, and drives the history of this world toward the goal destined by him (cf., e.g., Isa. 46:9-13 and other Scripture passages quoted above). Secondly, however, the Bible also casts light on the "instruments" of which YHWH makes use in his world dominion. These are invisible powers in the celestial spheres as well as visible powers on earth. I hope to show that often, according to the Bible, very different, much higher, much more essential matters are involved than current historiography seems to realize.

In my book *The Ninth King*, I have placed special emphasis

## PATTERNS, PURPOSE AND POWERS OF HISTORY

upon the influence of the higher (angelic and demonic) powers. A measure of one-sidedness cannot be avoided here. While in the past so much one-sided emphasis was laid on immanent forces in history, that is, upon action for which humans were responsible, in *The Ninth King* I also emphasized the transcendent forces. However, the great significance of human responsibility should not for a moment be overlooked. We see this already in the story of the Garden of Eden. How easy it is to attribute the whole fall of man exclusively to the devil (cf. John 8:44; 2 Cor. 11:3; Rev. 12:9). But in Scripture passages speaking of the Fall it is not only the devil's role which is underlined, but also human responsibility (e.g., Rom. 5:12-14). And the same is true for the whole history of mankind. Unfortunately, the activity of the spiritual powers has been underestimated to a large extent. But where they were recognized, this sometimes took place at the cost of human responsibility.

The two "forces," transcendent spiritual powers and immanent human choices, should not be played off against one another in such a way as to cancel each other out but they should be seen as completing each another. By the "spirit" of a given culture, we may often understand a very concrete transcendent power. But the Dutch historian and politician Guillaume Groen van Prinsterer (1801-1876; see chapter 1) was equally right when he, in speaking of the "spirit" of the French Revolution, did not think of the spiritual realm but primarily of the whole of human apostate choices. A "cultural force" can be a very concrete transcendent power; but at the same time it is *always* the power that consists of the free choices of responsible men. The French-Swiss Reformer John Calvin (1509-1564) somewhere calls the human heart an *idolorum fabricam*; that is a "workshop of idols." These idols can be very concrete demonic powers; but they can just as easily be the "idols" of our own pride and rebellion. Man submits to idolatrous powers outside him; but it is equally true that he *creates* idols in his own heart. The one thing needs to be emphasized without neglecting the other.

Besides, even when man "creates" his own idols, the objective "gods" outside him endeavor at the same time to make man the prisoner of his own "idols." And thus, man, in creating "idols" according to his own free responsibility and submitting to them, becomes the prisoner of the "gods" outside him after all. Man never falls helplessly and without the will to resist into the clutches of the evil powers, but always as a consequence of his own free choice. His responsibility is never switched off. Therefore, Adam's old excuse, "The serpent deceived me" (Gen. 3:13; cf. 1 Tim. 2:14), is never valid because, even where this is true, it is always man who, of his own free choice, *allowed* himself to be deceived.

## History and Mythology

In this context, it is necessary to say a few words about the relationship between history and mythology because many people would label a meta-history in which gods and other supernatural forces are involved "mythological." A myth is a story in which certain spiritual (religious, divine, demonic, angelic) powers are represented as concrete figures and forms, adopted either from the existing reality or from an imaginary one. For instance, in the mythologies of all ancient nations, as well as in the Bible, all kinds of monsters ("dragons" and the like) occur that are symbolic pictures of spiritual powers. Invisible angels and angelic princes in the invisible world are depicted as concrete monsters from the visible world, whether such monsters really exist in our world or not. These monsters are not "true" in the sense of "literally existing"—there are no literal dragons—but they are "true" in the sense that they refer to real spiritual powers. I have written at greater length about these matters in my book *The Ninth King*; here I will recall only some essential aspects.

The Bible tells us a lot about spiritual powers and angelic princes. These are demonic beings that in the invisible world may look like monsters such as dragons, and that are associated with natural elements such as sea, water, fire, and wind (*elemental spirits*). In my view, the names of the mythical monsters (Rahab, Leviathan) are the proper names of the relevant angelic princes. The biblical message is that God is mightier than all pagan angelic princes who intend to devour his people. I believe that in Scripture we are dealing with *inspired historiography*. Israel did not *adopt* its beliefs about the powers behind the scenes from the pagans, but *received* them from God through revelation. The biblical beliefs did not come from the pagans, but the pagan mythology in its kernel is rooted in a historical reality, which among the pagans was strongly corrupted and embellished, and has been handed down in pure form in Scripture alone.

Please note, we are not dealing with pious fantasy, but with concretely existing angelic powers. And we are not dealing here with adoptions, for Scripture itself knows very well the names of the relevant angelic princes. The fact that the pagan nations often know these names too does not necessarily indicate that Israel adopted these names from them, even if it could be demonstrated that the Jewish writings are much more recent than the pagan sources. Rather, this fact indicates that the Jewish and pagan writings are rooted in the same concrete experiences of reality. Whether we are considering the historical books or the poetic and prophetic books, most of what is referred to there as "mythical" elements in reality goes back to concretely existing spiritual realities, described at most in symbolic language.

## Fountains and Windows

A concrete example can be much more effective here than a long argument. For instance, in Genesis 7:11, which speaks of the "fountains of the great deep" (Heb., *tehôm*)" and the "windows of the heavens," historical criticism sees a clear example of mythical elements. In opposition to this claim, at least three attitudes are possible:

(a) Acceptance of this assertion, as a consequence of which, because of the mythical character of these elements, one immediately gets rid of their historical significance. In modernist theology, distinguishing mythical elements in the Old Testament, particularly in Genesis 1-11, went hand in hand with the denial of the historical trustworthiness of the relevant Bible stories.

(b) Strict rejection of the idea that we are dealing with any mythical elements at all. What is more, people emphasize the historical trustworthiness of the Scriptural data so forcefully that they are only prepared to read descriptions of certain astronomical and geological phenomena in the expressions I have referred to above. This is a kind of *eisegesis* ("reading into") that is just as bad as the modernist de-historicization of the Scripture passages concerned. In other words, the two are opposite expressions of the same modernist thought-attitude (scientism).

(c) Acceptance of the elements labeled as mythical (in the sense of representing meta-historical realities), without diminishing in any sense the historical trustworthiness of the relevant Bible story but, on the contrary, seeing in these elements references to invisible spiritual powers (chaos angels) which, under God's guidance, played a role in causing Noah's flood. Compare what I said about *Historie* and *Geschichte* in chapter 2.

Obviously, I prefer explanation (c). This has the advantage of taking into account, along with explanation (a), the reference to higher spiritual powers contained in the expressions mentioned, as well as adhering, along with explanation (b), to the concrete (meta-)historical reality to which these expressions, and the whole story of the flood, refer. With their "insights," historical criticism have booby-trapped the Bible and robbed the simple of their faith in the Bible's trustworthiness. In our efforts to avoid this, we should not fall into another, equally scientific approach of Scriptural data (the details given above as well as others) by reducing them to statements of a geological or geophysical nature. We should use the discoveries of the critical school, especially of form criticism, in order to deepen our own understanding of the higher realities described in Scripture, from a perspective that honors the Bible's own self-understanding. For the rest, I refer the reader again to my book *The Ninth King* for the way in which I have worked out these principles.

ALSO FROM THE AUTHOR
AT EVERY MAJOR ONLINE BOOK RETAILER

# Chapter Five
# MORE ABOUT BIBLICAL HISTORIOGRAPHY

In speaking of Western culture we realize that this culture is the spiritual heir of Hellenistic civilization and the culture of the Western Roman Empire, plus its Judeo-Christian heritage. (Hellenism was the culture and philosophy of the Greek Empire and its successor empires; it was a mixture of Greek thinking and local thought systems.) To this heritage, history has added significant Celtic, Germanic, and even Arab influences, spreading over Europe from the Middle East and Spain. The Greek and the Roman Empire play an important role in the Book of Daniel as the third and fourth empires in a series of four (see especially Dan. 2 and 7). We find extensive prophecies about these four ancient cultures. The Book of Daniel offers us a magnificent example of the various ways in which believing Jews and Christians can approach history.

## God's People in the Center

Daniel views the world empires at three "levels," so to speak. The first "level" is found in Daniel 2. Here, the four ancient world empires or world cultures are presented to the Babylonian king Nabu-kudurri-ussur (Nebuchadrezzar or -nezzar, c. 634-562 BC) in the form of an exceedingly impressive statue. In spite of modern liberal and alternative approaches, I cannot doubt for a second that the four parts of the image represent the (Neo-)Babylonian Empire, the Medo-Persian Empire, the Greco-Macedonian Empire including the Hellenistic empires resulting from it, and finally the Roman Empire (see Appendix 5 in my book *The Ninth King*).

However, the point that concerns me in particular now is that these four empires are presented to the king in such an impressive manner. This is the way in which man without God has always loved to view history: he sees "gold" and "silver," that is, mighty, magnificent empires and rulers, and he is hardly able to believe that history might be governed by anything other than such impressive kings and emperors. This is also the way in which history is generally taught in school; there, much of what we hear is limited to mighty statesmen and army generals. Let us remember what Thomas Carlyle (see chapter 1) said: "The history of the world is but the biography of great men." These are the heroes and the geniuses; they are either the great political or military figures, either the founders or conquerors of states or empires.

King Nebuchadnezzar must have understood very well what the message of his own dream in Daniel 2 was, for according to chapter 3 he built an impressive statue of gold, about thirty yards or twenty-seven meters high. It represented himself and his empire (not to mention his gods). He ignored the inferior metals, that is, the subsequent empires that his dream had indicated, as if the future belonged to him and his empire only. This is typical of so many dictators. They all dream that their empire will last a thousand years, whereas its real lifespan is always quite limited. Adolf Hitler dreamed of such a millennium for his *Third Reich*, but it lasted only twelve years (1933-1945).

Moreover, what is a thousand years? Remarkably enough, in 806, Charlemagne made a preliminary division of his enormous empire among his three (legitimate) sons, but as it turned out, only his son Louis the Pious survived. In 843, the three sons of Louis divided the Carolingian Empire among themselves with the Treaty of Verdun. Louis the German received the Eastern part, known as East Francia, which eventually became the medieval kingdom of Germany. This country formed the largest component of what was to be the Holy Roman Empire, although at times it also included kingdoms such as Italy, Bohemia, and Burgundy. This "Holy" Empire was dissolved in 1806—exactly one thousand years after 806—when the last (Austrian) emperor, Francis II, was defeated by Napoleon. During the last centuries, the power of the Holy Roman Emperor had already dwindled considerably. The Latin proverb sums it up beautifully: *Sic transit*

## MORE ABOUT BIBLICAL HISTORIOGRAPHY

*gloria mundi,* which means "Thus passes the glory of the world" (a phrase which can be found in Thomas à Kempis, 1418).

The Byzantine, or Christian Eastern Roman, Empire lasted even a little longer. It actually started in 395, when the Emperor Theodosius I definitively divided the Roman Empire between his two sons: the emperor Honorius in the West, and the emperor Arcadius in the East. The Eastern Roman Empire lasted until its capital, the proud city of Constantinople (afterwards called Istanbul), was captured by the Muslim Turks in 1453. That is a period of 1058 years. However, in the final centuries the empire had dwindled down, so that around 1450 it contained little more than Constantinople and its immediate surroundings, plus the Peloponnese peninsula. Again, thus passes the glory of mighty empires, "even" Christian ones. And what about the empire of those victorious Muslim Turks, the Ottoman Empire? It lasted from 1299 to 1922, that is 623 years. The Muslim caliphates (*khalîf* = "successor," i.e., of Muhammad) lasted from 632 to 1924, that is 1292 years—a long period; the Ottoman Empire was just one of these caliphates.

This is the clear divine message of Daniel 2: Your empire is tremendous, King Nebuchadnezzar, but its time is limited. As God said through the prophet Jeremiah, "I have given all these lands into the hand of Nebuchadnezzar, the king of Babylon, my servant, and I have given him also the beasts of the field to serve him. All the nations shall serve him and his son and his grandson, *until the time of his own land comes*. Then many nations and great kings shall make him their slave" (Jer. 27:6-7, italics added). After Nebuchadnezzar's empire, another one would follow, and then another, and yet another. Empires would come and go. They might last even more than a thousand years, but the decline and fall of each of these empires was *a priori* certain. Only the Fifth Empire, the Messianic Kingdom, "shall never be destroyed, nor shall the kingdom be left to another people. It shall break in pieces all these kingdoms and bring them to an end, and it shall stand forever" (Dan. 2:44).

## Four Beasts

In Daniel 7, the same four world empires—the (Neo-)Babylonian, the Medo-Persian, the Greco-Macedonian, and the Roman Empire —are viewed on a second, higher "level," closer to God's own mind. Again, they were presented in a dream; however, this time not to a pagan king, but to the prophet of the Lord, the God of Israel. And this man of God did not see a mighty statue, nor empires represented by precious metals, as earthly kings would like to see them. No, the prophet saw four powerful but ignorant beasts, namely, a lion, a bear, a leopard, and a "terrifying and dreadful and exceedingly strong" beast, respectively (in Rev. 13:2 they are viewed in reverse order). They were each characterized by what we associate with the images of beasts, namely, robbery, cruelty, tyranny, oppression. They were compared to beasts because they were "brutish and ignorant" (cf. Ps. 73:22). They did not know God but were driven only by their devilish animal instincts.

This is the true nature of cultures that do not submit to the Lord, the God of Israel. Heathen kings have no inkling of this nature—they cannot "see" such a dream—but the man of God can and does see it. That is, he sees the four empires as God sees them, and apparently as God sees *all* human empires and human dictators: they are brutish and ignorant beasts. If we think of the present, there are many examples: Manuel Noriega, Saddam Hussein, Muammar Gaddafi, Hosni Mubarak, Bashar al-Assad, Omar al-Bashir, Robert Mugabe, Viktor Yanukovych, Alexander Lukashenko, and so many more. How similar they are, and how similar is their fall will (probably) be, or at least the fall of their regimes after they have passed away.

Moreover, something comes to light in Daniel 7 that had not yet emerged in Daniel 2. In the chapter of the four beasts, it turns out that the people of Israel play a central role in the history of the world empires. It is the Son of Man—the Messiah of Israel—who will gain the victory over the four empires, but Israel will be closely involved in this victory: "the saints of the Most High shall receive the kingdom and possess the kingdom forever, forever and ever" (Dan. 7:18). "As I looked, this horn [i.e., the eschatological dictator] made war with the saints and prevailed over them, until the Ancient of Days came [i.e., in actuality, the coming of God in the person of the Messiah], and judgment was given for [or, to] the saints of the Most High, and the time came when the saints possessed the kingdom" (Dan. 7:21-22). "And the kingdom and the dominion and the greatness of the kingdoms under the whole heaven shall be given to the people of the saints of the Most High; their kingdom shall be an everlasting kingdom, and all dominions shall serve and obey them" (Dan. 7:27 note).

As we can see in these verses, the little nation of Israel turns out to be the pivot on which, according to the counsel and the election of God, the whole of world history turns. In the end, it is not only the Son of Man, or the Most High in the person of the Son of Man, who receives the Messianic Kingdom, but it is *his people* who receive the Kingdom together with him. In Daniel 7, only the man of God is aware of the future of God's people, and it must have been a tremendous comfort to him, lamenting as he was because of Israel's fate in the Babylonian Exile. The prophet also knew that the world empires without God would eventually perish, and that their judgment would be the more severe the more they have oppressed Israel, whereas eventually the people of Israel would be delivered, and would prevail.

Israel will be the center of the Messianic Kingdom, and has, since its beginning as a nation, always been the pivotal center of history. In our history textbooks on the ancient world, the history of Israel fills at best two pages (at least that was the case with my own school book around 1960, even though I was at a Christian school). Perhaps these few pages were mainly a concession to our own Judeo-Christian history, because for the rest Israel's role in ancient history was considered to be negligible. However, if we look at ancient history with the eyes of God, things look totally different.

## Abr(ah)am

I would like to illustrate this central point a little further before we come to the third and highest "level" in the Book of Daniel. To this end, I mention some other examples that show how in biblical historiography different things are pivotal than in common historiography. My first example comes from Genesis 14. Undoubtedly, before the episode described here many wars had already taken place on earth. However, the war of Genesis 14 is of great importance in salvational history, and worth mentioning, because God's elect, Lot and subsequently Abram, are involved in it.

The names of Amraphel and the other kings have been preserved for later generations only because they came into conflict with God's people. For a long time, it was customary to link the name Amraphel with Hammurabi, king of Babylonia (1792-1750 BC). This well-known king has become famous for Hammurabi's Code, one of the first written codes of laws preserved in history, which made the king a model for all later law-givers. There are striking parallels between this Code and the Torah of Israel, which have led to all kinds of speculation about the origin of the Torah. However this may be, none of this is found in Genesis 14. In our common textbooks, history revolves around the great powers, mighty kings, emperors and war lords. In God's way of describing history, everything revolves around his own people, even though they hardly find a place in the textbooks.

Interestingly, the great French rabbi Rashi (Rabbi Shlomo Yitzchaki, 1040-1105) told us that, according to an ancient Jewish tradition, Amraphel was the same as Nimrod, whom we know from Genesis 10:8-12. In that case, Abram's battle would be against what Nimrod stood for, namely, Assyria and Babylonia, as precursors of the later Assyrian and Babylonian Empires. Another rabbinical interpretation saw in the four kingdoms mentioned in Genesis 14, Shinar, Ellasar, Elam, and Goiim, descendents of Noah's sons, Shem, Ham and Japheth. After the flood, all mankind descended from these three sons, so that the suggestion is that this was a war between Abram and the rest of the world. In this way, the battle was a model for the rest of human history: God's people against the rest, or, in other words, a few Abels against a multitude of Cains. Usually, the Abels lose, but in the end they win. Thus, Abram's battle was a foreshadowing of the ultimate victory of God's people.

The great Catalan rabbi Nachmanides (1194-1270) suggested that the four kings represented the four empires that would oppress Israel from the seventh century BC onward (cf. Dan. 7). Again, Abr(ah)am is seen here as the representative of Israel in its centuries-long struggle with the Gentile nations. The fourth kingdom, Goiim (Heb. *goyyim*), very simply means "nations" or

## MORE ABOUT BIBLICAL HISTORIOGRAPHY

"Gentiles." With God's help, Abram and his small army (three hundred and eighteen men) are stronger than the four kingdoms. In the same way, Israel will triumph over the four world empires with the support of the God of Israel. We may think here of the four "horns" described in Zechariah 1:18-21, as representing four great enemies of Israel. The Targum, an Aramaic paraphrase of the Old Testament, reads "four kingdoms," which the medieval rabbis David Kimchi (1160-1235) and Isaac Abrabanel (1437-1508) identified as Babylonia, Persia, Greece and Rome.

In Genesis 14, it is important to take note of the two central figures: Abram and Melchizedek. Abram is a type of eschatological Israel—the Israel of Romans 11:26 ("in this way all Israel will be saved")—and the king-priest Melchizedek is a type of Jesus Christ, the King-Priest of the future Messianic kingdom (Heb. 7; cf. Ps. 110; Zech. 6:13). Melchizedek was a priest of the Most-High God, *El Elyon*, that is, the God who was exalted above all the gods of Canaan, and also above the gods of Shinar, Ellasar, Elam, and Goiim. Thus we see what history is: it is not only the continual conflict between Israel and the nations, but the struggle between the *God* of Israel and the *gods* of the nations. We can also think of what God said at Israel's exodus out of Egypt: "On all the gods of Egypt I will execute judgments" (Exod. 12:12; cf. Numb. 33:4). In this ongoing conflict, the ultimate victory will be gained in the person of the Son of Man, the Messiah of Israel.

## Cyrus

A second fascinating example is found in Isaiah 44:24-45:8. Here a prediction is made concerning the rise of the Persian king Cyrus (in Hebrew *Koresh*, and in Greek *Kyros*), who in 539 BC would conquer the Neo-Babylonian Empire and found the mighty Medo-Persian Empire. In Isaiah 44:28, the Lord calls Cyrus "my shepherd," who would "fulfill all my purpose." In Isaiah 45:1-3 Cyrus is called "his anointed;" the prophet predicted that he would subdue nations before God, and would break in pieces doors of bronze. And in fact, the Greek historian Herodotus tells us in his *History* about the hundred gates of bronze in the outer wall of the city of Babylon.

## PROBING THE PAST

God's first title for Cyrus, "my shepherd" (Heb. *ro<sup>c</sup>i*), is the same one that God used prophetically for the Messiah (Zech. 13:7; cf. Matt. 26:31), and that David used for the Lord (Ps. 23:1). And the second title, "his anointed" (Heb. *m'shikho*), is the same as "his Messiah." Although Cyrus was a pagan king, he was obviously a type of Christ as ruler of the world. Cyrus uttered a remarkably prophetic word, which immediately reminds us of the true Messiah himself: "The LORD, the God of heaven, *has given me all the kingdoms of the earth,* and he has charged me to build him a house at Jerusalem, which is in Judah. Whoever is among you of all his people, may his God be with him, and let him go up to Jerusalem, which is in Judah, and rebuild the house of the LORD, the God of Israel—he is the God who is in Jerusalem" (Ezra 1:2-3, italics added). It is the Messiah who will build the new Temple: "Behold, the man whose name is the Branch: for he shall branch out from his place, and he shall build the temple of the LORD" (Zech. 6:12).

As for the invitation to come to Jerusalem and worship God in his Temple, we are reminded of this prophecy: "The time is coming to gather all nations and tongues. And they shall come and shall see my glory, and I will set a sign among them. And from them I will send survivors to the nations, to Tarshish, Pul, and Lud, who draw the bow, to Tubal and Javan, to the coastlands far away, that have not heard my fame or seen my glory. And they shall declare my glory among the nations. And they shall bring all your brothers from all the nations as an offering to the LORD, on horses and in chariots and in litters and on mules and on dromedaries, to my holy mountain Jerusalem" (Isa. 66:18-20).

According to Isaiah 45:3-4, Cyrus would conquer tremendous riches—which indeed he did, as non-biblical history tells us—both in Babylon and in Lydia. In the latter country, he destroyed the power of the fabulously wealthy King Croesus. The Lord tells us why he granted all this to King Cyrus. He did it "for the sake of my servant Jacob, and Israel my chosen," and in order that Cyrus might know the Lord. It was Cyrus who allowed the Jews to return to their country and to rebuild the Temple, therefore, God rewarded him with a mighty empire. Please note: Cyrus did not *conquer* his gigantic kingdom by his own force, no, it was the Lord, the God of Israel, who gave it to him because of the good he had done to God's people.

## MORE ABOUT BIBLICAL HISTORIOGRAPHY

According to secular standards, this is absurd, but the prophet declares it here with great emphasis: Cyrus owes his empire to his benevolence with regard to the tiny nation of the Jews. He may not have known God, and he may never have thought of the connection between his kindness and its reward, but this is what is going on behind the scenes. The God *of Israel* gave Cyrus his enormous kingdom because of *Israel*. To any historian thinking in terms of physical causes and physical effects, which is characteristic of common historiography, and understandably so, this is not only an unproven thesis [hypothesis?] but also an extremely unlikely one. However, meta-history inevitably moves at a totally different "level." It takes account of factors of which common historiography has no idea. A Christian philosophy of history does this because it sees history in the light that God's revelation sheds on it.

## Xerxes

Let me give a third example. From secular history we know that the Persian king Xerxes I the Great, or Ahasuerus (518-465 BC: king from 486 BC), undertook an enormous expedition against Greece from the third to the sixth year of his reign (Second Greco-Persian War). This had been foretold by the Lord: "Three more kings shall arise in Persia, and a fourth shall be far richer than all of them. And when he has become strong through his riches, he shall stir up all against the kingdom of Greece" (Dan. 11:2). This war ended for the Persians in a terrible defeat, in the notorious Battle of Salamis (480 BC). If the expedition had ended in a different way, humanly speaking, the history of Europe might have followed taken a very different path. For our part of the world, therefore, the outcome of this war was of the greatest importance.

However, in the Book of Esther this expedition is quietly passed over. Apparently, God had very different priorities. In Esther 1:3, we hear about a great "feast" lasting a hundred and eighty days in the third year of the king, at which he "showed the riches of his royal glory and the splendor and pomp of his greatness for many days". In fact, this showing off cannot have been anything else than the preparation for the great war, but the Bible does not mention this detail. It mentions the "feast" because it was on this occasion that Queen Vashti lost her position as Queen Consort, so that it became necessary to replace her. However, the search for a new Queen Consort does not take place immediately. On the contrary, from this feast we skip immediately to the seventh year of Ahasuerus (Esther 2:16). We know from history that this was the period in which the Second Greco-Persian War was raging, but the Bible is completely silent about it. Scripture puts all the emphasis on the question of how the people of Israel fared in the period afterwards.

In Persian historiography, however, it is precisely the reverse. In the Persian chronicles, the spotlight falls on the war I mentioned, whereas Mordecai and Esther are entirely absent (although some have erroneously tried to equate Esther with Queen Amestris). To the world, the history of Israel at that time apparently had little value, but to God it is so important that he devoted a separate book of the Bible to it. The reason is obvious; if Haman, the "enemy of the Jews" (Esther 3:10; 8:1; 9:10, 24), had had his way, all Israel within the empire would have been exterminated. In a few words, the people's fate was decided: "If it please the king, let it be decreed that they be destroyed"; and the answer of the king was: "Do with them as it seems good to you" (Esther 3:9, 11). That's all. Please note that such wholesale destruction of Israel would have included the Jews who had returned to their homeland, because at that time, the country still belonged to the Medo-Persian Empire (cf. Neh. 9:36, where the Israelites are called "slaves" of the Persian king).

Imagine what the consequences might have been if Israel had been destroyed. In that case, the Messiah of Israel could never have been born. Ultimately, that would have been far more disastrous for the Western world, not to mention the rest of the world, than if the Persians had won the war against the Greeks. We might all have become "Persianized," but we, as well as the whole world, would still be lost. In God's view, the things that are mentioned in the Book of Esther are far more important than the things about which nothing is said. Taking all this into account, how differently we view world history! We learn to place the emphasis on very different things, simply by paying attention to the trials and tribulations of Israel, and later also of the Gentile followers of Jesus. In God's view, *they* are the heart of history, not the mighty kings and warlords.

## Copernicus

The various examples just listed give us an impression of the way God writes history, and of what his priorities are. Christian historiographers should learn from that. They should learn to discern God's priorities, that is, to look for the things in history that *he* would consider most significant. Of course, this is a subjective undertaking, but it is worth trying.

Let me give an example, which is based on the principle of synchronicity. In the following chapters I will say more about it. I adopted the principle from the Dutch psychologist and cultural philosopher Jan Hendrik van den Berg (1914-2012), who assigned great significance to the simultaneousness (synchronicity) of historic events. He pointed out that certain changes in the human cultural pattern are discontinuous, and at certain crucial moments in cultural history they simultaneously lead to changes within the special sciences as well as to closely related discoveries and renewals in very different cultural domains, both in the arts and in religious experience and the everyday pattern of life.

My example is the year 1543, first, because in that year—the year of his death—the Polish astronomer Nicolaus Copernicus (1473-1543) published his famous work *De Revolutionibus orbium coelectium* ("On the Revolutions of the Celestial Spheres"). This book laid the foundation for the modern heliocentric worldview, according to which the sun does not revolve around the earth, but the earth, along with the other planets, orbits the sun. The German polymath Johann Wolfgang von Goethe (1849-1932) has characterized this view as the "greatest, loftiest, farthest reaching discovery that Man has ever made." In a sense it might be seen as a shock for Christian faith because the earth was no longer viewed as the center of the universe, in seeming contradiction to Scripture. Therefore, many contemporaries, including the German Reformer Martin Luther (1483-1546), viewed Copernicus' theory as great foolishness. However, the English philosopher Frederick Copleston (1907-1994) pointed out that heliocentrism can also be viewed as a "lifting" of the earth, since it was promoted to the status of a celestial body. Aristotle had placed the imperfect "sublunar" earth in opposition to the "superlunar" heaven (sky), which was viewed as "perfect." Copernicus showed that the earth itself belongs to this "perfect" heaven (sky).

It is surely significant that in that same year 1543 the work of the Greek astronomer Archimedes (c. 287-c. 212 BC) was published in Venice in a Latin translation, and thus became available to Western scientists. Archimedes and Copernicus in particular became the two idols of Italian astronomer Galileo Galilei (1564-1642), and were to lay the astronomical and mathematical foundation for modern science. Only one year, later, in 1544, the new knowledge about the globe found its visible expression in the *Cosmographia Universalis*, an atlas by the German cosmographer Sebastian Münster (1488-1552). In the same year, 1544, there also appeared the first world map, made by Italian explorer Sebastiano Caboto (1484-1557). Here, one could finally see the earth as an "ordinary planet," as Copernicus had already described it; that is, a planet with an orbit around the sun, between the orbits of Venus and Mars.

For the first time, the earth's spherical shape became a tangible given with practical consequences. For instance, explorers sailing around the earth found out that, if they sailed West, they lost a day, whereas if they sailed East, they gained a day. The first world globes were constructed. Within a few years, Western Man became familiar with a totally new view of the world, which inevitably also meant a new view of himself. There is a tremendous difference between living on a geocentric earth, and living on a heliocentric earth, between living under the sky and being part of the sky.

## Vesalius

Whereas Copernicus in 1543 opened up the macrocosmos, so to speak, in the very same year, Andreas Vesalius (1514-1564), an anatomist and physiologist from Brussels, opened up the microcosm of the human body in his famous work *De humanis corporis fabrica* ("On the Fabric of the Human Body"). He had obtained the

## MORE ABOUT BIBLICAL HISTORIOGRAPHY

first accurate knowledge of human anatomy by dissecting human corpses. For a long time, his groundbreaking book would remain the textbook for human anatomy. It was as revealing as the work of Copernicus in offering modern Man the first accurate view of his "innermost being" (physically speaking, that is).

Vesalius was able to disprove the theories of Galen (129-c. 200/c. 216 AD), a famous Greek physician in the Roman Empire, on many points. This was unheard of. We can hardly imagine now what enormous authority the Greek and Roman thinkers and scientists possessed at that time. For one thousand four hundred years, nobody had dared to question the authority of Galen, especially because during most of that time, it was forbidden for religious reasons to dissect human bodies. In the time of Galen, it had been no different; his "human" anatomy was all based on the anatomy of animals such as dogs and apes. Later generations did not know this, however; Vesalius was the first to uncover Galen's secret.

When the Italian physician Mondino de Luzzi, or Mundinus (c. 1270-1327), began to carry out the first systematic dissections of the human body around 1300, this was a revolution. Yet, the authority of Galen was still so tremendous that Mundinus "saw" all the things that Galen had assumed were part of the human body—like the bone in the heart, the two lobes of the female uterus, the five lobes of the liver—but none of these imaginary things were actually there. Mundinus must be praised for his courage to dissect human bodies, but the time had not yet come for him to "see" for himself.

Vesalius was the first who dared to confront Galen point for point, "drawing for drawing." Yet, it took a century before the authority of Galen had entirely faded away. In the meantime, nevertheless, a new epoch had begun, in which, for the first time, thinkers dared to think for themselves. They found the courage to trust their own eyes and ears more than the great Greek and Roman scholars. Concretely, this means that, although for a thousand years scholars had "seen" this or that, the modern scholar did not see it and finally dared to say that it simply was *not* there. And, although for a thousand years, scholars had *not* seen this or that, the modern scholar *did* see it and finally ventured to say that it *was* there. And so the independently thinking individual was born. For the time being, this new attitude remained limited to the European elite; it was only during the time of the Enlightenment in the eighteenth century that it reached the masses.

Whereas Vesalius trusted his own *eyes* rather than the authority of Galen, the difference with Copernicus was that he trusted his own *thinking*. One could hardly say that Copernicus "saw" that the world was heliocentric rather than geocentric. *Epicycles* had been introduced into the geocentric model of the Greco-Roman astronomer Ptolemy (c. 90-c. 168 AD) as auxiliary hypotheses to explain the variations in speed and direction of the apparent motion of the various celestial bodies. Copernicus discovered that the need for these auxiliary hypotheses disappeared as soon as one started with a heliocentric model. The similarity between Copernicus and Vesalius was that both preferred their own seeing and thinking, respectively, to that of authorities who for more than a thousand years thought differently.

## The Reformation

We now come to the pivotal question: what do Copernicus and Vesalius have to do with a Christian view of history? The answer is that we cannot separate these intellectual developments from the religious developments which were occurring at the very same time. In 1517 the Lutheran Reformation had begun, and in 1521, at the German city of Worms, Luther had defended his new religious position before the young Holy Roman emperor Charles V and the representatives of the Roman Catholic Church. Luther openly declared that, if all popes and councils said A, and he found in his Bible B, he would choose to follow B. In other words, here was one man who dared to trust his own individual judgment over the opinion of the majority. This is precisely the same thing that we found in such men as Copernicus and Vesalius.

This new emphasis upon the *independently thinking individual* was a consequence of the Renaissance. As I said, this is *the* characteristic of the modern world: Man begins to think for himself, and no longer relies purely on the authority of others. Luther, Copernicus and Vesalius were products of this same development.

## MORE ABOUT BIBLICAL HISTORIOGRAPHY

All three broke with what tradition had always said about what people should believe. Copernicus said: The world is very different from what we thought for so long. Vesalius said: The human body is very different from what we thought for so long. Luther said: The Bible says something very different from what we thought for so long. All three found things out for themselves, and had the courage to speak up against all the odds. At that time, this was still a matter limited to the intellectual elite; but only a few centuries later, during the time of the Enlightenment this attitude would reach the European masses.

For the fledgling Reformation movement, the period from 1542 to 1545 was crucial. In July 1542 the preparations were begun for the Roman Catholic Council of Trent, which actually started in 1545. The purpose of the Council was to restore the unity within the Church by condemning the Lutheran Reformation in the strongest terms, but also by creating its own, *internal* reformation of the Roman Catholic Church. The Council marked the lasting separation between Catholics and Protestants, and thus the independent position first of German Protestantism, and later of Protestants in Europe and worldwide.

The Council's massive attack on Protestantism caused Luther's harsh retaliation in 1544, in his work *Wider das Papsttum zu Rom, vom Teufel gestiftet* ("Against the Roman Papacy, an Institution of the Devil"). In that same year, Albrecht, Duke of Prussia, founded the German Protestant University of Königsberg (today the Russian city of Kaliningrad), where two centuries later the great German philosopher Immanuel Kant (1724-1804) would teach. In the same year, the world's first Protestant church was built near Hartenfels Castle in the German town of Torgau. Protestantism would remain and has lasted to this very day, just as the new insights of modern science have endured through people such as Copernicus and Vesalius.

First, around 1543, the earth was discovered to be a true globe and a planet. Second, the world of the human body was opened up. Third, the independent world of Protestant thinking and church life began. Within a few years, three new "realms" had been disclosed: a new view of the world, a new view of the human body, and a new view of the Bible, and thus of religion.

## PROBING THE PAST

Three factors are simultaneously interconnected here: *cosmos, Man and God*. This cannot be a coincidence. It is especially Christian historical science that may be expected to have an eye for such striking connections. The three factors, now formulated as cosmos, soul and God, became three central motifs in the thought of the German philosopher Christian Wolff (1679-1754), and following him, in the thought of the German philosopher Immanuel Kant (see above).

I repeat that the three factors, cosmos, Man and God, and the new light that was thrown upon them, seem to be interrelated through the same phenomenon: *the freedom of thought gradually acquired by Western Man since the Renaissance*. This freedom led to a totally new way of looking at the world, at oneself and at God. Thus, the discoveries of Copernicus and Vesalius were of the same category, and equally important, as was the beginning of independent Protestantism. Modern Man had begun to think for himself, both in the religious and in the secular domain, and he has never given up this new ability to this day.

## Invisible Powers

We now finally arrive at the third and highest "level" of consideration in the Book of Daniel, namely, in Daniel 10. In Daniel 7, we get a glimpse of the true nature of the godless cultures, but we are not yet given a good look behind the scenes. This does not happen until we get to Daniel 10. There, the prophet meets a celestial being who reports to him about an encounter between him (the being) and the "prince of the kingdom of Persia" (or, the "prince of Persia"; Dan. 10:13, 20). He also speaks about the "prince of Greece" (Dan. 10:20), and in particular about "Michael, one of the chief princes," or, "Michael, your prince," "Michael, the great prince who has charge of your people," that is, the prince of Israel (Dan.10:13, 21; 12:1).

It is obvious that Daniel 10 does not deal with earthly princes but with invisible powers in the spiritual realm, angelic powers, which turn out to be the guiding forces behind the various empires. It is not the earthly rulers but apparently these celestial beings who are the actual rulers behind the scenes, who dominate

## MORE ABOUT BIBLICAL HISTORIOGRAPHY

and manipulate the history of their respective empires and nations. I have dealt extensively with these powers and their influence in my book *The Ninth King*.

Here is another point is of great significance. These celestial beings turn out to be hostile toward the celestial messenger appearing to Daniel, as well as toward Michael, the "prince" of Israel, and thus toward Israel itself. Here we receive the deepest insight concerning the true nature of the four world empires. Apparently, they were not just ignorant beasts as such, but were governed by invisible angelic powers. Moreover, these spiritual powers apparently did not primarily fight one another but first and foremost aimed at Israel. In "common" history what was going on first of all seemed to be a war between Persia and Greece (334-333 BC). But that was, so to speak, nothing but a chess match between two black kings.

To refine the picture of the chessboard, imagine a two-tiered chessboard, the lower board representing the earth, and the higher board representing the invisible celestial world (the "heavenly places" of Eph. 1:3, 20: 2:6; 3:10; 6:12). The two black armies (e.g., Persia and Greece) fight on the lower board, with a few white pawns in between, representing God's people, sandwiched between these two antagonistic powers, who are hostile to one another but especially to God's people. The *real* battle in history, however, is fought on the higher board, between all black celestial princes on one side and the great White King on the other side. In the cases of Cyrus and Ahasuerus we saw that it is not the mutual conflicts between the cultures which are of decisive significance in history, but their acceptance or rejection of Israel, and thus of the Lord. No matter how strange this may seem to the average historian, Israel is the pivot of world history.

In *The Ninth King* I have investigated what Scripture has to tell us further about the invisible powers in the celestial realm, which, under God's universal dominion, determine world history. In Hebrew, the word for "prince" is *sar*. In Jewish tradition this is a well-known term for the angelic princes of the various nations. The same word is used many times for an earthly "prince," but a few times also for celestial "princes." Apart from Daniel 10:13, 20 and 12:1, this is the case in Joshua 5:14, where we hear about "the

Prince of the army of the LORD," that is, a celestial prince, who was placed as commander over a whole army of celestial beings. The war of Israel against Canaan was not only a battle between two earthly nations but in fact a spiritual conflict between two invisible powers: the army of the Lord and the evil spiritual army behind the Canaanite nations, the army of the Canaanite "gods," just as the exodus had been a war between the God of Israel and the gods of Egypt (Exod. 12:12).

A few times we receive insight similar to the kind Joshua had into God's army in the "higher world," in particular when people belonging to God get into a conflict situation. There is, for instance, the example of Jacob: "Jacob went on his way, and the angels of God met him. And when Jacob saw them he said, 'This is God's camp!'" (Gen. 32:1-2). We can also think of Elisha when the Syrians were about to attack. He "said [to his servant], 'Do not be afraid, for those who are with us are more than those who are with them.' Then Elisha prayed and said, 'O LORD, please open his eyes that he may see.' So the LORD opened the eyes of the young man, and he saw, and behold, the mountain was full of horses and chariots of fire all around Elisha" (2 Kings 6:16-17; also compare 7:6, "For the Lord had made the army of the Syrians hear the sound of chariots and of horses").

## Daniel 8

There is one more special chapter in the Book of Daniel that sheds light on the way God views history, namely, Daniel 8. The periscope title in several Bible translations is something like this: "Daniel's Vision of the Ram and the Goat." This is understandable because a large part of the chapter is devoted to the great clash between the ram and the goat: "As for the ram that you saw with the two horns, these are the kings of Media and Persia. And the goat is the king of Greece. And the great horn between his eyes is the first king," that is, Alexander the Great (v. 20-21). Daniel 8 describes the collision of the two, as well as the triumph of Alexander over the Persian Empire. It further describes how, out of the Greek Empire (after Alexander's sudden death), four smaller kingdoms came forth: "As for the horn that was broken [i.e., Alex-

## MORE ABOUT BIBLICAL HISTORIOGRAPHY

ander], in place of which four others arose, four kingdoms shall arise from his nation, but not with his power" (v. 22).

One of these four Hellenistic kingdoms was the Seleucid Empire, including present-day Syria and Iran, and parts of Turkey, Iraq, and Afghanistan. Its most notorious king was Antiochus IV Epiphanes (215-164 BC, reigned from 175 BC). At that time, the land of Israel was part of the Seleucid Empire, and this is why this King Antiochus gets so much attention in the Book of Daniel (also see 7:23-25; 11:21-35). In 167 BC, Antiochus desecrated the Temple at Jerusalem, erected an image of Zeus in it, and had pigs sacrificed on the brazen altar. This led to the famous revolt of the priest Mattathias ben Johanan and his five sons, three of whom were called Maccabaeus (from Hebrew *makkabi*, "hammer"). Because of the insurrection, which became known as the Maccabean Revolt, the family managed to restore the Temple in 165 BC, and re-dedicate it to the service of the Lord.

Although the clash between Persia and Greece is described rather extensively, the real point of the chapter is to look at the Seleucid Empire, and to see what King Antiochus IV did to Israel, and thus to the God of Israel. In Daniel 11, the kings of the Seleucid and Ptolemaic Empires are called "the king of the North" and "the king of the South" respectively, because everything in this Book is viewed from the standpoint of Israel.

As I said, the periscope title above Daniel 8 is: "Daniel's Vision of the Ram and the Goat." But now consider the fact that God called the vision: the "vision of the evenings and the mornings" (v. 26). This is explained to the prophet in verse 13-14: "'For how long is the vision concerning the regular burnt offering, the transgression that makes desolate, and the giving over of the sanctuary and host to be trampled underfoot?" And he said to me, "For 2,300 evenings and mornings. Then the sanctuary shall be restored to its rightful state." The vision of Daniel 8 is *not* primarily about the ram and the goat but about the 2,300 "evenings and mornings" when no burnt offerings could be brought to the Lord. Some explain this as 2,300 twenty-four hour days, others as 1,150 days consisting of 1,150 evenings and 1,150 mornings, but this is of no concern to us right now. The point is that the main point of the chapter is this: for 2,300 (or 1,150) days the sacrifices have been stopped (cf. 9:26, the enemy "shall put an end to sacrifice and offering").

This is how the Lord views history: those 6,400 (or 2,300) burnt offerings that were withheld from God, so that his blessing could not rest on Israel (cf. Exod. 29:42-46), are of greater meta-historic significance than all kinds of "great" events on the world stage. Far more than most historians realize, God's blessing upon the world depends on this blessing upon Israel, as God told Abraham: "In your offspring shall all the nations of the earth be blessed" (Gen. 22:18). I will pick up this theme again when we come to the Axial Age and the significance of the *Shekhinah* for world history (chapter 10).

## A Final Remark on Angeology

In the Pentateuch, the Lord himself is still the Captain of his people (cf. Exod. 32:34; 33:2, 12-17), whereas in Daniel 10-12 it is the archangel Michael who is Israel's prince. These are not necessarily two contradictory representations, but redemptive-historical changes in the spiritual development of Israel. That is, at the fall of Jerusalem (586 BC) the *Shekhinah* had withdrawn from the Temple to heaven (for more detail, see chapter 10), and after the Babylonian Exile we do not hear about the return of the *Shekhinah* to the rebuilt temple. Apparently from 586 BC onward, Israel was no longer under the immediate guidance of the Lord, but was placed under a guardian angel, just like all the other nations—although Israel's guardian angel was still the most powerful of them all. Michael is the only "archangel" mentioned in the Bible (1 Thess. 4:16; Jude 9).

Every angelological study endeavors to tell us as much as possible about these celestial beings, whereas it is striking how very little Scripture actually tells us about angels and demons, i.e. fallen angels. Many questions have been asked about angels and demons that have led to an enormous amount of speculation, both by Jews and by Christians. But in Scripture these questions are simply not answered. I will just give a few examples of these questions, such as: How were angels created? When were they created? Before the first day of creation? On the first day? On the second day? What exactly are all their functions? How, when and why have certain groups of angels "fallen"? Did all the "fallen" angels "fall" at the same time, or was there more than one fall among the angels? Do all the fallen angels belong to Satan (cf. Matt. 25:41; 2 Cor. 12:7; Rev. 12:9)? To all these questions we receive no answer, or just a minimal one. Interpreters must therefore beware of any excessive speculation, i.e., going beyond what Scripture tells us.

However, we are allowed to thoroughly examine and fully exploit the few data that Scripture does provide us. No fear of speculation should make us reluctant to use what is actually revealed in Scripture, as has happened too often. In this regard, we should also consider that the limited data in the later Books of the Old and in those of the New Testament cannot be separated from the Jewish pseudepigraphic and apocalyptic literature, which tells us much more about angels. These writings are not inspired and certainly not free of speculation; they were written by men with the "veil" upon their heart, of which Paul speaks (2 Cor. 3:15). However, this does not mean that everything that is found in these texts is wrong. The Jews were the first to interpret the biblical texts concerned, and if at times they erred, so did the later Christian interpreters. Those who take these early Jewish views seriously cannot deny that they form a useful source of data, which can help us to see the biblical data in a clearer perspective. What this perspective may look like has been worked out in my book *The Ninth King*.

## Chapter Six
# THE EPOCHS OF WORLD HISTORY

History is a continuum of facts and events, which presents itself to us as a confusing and overwhelming labyrinth. One method by which historians try to find a pathway through this labyrinth is by dividing it up into periods, as we have seen in previous chapters. Theologians sometimes love to do the same thing when it comes to salvational history. Scripture itself sets the precedent, for example in Daniel 2 and 7, where history, from the fall of Jerusalem until the end time, is divided up into four epochs. These are those of the four Gentile world-empires to come, followed by a Fifth Era, that of the Messiah.

There are many ways to divide history into distinct epochs. In the past, many suggestions have been made by theologians and Christian historians as to the epoch in which we are living today. Let me mention a number of these various views.

### Are We Living in the "Third Era"?

First, the idea of a Third Epoch fits very well into the common anti-dispensationalist or amillennialist view of eschatology. For instance, the American theologian Floyd E. Hamilton (1924-2013) distinguished three epochs: the pre-Mosaic, the Mosaic, and the New Testament eras. In this respect, he followed the second-century church father Irenaeus, who spoke of three "covenants," the first characterized by the law written in the heart (i.e., before Sinai), the second by the law as an external commandment given at Sinai, and the third by the law restored to the heart through the operation of the Holy Spirit (cf. Rom. 5:12-21). The church father Augustine (354-430) used the same tripartite structure. Similarly, Johannes Cocceius (1603-1669), a Dutch theologian of German descent, distinguished three dispensations of the covenant of grace, the first *ante legem* ("before the law [was given]"), the second *sub lege* ("under the law"), and the third *post legem* ("after the law"). In contrast to this, other Reformational theologians, such as the Dutch-American theologian Louis Berkhof (1873-1957), preferred to distinguish only two dispensations, those of the Old and New Testaments.

The scheme of three dispensations became especially interesting when some theologians began to link it with three periods of two thousand years each. This view was associated with a very common idea in church history, namely, that the Old Testament period had lasted four thousand years. According to the calculations of the English bishop James Ussher (1581-1656), the creation had taken place in the night preceding the 23rd of October in the year 4004 BC. This date was included in the margin of the Authorized Version, or King James Bible. If we assume that Christ was born in the fourth year before the Christian era, this means that there were precisely four thousand years between the creation and the birth of Christ. Other Reformational writers arrived at slightly different dates for the creation of the world: Martin Luther (3961 BC); Philipp Melanchthon (3964 BC); Johannes Kepler (3984 or 3993 BC?); Joseph B. Lightfoot (3960 BC); John Playfair (4008 BC); Joseph Scaliger (3950 BC); Johann A. Bengel (3943 BC).

Even in the twentieth century, we can find similar numbers. Johannes C. Sikkel assumes that Adam was created in 4220 BC. The great theologian Herman Bavinck mentioned attempts to elongate the Old Testament by a few thousand years, but he had no difficulty assuming that Noah's flood was in 2348 BC, implying that Adam might have been created in 2348 + 1656 = 4004 BC.

## The *Dictum Eliae*

In 1532, the German astrologer and historian Johannes Carion (1499-1537) published a chronicle, of which a great part relies on the lectures given by Luther's co-worker, Philipp Melanchthon (1497-1560). This chronicle distinguishes three epochs of two thousand years each. Luther assumed that Abraham was born around 2000 BC, which neatly divided the period of four thousand years

## THE EPOCHS OF WORLD HISTORY

into two equal parts. Interestingly, this division was based upon the so-called *Traditio Domus Eliae,* or *Dictum Eliae,* that is, a proverb from the school of Elijah. The oldest written version is found in the Talmud (Sanhedrin 97a [cf. 97b], Avodah Zarah 9a).

In 1531, Melanchthon wrote that the *Dictum Eliae* was very famous among the rabbis, and was generally accepted by the Jews. Both Luther and Melanchthon referred to Paul of Burgos (1353-1435), a converted Spanish Jew, who quoted the *Dictum Eliae* from rabbinical sources. The *Dictum* was also quoted by the Italian philosopher Giovanni Pico della Mirandola (1463-1494) and the German theologian Andreas Osiander (1498-1552). The Dictum says:

> *Sex millia annorum mundus, et deinde conflagratio [or, destructio].*
> *Duo millia inane [or, sine lege],*
> *Duo millia lex,*
> *Duo millia Messiae.*
> *Et propter peccata nostra, quae multa et magna sunt,*
> *deerunt anni qui deerunt.*

That is, world history will last six thousand years, consisting of two thousand years which are "empty" (or, without law), two thousand years under the law, and two thousand years which are the epoch of the Messiah. Because of our many and great sins, says the proverb in Melanchthon's version, a number of years will drop out. That is, Christ was supposed to have come again before the year 2000. In the Talmud's version, however, the words imply that the Messianic era should have started already, but that it was delayed because of "our many and great sins." This suggests that these words of the Talmud words were first formulated shortly after the year 240 A.D., when, according to Jewish calculation, the period of four thousand years since creation had ended. I will come back to this idea of six thousand years of world history when I discuss the "Sixth Era."

It may seem strange that Melanchthon based such an important view concerning the tripartite division of world history on a single extra-biblical source. However, he believed there was some corroboration for his view in Daniel. In Daniel 12:11-12, two periods are mentioned, one of 1290 days and another one of 1335 days. Melanchthon was convinced that these "days" had to be read as years, that the two numbers had to be added, and that the total number referred to the end of times. Thus, he believed that 2625 years would elapse between Daniel and the end times; there was about six hundred years between Daniel and the birth of Christ, leaving two thousand years for the period between Christ's birth and his second coming. This interpretation was rejected by the French-Swiss Reformer John Calvin (1509-1564), although he too made the remark that the world was drawing toward its end although it had not yet reached the end of the six thousand years.

Somewhat later, the German theologian Andreas Musculus (1514-1581), in his tract, *Vom jüngsten Tage* ("About the Last Day"), also referred to the *Dictum of Elijah* as evidence that the world would not endure longer than six thousand years. He added that, because the world had lasted already for 5556 years, it should have about five hundred years more to go, according to Elijah's prophecy. So apparently he too accepted the theory that world history would end around the year 2000. Around the same time, the famous English theologian Hugh Latimer (c. 1487-1555) adhered to the six thousand years theory, and thus, when he was writing in 1552, he stated that "there is no more left but four hundred and forty-eight [years]," i.e., until 2000, although he also believed that the time would be shortened. A century and a half later, Robert Fleming (c. 1660-1716), a pastor of Scottish descent in the Dutch cities of Leyden and Rotterdam, wrote that he expected the destruction of the "Papal Kingdom" in the year 2000. In that year, Christ would return and the world would enter into that glorious "sabbatical millenary," when "the saints shall reign on the earth, in a peaceable manner for a thousand years more."

## Joachim of Fiore

The best known tripartite division of history is the one designed by a twelfth-century monk, Joachim of Fiore. He claimed that during the night before Easter he had received a vision in which God had unfolded to him his plan for history. After the empire of the Father (that of the law, i.e., from Abraham to Christ) and

## THE EPOCHS OF WORLD HISTORY

that of the Son (the empire of the gospel), he saw a "third empire" arising, the millennial kingdom of the Holy Spirit, the kingdom of love and freedom, in which the corrupt church was to be restored in its original purity. In Joachim's view, the unit of which these epochs are made up is the generation. Matthew 1:17 tells us that forty-two generations elapsed between Abraham and Christ; Joachim believed that the second epoch would include the same number of generations.

Joachim did not try to calculate the beginning of the Third Epoch, but his followers did. Assuming thirty years for a generation, they expected the kingdom of the Holy Spirit to arrive in the year (42 x 30 =) 1260. Of course, the numbers 42 and 1260 strike us immediately: Revelation 11:2-3 speaks of 42 months, that is, 42 x 30 = 1260 days; the Joachimites turned this into 1260 years. They linked this with the Holy Roman Emperor Frederick II (1212-1250), who was exceptionally gifted both politically and scientifically, and who was the "emperor of peace" (the German name Friedrich is derived from the word *Friede*, meaning "peace"!), whom they nevertheless regarded as the Antichrist.

This astonishing person, called *stupor mundi* ("the amazement of the world"), actually exhibited a kind of "end time" character. This came to light, among other things, in his ardent conflict with Pope Gregory IX, in which each of them depicted the other as the Antichrist. When, after Frederick's death, apparently the Third Era did not begin, some Joachimites believed that the start of this Third Epoch should be enforced with violence. One of the most famous of these fanatics was Fra Dolcino, who shortly after 1300 announced the church of the Spirit, implying thereby the end of the church of the flesh, and, hidden in the mountains with his followers, he awaited the appearance of a saving emperor and a holy pope. (To be sure, Fra Dolcino himself worked with a scheme of four epochs; his system assumed that the Third Era had begun with the Emperor Constantine and Pope Sylvester.) In 1307 he and his followers were all killed in a most cruel way. (Umberto Eco's novel, *The Name of the Rose* [1980], contains many references to Fra Dolcino.)

In fact, Joachim was a forerunner of the post-millennialists. These are Christians who believe in a future millennial Kingdom, which does not follow the second coming of Christ but precedes it (post means that the second coming takes place after the millennium). Later German philosophers, such as the Enlightenment thinker Gotthold E. Lessing (1729-1781), and the German philosopher Friedrich Schelling (1775-1854), each in their own way played with the notion of a Third Empire. Lessing found that the idea of a triple empire was not without its attractions, but he blamed Joachim and his associates for proclaiming the Third Empire as being so near. Schelling saw, after a *Petrine* (Roman Catholic) and a *Pauline* (Germanic Protestant) empire, a third *Johannine* empire coming up, which would acknowledge only one world religion of love.

The German philosopher Georg Hegel (see above) inspired quite a few philosophers of history with his dialectic concept of *thesis, antithesis,* and *synthesis*. Thus, the Norwegian playwright Henrik Ibsen (1826-1906) spoke of a Third Empire which would be a synthesis of ancient culture (thesis) and Christianity (antithesis), and the Russian writer Dmitry R. Mereshovski (1865-1941) saw a Third Empire as a synthesis of religion and science. In the works of the Russian novelist Fyodor M. Dostoyevski (1821-1881) and the German philosopher of history Oswald Spengler (1880-1936) we encounter similar ideas.

The idea of a Third Era has become well known in the twentieth century through the "Third Reich" of German National Socialism. This was a third empire after the first one, the Holy Roman Empire of the German nation, and the second one, the Lesser German Empire of the German emperors of the nineteenth and twentieth century. The person who most influenced the National Socialist idea of the Third Empire, albeit inadvertently, was the German political writer, Arthur Moeller van den Bruck (1876-1925), who in 1923, two years before his suicide, published his book, *Das dritte Reich* ("The Third Empire"). He too interpreted the concept of a Third Empire in a Hegelian dialectic sense, namely, as an eschatological and millennialist synthesis of the Holy Roman Empire (thesis) and the "second" German empire (antithesis). In this sense, the term was adopted by the National Socialists, although they gave it a form very different from what the writer had intended. By the *Third Reich*, the Nazis meant the "millennial empire" (compare Joachim!), which they themselves founded as the successor to the first and second empires in 1933.

## Are We Living in the "Fourth Era"?

Forty years ago, I described a view in which the seven days of creation were considered to be "types" of seven epochs of salvational history. This view had been presented before by writers such as the Anglo-Saxon theologians and Bible teachers Andrew Jukes (1815-1901), Frederick W. Grant (1834-1902), Philip Mauro (1859-1952) and Algernon J. Pollock (1864-1957). In this dispensational view, the fourth day, on which the celestial bodies were created, represented the present epoch of grace, that is, the era of the Christian Church. Christ is the sun of righteousness (Mal. 4:2), the light that came into the world (John 12:4, 6). As long as this light was in the world, it was "day," says Jesus in John 9:4-5. After a glorious "sunset" (so to speak), the "night" came, in which the only light came from the moon and the stars. The Church has no light of itself but, just as the moon reflects the light of the sun, the Church spreads the divine light which it receives from Christ (cf. Matt. 5:14; 2 Cor. 3:18). In Philippians 2:15, Christians are compared to celestial bodies, which must give light in the darkness.

I will leave this view now, and turn to Daniel 2 and 7, which I have already mentioned several times previously. Let us now compare these chapters in Daniel to Revelation 17:7-9. Here, the Apostle John gives an explanation of the "beast," the eschatological world power, which is destroyed by Christ at his second coming. Verse 10 says that the seven heads of the beast are seven "kings." As is the case with each element in Revelation, there are many interpretations for this one as well. I myself prefer, along with many commentators, to interpret these seven "kings" as seven personified kingdoms. These seven successive empires, leading to the "beastly" world power of the latter days, would then be: Egypt, Assyria, (Neo-) Babylonia, Medo-Persia, Greece-Macedonia, the Roman Empire, and a seventh empire (for this, I refer the reader once more to *The Ninth King*). Some interpreters (Seakle Greijdanus, William Hendriksen) think of Old-Babylonia rather than of Egypt but, in my opinion, this empire lies outside the scope of Scripture.

## PROBING THE PAST

The text of verses 10-14 can now be paraphrased as follows. The seven heads of the beast are seven kingdoms. Five of these empires, from the Egyptian to the Greco-Macedonian Empire, had already perished by the time of the Apostle John, the sixth (the Roman Empire) still existed at the time of the author, the seventh empire had not yet come, and when it did, it would last only a short while. The beast itself is the eighth world empire, as well as the head of that empire, but it is a revival of one of the previous seven. It will ultimately be destroyed, for it will perish by the hand of the Lamb, who is God's Messiah, the King of kings (Rev. 17:14; 19:11-21). After the eight preceding kings, the Messiah is the Ninth King (cf. the title of my book to which I have referred above).

The fact that we are dealing symbolically here with seven heads of the *one* beast which itself is "the eighth" signifies that in the beast the continuity of the seven previous empires becomes clear. They are the beast's heads because he includes in himself all these previous empires. In the same way, the beast in Revelation 13 exhibits the features of three previous empires especially: the leopard, the bear, and the lion. According to Daniel 7:4-6, these are (in reverse chronological order) the Greco-Macedonian, Medo-Persian, and Babylonian Empires. The beast itself is the revived Roman Empire. This is the meaning of the statement that the beast is itself "the eighth," but is "of the seven," namely, a revival of the sixth or Roman Empire.

Some commentators have argued that "king" cannot mean "kingdom." However, in Daniel 7:17, the four "beasts" (i.e., empires) actually bear the title of "kings." But perhaps we should answer this objection in another way, i.e., by thinking in Revelation 17 especially of the *angelic princes* who represent the successive empires, just as they did in Daniel 10. In Scripture, the world empires are usually characterized by one specific earthly prince. These are, respectively: the Pharaoh of the Exodus (Egypt); Sennacherib (Assyria); Nebuchadnezzar (Babylonia); Cyrus, and possibly Ahasuerus as well (Persia); Alexander the Great (Greece-Macedonia); Augustus, and possibly Nero as well (Rome); and the "beast" (the eighth king) of Revelation. Behind each of these earthly princes there is a spiritual power, an "angelic prince." To what we just said about the "continuity" of the succession of world empires, we can now add that this involves the fact that hiding behind the world empires is *one and the same* principal angelic power, called the devil and Satan (Rev. 12:9; 20:2).

The Scottish historian John Adam Cramb (1862-1913) once said that world empires are "successive incarnations of the divine ideas." I would like to rephrase this in the following way: world empires are successive "incarnations" of concrete divine powers. And Britain's prime minister, Lord Rosebery (1847-1929), said of these empires that they were "not built by saints and angels, but the work of man's hands"; but he adds, "human and yet not entirely human, for even the most inattentive and cynical must see the finger of the Divine." I would like to restate this as follows: world empires are built by man's hands, which, however—without taking anything away of human responsibility—are guided by "divine" (read, angelic) powers, over which is the God of gods.

## A Jewish View

The idea of seven world empires is supported by Jewish tradition, which says that Israel in total has known six exiles. These exiles occurred in the Egyptian, Assyrian, Babylonian, Medo-Persian, Greek, and "Edomite" (= Roman) Empires. In the rabbinical literature, "Edom" is the code-name for the Roman Empire, both in its earlier pagan form and in its later Christian manifestation. Over time, the name was even used to designate Christendom in general. According to some Christian thinkers, the whole his-tory of the Western world, viewed from a meta-historical perspec-tive, can be seen as the struggle between Jacob and Esau, that is, between the *God* of Jacob and the *god* of Esau, i.e., Edom, or the (apostate) "Christian" world (for more details, see *The Ninth King*). Of course, there have been many more mighty empires in world history. We can think, for instance, of ancient China and India, the Inca Empire, the Mongolian and African empires, the Russian Empire (later extended to become the Soviet Union), etc. But the seven world empires we are discussing here share one significant feature: they each exhibited a close relationship with God's chosen people, Israel. Things which have hardly any im-

## PROBING THE PAST

portance in secular historiography are of the greatest importance to God; in his historiography, Israel is always the point of reference. We have already seen some examples of this. Israel has been under the authority of all the seven empires listed. Even today, the state of Israel would have no place without the support of the Western world, which is the cultural and spiritual heir of the ancient Roman Empire.

In *The Ninth King*, I have described certain parallels between the first empire (Egypt) and the eighth empire (eschatological "Rome"), and also between the third (Babylon) and the eighth empires. Moreover, I have argued that the greatest catastrophes occurred to Israel during the seventh and eighth empires. The seventh is the Germanic Empire, which reached what I believe to be its lowest point with the idolatrous National Socialism; under this regime, Israel experienced the catastrophe of the Holocaust. The eighth empire will be that of the Antichrist. The Ninth King is the one who, in Revelation 17:14, is called "the Lamb" and "Lord of lords and King of kings." It is only under his rule that all of Israel's exiles and tribulations will come to an end.

"(World) empires" in the meaning here intended are not common countries or states. A (world) empire includes a number of various countries, which each retain their own cultural character even though they have been brought together under one central ruler. We speak of a world empire only if it forms a central power in the world, which is supreme over other countries and empires. The idea that there have been several such successive world empires is deeply rooted in European history, as we will see in greater depth. Traditionally this phenomenon has been called the *translatio imperii*, the "transference of the world empire." Such a *translatio* is precisely what the prophet presents to Nebuchadnezzar in Daniel 2: the power is transferred from the first empire to the second, and from the second to the third, etc.

In Europe, it was usually believed that this transference moved from the East to the West: from Mesopotamia to Greece, from Greece to Rome, from Rome to Western Europe, from Europe to (North) America. This idea certainly does not fit into the scheme of seven world empires as we see it: from Egypt to Assyria is north-eastward, from Assyria to Babylon is southward, and

## THE EPOCHS OF WORLD HISTORY

from Babylon to Susa is eastward. Only the movements from Susa to Macedonia (or Athens), and from there to Rome, are westward. That is also true for the movement from Europe to America. The eighth empire, that of the beast, is indeed explicitly a revival of the ancient Roman Empire, but America, as the most powerful co-heir of Rome, could easily be included in this (see *The Ninth King*, chapter 9). However, the question whether the center of power will be established in Rome (Brussels?) or in Washington cannot be answered with any certainty at present.

## The Four Middle Empires

In the summary given of the seven world empires the Roman Empire is the sixth. In the summing-up of the four world empires in Daniel 2 and 7, the Roman Empire comes fourth. And in the German tradition, the Roman Empire lives on in the First, Second and Third Reichs; these are the Holy Roman Empire of the German nation ([800]-962-1806), the German Empire of the Hohenzollern emperors (1871-1918), and the Nazi Empire (1933-1945), respectively. We should therefore take great care in numbering the empires (see the following scheme):

> Numbering of the Empires
> 1. Egypt
> 2. Assyria
> 3. = I. Babylon
> 4. = II. Medo-Persia
> 5. = III. Greece
> 6. = IV. Rome
>         i. Holy Roman Empire
>         ii. Lesser German Empire
> 7.        iii. Third Reich
> 8. Empire of the Antichrist
> 9. = V. Empire of Messiah

Arabic numerals: numbering of Revelation 17.
Large Roman numerals: numbering of Daniel 2 and 7.
Small Roman numerals: numbering of German history.

## PROBING THE PAST

In the series of the seven world empires plus "the eighth," the four empires which are exactly in the middle take up a special place. They are preceded by the Egyptian and Assyrian Empires, and followed by the "seventh" (Germanic) Empire and the eighth empire of the Antichrist. Today we also find other, liberal views on the identity of the four empires in Daniel 2 and 7 (see *The Ninth King*, Appendix 5). However, for many centuries it was firmly believed by both Jews and Christians that these four empires were the Babylonian, Medo-Persian, Greek, and Roman Empires. As such, throughout the Christian era they have particularly stirred the imagination.

In this connection, time and again some key questions arose. In Daniel 2 and 7, we read how the fourth (Roman) Empire is immediately superseded by a new, a "fifth," empire, which is that of the Messiah. There is no doubt that this, too, is an "intra-temporal" (immanent) empire, which as such directly follows the previous four empires in this world. This "chiliast" or "millennialist" view was already held by church fathers such as Irenaeus, Tertullian, Commodian, and Lactantius. The American philosopher of history Ernest L. Tuveson (1915-1996) said that the doctrine of the millennial kingdom seems to have been very strong until late in the reign of Constantine.

However, what is the nature of this fifth empire? Is it a Christian "empire" in Europe, which has existed in numerous forms since the fall of the Western Roman Empire in 476, or even since the fourth century, when the Roman Empire became Christian? Or is it an empire that will only emerge at the second coming of Christ? How will the Messianic Empire seamlessly follow the fourth empire, Rome? Did this transition take place already under Constantine the Great? Or did it occur after the fall of Rome, at the rise of the Carolingian Empire in the eighth century? Or is it rather the case that, since the Messianic Empire will only arise after the second coming of Christ, it is precisely the Roman Empire which lives on in Europe in various forms until the present day? In brief, do we live today under the fourth or under the fifth empire of Daniel?

## Fourth and Fifth Empires

In this study, a clear answer is given to this question. According to Daniel 7, in comparison with Daniel 2, it is no less than the Son of

## THE EPOCHS OF WORLD HISTORY

Man, the One who comes with the clouds of heaven, who brings the fourth empire to a *radical* and *sudden* end, and immediately after this empire establishes the fifth and last intra-temporal empire. If we consider this, it must be crystal clear that the fourth empire has not yet come to an end yet, and that the empire of the Son of Man will only emerge at his second coming (this was also the view of all the Greek church fathers and almost all the Latin ones, *including* Augustine). We can therefore conclude that we live during the time of the fourth empire; more precisely: during the time between the apparent fall of the Roman Empire and its revival in the last days.

The Romans themselves, at the summit of their world power, viewed their empire, which actually included almost the entire world known at the time, as the ultimate empire. They could hardly believe that their empire would ever perish, and that another one would take its place. In their opinion, the *translatio imperii* had come to an end in the Roman Empire, as the poet Virgil (70-19 BC), among others, expressed it in his pastoral poems. Jupiter was the god of that empire, and Virgil was his prophet, when he allegedly received the following words from Jupiter: *imperium sine fine dedi*, "I gave [you] an empire without end." It is striking that we find similar words in Daniel 2:44 and 7:14, 18, 27, but there the "empire without end" is not the fourth empire but the fifth! This is the Kingdom of the Son of Man.

Of course, the Roman Christians knew about this fifth empire. But they had remained Roman enough to believe that the glory of Rome would continue at least until the coming of that fifth empire. The famous Christian historiographer Orosius (c. 375-418), a student of Augustine, expressed it this way: *Quando cadet Roma, cadet et mundus* ("When Rome falls, the world falls too"). In some sense he was right. Even if Revelation 17 tells us that there is a seventh and an eighth king after the sixth (Roman) king, those seventh and eighth kingdoms are nothing but revivals of the sixth empire. In this sense, the Christian knows that he lives under the "last" empire before the second coming of Christ. Therefore the Christian lives *circa finem*, near the end of times, as the medieval Otto bishop of Freising (c. 1114-1158) put it because of the fact that the *translatio imperii*, the succession of the world empires, was now completed (cf. 1 Cor. 10:11, which speaks of "us, on whom the end of ages has come").

PROBING THE PAST

## More on the *Translatio Imperii*

Other Reformers have better understood that, up to their own time, the "stone" of Daniel 2 had never become "a great mountain," and that the ideal of a "Roman" Empire in Europe had not yet died out completely. It is one of the particular aims of my book *The Ninth King* to shed light on this "Roman ideal." It lived on in the empire of the Carolingians (during the reign of Charlemagne in particular), in the Holy Roman Empire (particularly under the Ottonian dynasty), in the world empire of the Habsburg ruler Charles V, in the Renaissance "empires" of letters and scholars, in the Napoleonic Empire, and similarly in the Second (German imperial) and the Third Reichs which were viewed as successors to the First (Holy Roman) Empire. Each time the Roman ideal re-emerged, people spoke of a renaissance, a "rebirth," *of ancient (Roman) Man*: this occurred in the Carolingian renaissance (c. 800), the Ottonian renaissance (c. 1000), the twelfth-century renaissance, and finally *the* Renaissance (flourishing in the fifteenth century).

Philipp Melanchthon (1497-1560) fully accepted and elaborated the idea of the four world empires and that of the *translatio imperii*. According to him, too, after the fall of the Western Roman Empire in 476, the "fourth empire" lived on in the Carolingian and Ottonian Empires, etc. It is significant that, in his opinion, the "fifth empire" in Daniel 2 and 7 is not a "Christian" empire in which we would supposedly still be living today, but one that will arise at the last day, the second coming of Messiah, the resurrection of the dead and the end of (the present) times. In this connection, Melanchthon had to account, of course, for the fragmentation of the empire and the rise of the national states. He found the explanation for this in the Roman feet of the image of Daniel 2, which were partly of iron, partly of clay.

Martin Luther (1483-1546) also spoke explicitly of the *translatio* of the Roman Empire, *von den Griechen auf die Deutschen*, "from the Greeks [i.e., the Eastern Romans] to the Germans [i.e., the Carolingians and Ottonians]." He applied the feet partly of iron, partly of clay, to the strong and the weak emperors. He expressly stated that the Roman Empire was the last empire, and that Christ alone would break it down and replace it by his own empire. In his view based on the Book of Daniel, the Turkish Empire rapidly rising in his days could not possibly form a fifth empire before the second coming of Christ; it was only a forerunner of the anti-Christian empire of the last days. Shortly after the empire of the Turks ended—that is in retrospect only at the end of the First World War (1917-18)!—the last day would arrive. This is an extremely fascinating view—despite the fact that since the end of the First World War almost another century has passed.

## Are We Living in the "Fifth Era"?

The interpretation of John Calvin (1509-1564) concerning the fifth empire in Daniel 2 and 7 was totally different. According to him, the four world empires would not come to an end at the Second Coming, because they had already come to an end by the time of the first coming of Jesus Christ. Since that event, we are living under the "fifth" empire, the ecclesiastical empire of Jesus Christ, as he put it. It is no wonder that outside Calvinistic circles this interpretation has gained hardly any following because of the mind-boggling exegetical gymnastics involved.

First, the stone in Daniel 2 destroys the Roman Empire in one strike, whereas at the birth or the ascension of Christ, or at the day of Pentecost (Acts 2), the Roman Empire showed not the least sign of falling.

Second, the ideal of a *Roman* Empire in Europe never fully died out, even after it had turned Christian. It simply became the Christian Roman Empire, or even the *Holy* Roman Empire, which formally lasted until 1806.

Third, in church history, a true world empire ruled according to the mind of Christ has simply never existed.

Fourth, even when the Western Roman Empire was destroyed, this was not brought about by orthodox Christianity, but by pagan or Arian Germanic tribes.

Fifth, no matter how "heavenly" and "spiritual" the "fifth empire" of Christ may be, if we follow the basic idea of Daniel 2 and 7 it must be viewed, too, as an earthly, intra-temporal, political empire, and cannot be viewed as a *spiritual,* religious, supratemporal empire in opposition to the four earthly, intra-temporal, political empires.

Sixth, in Daniel 7:13 the Messianic Kingdom clearly emerges, not at the birth or ascension of the Messiah, but at his coming with the clouds (cf. Matt. 24:30; 26:64; Rev. 1:7).

Therefore, the only possible conclusion is that Calvin was wrong, and the majority of commentators were and are right. The fifth empire, that of the Messiah, begins only at the Second Coming of Jesus Christ.

## Are We Living in the "Sixth Era"?

In the traditional dispensational view within certain Evangelical circles, the present dispensation of the Church is the sixth one. Dispensationalism as a theological paradigm is based upon a strong notion of discontinuity between the successive phases of salvational history. Consequently, this history is viewed as divided up into a number of so-called "dispensations," distinct epochs in which God supposedly dealt and deals with mankind according to rather different principles.

The *Scofield Reference Bible* distinguishes seven successive dispensations:

1. The dispensation of Innocence (from creation to the Fall into sin),
2. The dispensation of Conscience (from the Fall to the Flood),
3. The dispensation of Human Government (from the Flood to Abraham),
4. The dispensation of Promise (from Abraham to Moses),
5. The dispensation of the Law (from Moses to the first com ing of Christ),
6. The dispensation of Grace (From Christ's first coming to his second coming),
7. The dispensation of the Millennial Kingdom (to the eternal state).

The weakness of such a system is that various authors arrive at quite different schemes. For instance, the Bible teacher John Ashton Savage (1818-1900) also saw the present dispensation as the Sixth Era, but he started his series of dispensations only at

## THE EPOCHS OF WORLD HISTORY

the Fall, and split Scofield's dispensation of the Law up into two parts: from Moses to the Babylonian captivity, and from the captivity to Christ.

When we think of a Sixth Epoch, quite a different scheme comes to mind as well, one that is particularly linked to the year 2000. I already gave Melanchthon's version of the *Dictum Eliae*, which says that, because of our many and great sins, a number of years would drop out. But Instead of these lines, Martin Luther offers us a rather different version:

*Isti sunt Sex dies hebdomadae coram Deo,*
*Septimus Dies Sabbatum aeternum est.*

That is, Luther compares the six thousand years with the six weekdays "before God," that is, the days of creation, followed by the seventh "day" of God's eternal rest. Luther quoted Psalm 90:4 ("A thousand years in your sight are but as yesterday when it is past") and 2 Peter 3:8 ("With the Lord one day is as a thousand years") in order to claim that, since God had created the world in six days, the history of the world was going to last six millennia.

This was an ancient idea, which already occurs in the Slavonic book of Enoch (32:2; 33:1-2), where God mysteriously says, "I blessed the seventh day, which is the Sabbath, on which [Adam] rested from his works. And I appointed the eighth day also, that the eighth day should be the first-created after my work, and that the first seven revolve in the form of the seventh thousand, and that at the beginning of the eighth thousand there should be a time of not-counting, endless, with neither years, nor months nor weeks nor days nor hours." This seems to point to six thousand years of labor and toil until the judgment, followed by a millennium of rest and blessedness, and afterwards the eighth eternal day.

The idea recurred in later rabbinical writing, such as that of Abraham bar Hiyya ha-Nasi (c. 1100) and that of Nachmanides (or Ramban, c. 1250). Both rabbis asserted that the Messiah would come at the end of the six thousand years. The same idea was found in the *Zohar*, the famous Cabbalistic work of Moses de León (written in the thirteenth century but allegedly going back to the second-century Rabbi Shimon bar Yochai).

## PROBING THE PAST

## Early Millennialism

Already at an early stage, this millennialist view crept into Christian thinking. In the Epistle of Barnabas (around 100 AD) it is said: "Note, children, what this 'He was ready in six days' implies. It means: the Lord will complete all in six days. With the Lord, one day means thousand years. Thus, all will be completed in six days, that is, in six thousand years, children. And he rested at the seventh day. That means, when his Son is come and the time of lawlessness is finished, and he will judge the wicked and will change the sun, the moon and the stars, then he will certainly rest at that day" (15:3-5). Similarly, the church father Irenaeus (d. 202) wrote in his *Adversus Haereses*, "If the days of the Lord are as a thousand years, and creation is completed in six days, then apparently its completion is the year 6000." And, "For the righteous, he will allow the times of the empire to arrive, that is, the rest, the holy seventh day." The same view is encountered with church fathers such as Hippolytus, Lactantius, Hilary, Cyprian, Ambrose, Jerome, and Augustine. They expected a millennial period of peace and righteousness, although they had no place for ethnic Israel in it, and often took the seventh "thousand" to mean "everlasting."

Obviously, the comparison to the six days of creation not only suggested that world history would last seven thousand years, but also that it should be divided up into seven periods of one thousand years each. Thus, the Christian scholar Sextus Julius Africanus (c. 160-c. 240) wrote a five-volume *Chronographia*, in which he attempted to synchronize sacred and profane history, and to divide history up into six periods of a thousand years. Precisely in the middle of the six thousand years, that is, in the year 3000 after creation, he placed the death of Peleg (Gen. 10:25); the name Peleg, which probably means "division," was even interpreted to mean *to hèmisu*, "the half."

Just like several other church fathers, Sextus Julius Africanus believed Christ to have been born in the year 5500 after creation—a number based on Septuagint chronology—which left precisely one twelfth of world history remaining. Support for this idea was found, for instance, by Origen, in the parable of the vineyard in Matthew 20:1-16. The twelve hours of the "day" mentioned there

## THE EPOCHS OF WORLD HISTORY

allegedly represented the whole of world history. The "last hour," being the hour of grace (Matt. 20:6, 9), had begun with the coming of Christ (1 John 2:18). So, several fathers expected the second coming of Christ to come in 500 AD. This meant that, just as the rabbis had been nervous around 240 A.D. (see above), tensions arose among some fathers when the year 500 came near.

A wiser approach was followed by Augustine. He rigorously broke away from the idea of six periods of precisely one thousand years each. However, he retained the interpretation of the days of creation as epochs of world history, although he assumed that each epoch was of a different length (*De Civitate Dei* XXII, 30). Thus, he considered the first period to include the 1656 years between the creation of Adam and Noah's flood. He arrived at roughly the same scheme that Savage followed many centuries later (see above): Adam – Noah – Abraham – David [Savage: Moses] – Babylonian Captivity – Christ – the *eschaton*.

The great difference from the later dispensationalists was that, for Augustine, the seventh "day" was the "eternal state" (the new heavens and the new earth), whereas for the dispensationalists this "day" was the millennial Messianic Kingdom, followed by a new eighth "day," the eternal state. Augustine found the basis for this division partly in the genealogy of Matthew 1, which is divided into three parts: from Abraham to David, from David to the Babylonian Captivity, and from the Captivity to Christ. Augustine explicitly said: "We now live in the Sixth Era." The fact that he rejected the idea of six epochs of exactly one thousand years each had the advantage that it emphasized the inability to pinpoint the year of Christ's second coming. Augustine quoted Acts 1:7 to show the impossibility of such a calculation. Thus, in his view we are still living in the sixth epoch.

Augustine's view gained a fairly large following. Paulus Orosius, the fifth-century historian, adopted it in his *Adversum Paganos* ("Against the Pagans"). The seventh-century Isidore of Seville used it in his *Etymologiarum sive originum libri viginti* ("Twenty Books of Etymologies or Orgins"). And the eighth-century English historian, the Venerable Bede did the same in his *De sex aetatibus* ("On the Six Epochs") and his *De ratione temporum* ("On the Reckoning of the Times"). Throughout the Middle Ages, the idea

## PROBING THE PAST

of the *aetates mundi* ("epochs of the world") based upon the days of creation remained a well-known theme.

## Are We Living in the "Seventh Era"?

Let us now come back for a moment to the matter of the four world empires. Not all authors have viewed the empires after the fall of the Western Roman Empire as variations on the Roman Empire. The "Monk of Saint Gall," an anonymous medieval chronicler (usually identified with Notker Balbulus, "the Stammerer," c. 840-912), saw, as it were, a new succession of empires arising after Rome. About the image which Nebuchadnezzar saw (Dan. 2) he wrote: "When the Almighty, who governs all and determines the destiny of kingdoms and epochs, had broken the feet of iron and clay of that wondrous image, that is, the Romans, he erected in the land of the Franks, by means of the renowned Charles, another no less wondrous image with a head of gold." Such a *translatio* had taken place before, when Constantine transferred the empire to the Greeks at Constantinople. Now the pope, on the basis of an authority founded on the see of "Peter," transferred the empire from the Greeks (i.e., the still surviving Eastern Roman Empire) to the Franks. This was what was called a *renovatio imperii Romani*, "renewal of the Roman Empire" (as Charlemagne wrote in his imperial bull) under Frankish authority.

So here we have Charlemagne (742-814) as a new golden head! But could a Christian such as the Monk of Saint Gall have wished to contradict Daniel 2? After the Roman Empire, the Kingdom of the Son of Man arrives, that is certain from the outset. And thus, a new image of which Charlemagne would be the golden head is conceivable only within the framework of the Roman Empire as it survives in different (Christianized) variations. Many authors throughout the history of the church have preferred such a solution. Thus, in the twelfth century, Otto, bishop of Freising distinguishes not only the four world empires, but also four epochs in world history, in such a way that the four world empires together form the first epoch of world history, the period until the birth of Christ. Since then, three epochs have supposedly followed. The fourth and last period—or, in the total series, the seventh em-

## THE EPOCHS OF WORLD HISTORY

pire—was supposed to have begun with the emperor Theodosius I, who on November 8, 392, elevated Christianity to the state religion and forbade all pagan worship. However, these latter epochs also include stages of the Roman Empire. This empire in its fourth and last stage has become a "Christian" empire, which will supposedly last until the Second Coming of Christ.

Just as I had a question for the monk, I have one for the bishop. Will the "Christian" empire really last until the Second Coming? Will there not be, just before the coming of Christ, an anti-Christian empire on earth? And when will that *anti*-Christian empire begin, or has it already begun in secularized Europe and North America? Could we not, with the same right, defend the thesis that this empire, so hostile to God, already began with the "Christianization" of the Roman Empire, the blending of church and state (to the detriment of the church)? This too is a question that is of essential significance for any Christian view of history; I have dealt with it extensively in my *The Ninth King*.

In European history, whenever an important empire approached its end, these kinds of eschatological questions emerged. When the house of the Holy Roman Hohenstaufen Emperors died out in 1254 with Conrad IV (1228-1254), many voices were raised in Germany warning that the fall of this empire would usher in the empire of the Antichrist. And just as it was believed that in the year 1000 history would come to an end and Christ would return, the same rumors arose everywhere in Christendom when the world was facing the year 2000.

## Are We Living in the "Eighth Era"?

Let us come back to the text of Revelation 17:10-14, where we hear about the beast, which is not only the eighth world empire but its head, as well as being a revival of one of the previous seven empires. Ultimately, it will be destroyed, for it will perish by the hand of the Lamb, who is the King of kings. After the well-known series of seven empires, there is an eighth, namely, that of the Antichrist, who will persecute God's people in a way that has hardly ever occurred before. The Ninth King is he who, at the end of our passage, is called "the Lamb" and "Lord of lords and King of

## PROBING THE PAST

kings." Only under him will all of Israel's exiles and tribulations come to an end.

The idea that there are several successive world empires in history is deeply rooted in European history. As I have said earlier, this phenomenon is traditionally called *the translatio imperii*, the "transference of the world-empire." As far as can be ascertained, the idea of the transition of one empire to its successor was expressed first in a writing attributed to Demetrius of Phaleron (c. 300 BC). He claimed that the idea of four world empires had first been launched by the Greek politician and historian Zenon of Rhodes shortly after the battle of Magnesia (190 BC). Already at that period, the fourth empire would have been Rome.

What is left is the eighth empire, the empire of the Antichrist. Some who see the power of Antichrist looming today might argue that we already live in the eighth era, or that we are on the brink of it. If this is true, we have all the more reason to look forward to the imminent coming of the Ninth King. In the nineteenth century, new interest for prophetic epochs and dispensations sprang up. However, we would do well not to be carried away by speculations. Christians who looked forward to the Lord's coming have always clung to his word: "Behold, I am coming soon!" (Rev. 22:7, 12, 20).

**ALSO FROM THE AUTHOR
AT EVERY MAJOR ONLINE BOOK RETAILER**

## Chapter Seven
# THE PROVIDENCE OF GOD

In previous chapters we have seen that Christians believe in some design, end-purpose, teleology, which history exhibits. History has a goal, and that goal is the ultimate establishment of the Kingdom of God (see chapter 8). Many details in history can be understood within their limited context without knowing about this ultimate goal. But to understand the overall picture, it is indispensable to know the biblical truth about the Kingdom of God. No Christian view of history can be complete without having some understanding of the Kingdom.

The Kingdom of God is, apart from the divine persons themselves (Father, Son, Holy Spirit), the most comprehensive subject of the entire Bible. Holy Scripture is, so to speak, the Book about the Kingdom of God, to which people have looked forward from the outset. The Kingdom has, to some extent, become reality in Jesus Christ at his First Coming, and will become full reality at his Second Coming. You can follow the thread of the Kingdom from book to book in the Bible. Scripture's central topic is always "the mystery of His [i.e., God's] will, according to His good pleasure which He purposed in Himself, that in the dispensation of the fullness of the times He might gather together in one all things in Christ, both which are in heaven and which are on earth" (Eph. 1:9-10 NKJV).

## The Hidden God

In its most elementary form, the Kingdom of God is nothing other than the general dominion of God. God reigns over the heavens and the earth; he reigns over what he has created. One does not always easily recognize that God holds sway, and if you close your eyes to it, you might even deny it. Many historians do not perceive anything of God's dominion in history, and do not even *want* to see it. Even believers may sometimes have difficulty accepting it. Especially when they have to suffer, they may feel that God has lost control over things, or even that there is no God at all who guides things. God often resembles the remote, mysterious, inaccessible, and perhaps even non-existing authorities in the novels of the German-Czech novelist of Jewish descent, Franz Kafka (1883-1924), such as *The Trial* and *The Castle*.

It is only through faith that we know that behind the scenes of all things that happen the dominion of God is concealed. Only through faith do we know that God is there, that we can trust him, and that he never loses control. Many people will argue that, if God is really there in history, and if it is even essential to assume this in order to acquire a proper perspective on history, at least one should say that God has done his best to remain as hidden as possible. They might even argue that assuming the presence of God in history does not add anything to our understanding of history because God has hidden himself so effectively. To take a parallel: what does it add to our physical understanding of earth, water, fire and air if we attach the idea of *elemental spirits* to them, as the Bible and Jewish literature do?

This idea of the *deus absconditus*, the "hidden God," has occupied the mind of many philosophers and theologians throughout the ages. The expression has several quite distinct meanings. The first is the *ontological* meaning. God is the Creator, and we are, and always will remain, his creatures. As such, there is an ontic separation between him and us, which can never be bridged. Perhaps this is the meaning of the expression "your Father who is in secret" (Matt. 6:6, 18), that is, who cannot been seen (cf. Exod. 33:20; Deut. 5:26; Judg. 5:22-23; 13:22). Among many other things, it means that we cannot really understand the depths of his being: "the Spirit searches everything, even the depths of God. For who knows a person's thoughts except the spirit of that person, which is in him? So also no one comprehends the thoughts of God except the Spirit of God" (1 Cor. 2:10-11).

The second meaning of the "hidden God" is the *hamartiological* meaning (hamartiology is the theological doctrine of sin). Even if Man had never sinned, there would have been an ontic separation between him and God. But from the moment that he fell into sin,

# THE PROVIDENCE OF GOD

there is also a hamartiological separation. The prophet tells the apostate people: "Your iniquities have made a separation between you and your God, and your sins have hidden his face from you so that he does not hear" (Isa. 59:2). In the Garden of Eden, Adam and Eve hid from God after they had sinned. But it is equally true that God hides himself from humans when they rebel against him.

We find this thought in many passages of the Bible: "When he is quiet, who can condemn? When he hides his face, who can behold him, whether it be a nation or a man?" (Job 34:29). "Hide not your face from me. Turn not your servant away in anger" (Ps. 27:9a); "I will wait for the LORD, who is hiding his face from the house of Jacob" (Isa. 8:17). "In overflowing anger for a moment I hid my face from you" (Isa. 54:8). "Because of the iniquity of his unjust gain I was angry, I struck him; I hid my face and was angry" (Isa. 57:17). "I dealt with them according to their uncleanness and their transgressions, and hid my face from them" (Ezek. 39:24; cf. v. 29). God "will hide his face from them at that time, because they have made their deeds evil" (Micah 3:4).

Instead of complaining about God's apparent absence in history, people should wonder instead whether Man's rebellion might not be a good reason for this. The rebellious person may even be *happy* that God is apparently hidden because this gives him the opportunity to sin freely: "In the pride of his face the wicked does not seek him; all his thoughts are, 'There is no God'... He says in his heart, 'God has forgotten, he has hidden his face, he will never see it'" (Ps. 10:4, 11).

There is a third important meaning of the "hidden God," and that is the *soteriological* one (soteriology is the theological doctrine of salvation). It means that God may (seem to) hide himself from his faithful ones, in order to test and educate them through their sufferings, before he finally reveals himself again to them, to order to save them. We often hear the faithful complain about this "hiddenness" of God: "Why do you hide your face and count me as your enemy?" (Job 13:24). "Why, O LORD, do you stand far away? Why do you hide yourself in times of trouble?" (Ps. 10:1; cf. 13:1; 44:24; 69:17; 88:14; 89:46; 102:2; 143:7); "you hid your face; I was dismayed" (30:7b). "Give ear to my prayer, O God, and hide

**PROBING THE PAST**

not yourself from my plea for mercy!" (55:1). "Truly, you are a God who hides himself, O God of Israel, the Savior... But Israel is saved by the LORD with everlasting salvation" (Isa. 45:15-17).

## God's Providence

Hidden or not, God reigns nonetheless. The first time that the Bible speaks of God's reign is after the Israelites have left Egypt and have crossed the Red Sea. On the other shore they sing their great song of deliverance. At the end of it, we hear this shout of triumph: "The LORD will reign forever and ever," or, in the present tense, "The LORD reigns forever and ever." "To reign" (Heb., m-l-k) could also be rendered as, "is King (mèlekh)" (Exod. 15:18). God shows his Kingship in the way he has triumphed over Egypt, and even over her gods (Exod. 12:12; Num. 33:4): "Truly, your God is God of gods and Lord of kings," says King Nebuchadnezzar to the prophet Daniel (Dan. 2:47).

Speaking of "shouting" at the Red Sea, the false prophet Balaam said of Israel: "The LORD their God is with them, and the shout of a king is among them" (Num. 23:21). The "shout" (Heb. t'ru'ah) is the sounding of the sacred trumpets (Num. 10:1-10) in honor of God, the great King of Israel, and of his kingship, referring to the dominion of God, primarily over Israel and secondarily over all the earth. First, there was nothing to rule over, but God created this world, and put it, so to speak, in subjection under his own feet. This world is *his* world.

In the Psalms, we hear many times that God is King, that he rules over all things, that everything is subjected to him, and that his dominion is over all things. Here are some examples: "For the LORD is a great God, and a great King above all gods. In his hand are the depths of the earth; the heights of the mountains are his also. The sea is his, for he made it, and his hands formed the dry land" (Ps. 95:3-5; cf. 97:1). "I will extol you, my God and King, and bless your name forever and ever... All your works shall give thanks to you, O LORD, and all your saints shall bless you! They shall speak of the glory of your kingdom and tell of your power, to make known to the children of man your mighty deeds, and the glorious splendor of your kingdom. Your kingdom is an ev-

# THE PROVIDENCE OF GOD

erlasting kingdom, and your dominion endures throughout all generations." (Ps. 145:1, 10-13).

Theologians usually speak of God's "providence." That is, whatever happens in this world, God is "providing," taking care. This is in line with several passages of Scripture: "Who provides for the raven its prey, when its young ones cry to God for help, and wander about for lack of food?" (Job 38:41). "You visit the earth and water it; you greatly enrich it; the river of God is full of water; you provide their grain, for so you have prepared it" (Ps. 65:9); "in your goodness, O God, you provided for the needy" (Ps. 68:10). "He provides food for those who fear him; he remembers his covenant forever" (Ps. 111:5). "I will provide for them renowned plantations so that they shall no more be consumed with hunger in the land" (Ezek. 34:29); "As for the rich in this present age, charge them... to set their hopes... on God, who richly provides us with everything to enjoy" (1 Tim. 6:17).

## God's Ways

More precisely, what is meant by God's providence is that in all things that happen God's reigning hand is present in some way or another. This is not exactly identical with the Kingdom as such. It is not difficult to imagine a king who has supreme authority but does not occupy himself with all the details of what happens within his kingdom. Still less would he be involved in all that happens, or even *direct* all events in his kingdom. But with God it is different. His Kingdom involves his "hand" being in some way present in all events within his domain, whether they are good or bad. He may never be called the direct *cause* of bad things, but at the same time we must say that even the worst things are under his control. He allows or permits them, without being responsible for them. (I will come back to this important point below.)

God's Kingdom, or God's providence, involves his allowing or permitting the actions of others, humans or angels, but in particular his own active doing, according to his own sovereign will: "For he [i.e., God] will complete what he appoints for me [i.e., Job], and many such things are in his mind" (Job 23:14). "The works of his hands are faithful and just; all his precepts are trustworthy;

they are established forever and ever, to be performed with faithfulness and uprightness" (Ps. 111:7-8). "Our God is in the heavens; he does all that he pleases" (115:3). "I form light and create darkness, I make well-being and create calamity, I am the LORD, who does all these things" (Isa. 45:7). "My counsel shall stand, and I will accomplish all my purpose" (Isa. 46:10). "In a time of favor I have answered you; in a day of salvation I have helped you" (Isa. 49:8). "Does disaster come to a city, unless the LORD has done it?" (Amos 3:6b; about this verse, see chapter 3).

Personally, I prefer the word "ways" to the term "providence," because the former term also includes God's sustaining his creation. Here are some examples: "[P]lease show me now your ways, that I may know you in order to find favor in your sight" (Exod. 33:13). "The Rock, his work is perfect, for all his ways are justice" (Deut. 32:4). "His ways prosper at all times" (Ps. 10:5). "He made known his ways to Moses, his acts to the people of Israel" (Ps. 103:7). (These verses must be distinguished from those in which God's "ways" simply mean his "commandments.")

When I use the word "ways," I think of God's doings in history—which by definition is always *salvational* history—in permanent relationship to his *counsel*. His "ways" are the strategies through which he realizes his eternal counsel. His counsel is well established beforehand, but in his ways, there is permanent interaction with the free acts—whether good or bad—of humans. It is very important to understand this correctly. On the one hand, in Hyper-Calvinism, *all* that happens is part of God's counsel. On the other hand, in what we call process theology (Charles Hartshorne, John B. Cobb), *all* that happens belongs to God's ways (and Man's ways).

I am convinced that the truth lies in the middle. The outcome of history (or of certain events within history) has been determined by God beforehand in his counsel, whereas all other events belong to his ways. God's counsel *precedes* human history, whereas his *ways* are discerned *within* history and continually change *with* it. God's counsel is *transcendent*, while his ways, as accomplished within history, are *immanent*. In a very broad sense, Christians might define historical science as the scholarly investigation of God's ways in history. I will try to explain this.

## THE PROVIDENCE OF GOD

## Counsel *versus* Ways

Let me give some biblical examples of the important difference between God's counsel and his ways. God's *counsel* comes to light in his promises and prophecies, pointing forward to the final goal of his ways. In the diversity of, and modifications in, the manner in which this final goal is reached, God's *ways* become manifest:

(a) It was part of God's *counsel* that he gave to Abraham a rich offspring through his son Isaac, offspring to whom he entrusted his promises and blessings. It belonged to God's *ways* that even after Abraham, following a path of disobedience and disbelief, had fathered Ishmael by Hagar, God also gave blessings to this son (Gen. 17:20).

(b) It belonged to God's *counsel* that Moses led the people of Israel out of Egypt. It belonged to his *ways* that, when Moses opposed his calling and God became angry with him, he sent his brother Aaron to be with him (Exod. 4:10-15).

(c) It belonged to God's *counsel* that Israel entered the Promised Land and possessed it. It belonged to God's *ways* that it took forty years to reach this goal, as a consequence of Israel's rebellion (cf. 1 Cor. 10:5). For this reason, he decided that the people would arrive in the land only after all the older generation had died in the wilderness (Num. 14:28-35).

(d) It belonged to God's *counsel* to place the house of David over Israel; it was not Saul but David who was the "man after God's own heart" (1 Sam. 13:14). It belonged to God's *ways* (1) to make a "detour" via Saul—Saul was indeed chosen by God but entirely because of the sinful wishes of the people (1 Sam. 8:7-9)—and, afterwards, (2) to limit the authority of David's house temporarily to the two tribes (2 Sam. 2:4, 11; 5:1-5).

(e) It belongs very generally to God's *counsel* that Israel in the end will receive the fulfillment of all God's prophecies, and that for this reason the people are time and again delivered from their enemies. Thus, there was no chance that, for instance, the plan of Haman, the "enemy of the Jews" (Esther 3:10 etc.), to exterminate Israel could ever be successful. But the *way* in which this plan would fail was not certain. We see this very strikingly in Mordecai's appeal to Esther: "For if you keep silent at this time, relief and deliverance will rise for the Jews from another place, but you and your father's house will perish. And who knows whether you have not come to the kingdom for such a time as this?" (Est. 4:14). That is: "Ask yourself, Esther, whether God might not have placed you in this special position (Queen Consort of the Persian King Ahasuerus) in order to deliver his people through you. But know at the same time that God does not depend on you, so that if you are not prepared to do it, he will find another *way* to realize his *counsel*.

(f) It belonged to God's *counsel* that Jesus was to be born of the house of David, and thus of the tribe of Judah, and thus of Abraham. It belonged to God's *ways* that, in interaction with the (often evil) deeds of humans committed on their own responsibility and with their own freedom of choice, in Jesus' genealogy we find women such as Tamar and Rahab, who both prostituted themselves, or Ruth the Moabite (i.e., a member of a cursed nation), or Bathsheba, with whom David had an adulterous affair (Matt. 1:1-17). All these sins were definitely *not* part of God's counsel; but in his *ways*, he used them to reach his goal.

(g) It was "according to the definite plan (*counsel*) and foreknowledge of God" that Jesus was "delivered up" to be crucified (Acts 2:23). It belonged to God's *ways* that Caiaphas, Herod, and Pilate actually carried out this counsel, entirely on their own responsibility and using their own free choice. This is, I believe, the deeper meaning of Jesus' prayer in Gethsemane: "My Father, if this cannot pass unless I drink it, your will be done" (Matt. 26:42; cf. Luke 22:42). God's *counsel* was definite, and was entirely known to Jesus, who himself said: "[T]he Son of Man came… to give his life as a ransom for many" (Matt. 20:28). But even so, in Gethsemane he could still ask whether there was another *way* in which this counsel could be fulfilled. If Hyper-Calvinists or process theologians were right, and God's counsel and ways were identical, and (as Hyper-Calvinists would say) all events were determined beforehand, in my view Jesus' question would be incomprehensible.

## THE PROVIDENCE OF GOD

## A Mystery

We must remember that the distinction between God's counsels and God's ways as I have just explained it is a theological model. There are no Bible verses which explicitly state, "*This* is God's counsel, and *that* belongs to God's ways." The model helps us to distinguish between the two in the sense that, on the one hand, history in its entirety is *not* trapped within God's counsel, and on the other hand, there *are* definitely counsels of God that are worked out in and through history. However, the model does not necessarily solve all problems. It is only an aid to understanding some aspects of how God's hand is visible in history. But no model could ever solve, or take away, the essential biblical paradox between God's sovereignty on the one hand, and Man's responsibility on the other.

Let us think again of the Fall of Man into sin, as described in Genesis 3. On the one hand, I feel we cannot possibly say that the Fall as such was part of God's counsel, because this would make God responsible for Man's sin. We are never allowed to suggest that Man *had no choice* but to sin because the Fall had been predestined by God. On the other hand, we have seen above in chapter 3 that, as a consequence of the Fall, God is accompanying us on our way to the best of all possible worlds, which without the Fall would not have been possible. This is a mystery that we will never be able to grasp fully. The paradox is this: God does not want sin—but through Man's Fall into sin a perfect, holy, peaceful and righteous world has become possible, a world that will be far better than the innocent one that Adam had lost.

It is similar with all rebellion of Man. God does not *decide* this rebellion—it is not part of his counsel—but he can, and does, *predict* this rebellion, which is something very different. There is a fundamental difference between God's *foreknowing* and God's *foreordaining* (i.e., predestination) (Rom. 8:29). There are things that God did not decide, things that are the products of the free choice of humans. But God can know them beforehand, and predict them; in fact, he often does so. I am well aware of the philosophical problems involved in this distinction, because, if God *knows* beforehand that something will happen, allegedly this thing *must*

## PROBING THE PAST

necessarily happen. I do not agree with this—the fallacy is based on conceptualizing terms like foreknowledge—but I will not go into this theological-philosophical problem here (if you can read Dutch, see my book *Het plan van God*.)

An interesting biblical example is the Pharaoh of Egypt in the time of Moses. God tells Moses several times beforehand that Pharaoh will not listen to him (Exod. 7:4; 11:9). Some may argue that Pharaoh had no real choice because the Lord hardened his heart so that he *could* no longer repent (Exod. 4:21; 7:3; 9:12; 10:1, 20, 27; 11:10; 14:4, 8). Such people overlook the fact that at first it was Pharaoh *himself* who hardened his heart (7:13, 22; 8:19; 9:35). It was only after Pharaoh had rejected the Lord time and again that the moment inevitably came when the Lord rejected *him*. The Lord had predicted this beforehand because he knew Pharaoh's heart. But God did not *predestine* Pharaoh to be his enemy. The thought alone would be terrible. Even though Proverbs 16:4 says, "The LORD has made everything for its purpose, even the wicked for the day of trouble," this does not mean that certain people have been predestined *beforehand* to be wicked, and thus to be rejected. What the verse says is that, if people show themselves to be wicked, and persist in this way, they must realize what their destination will be: eternal damnation.

Compare this with the striking statement of Jesus: "Did I not choose you, the Twelve? And yet one of you [i.e., Judas] is a devil" (John 6:70). Please note, first, that this verse does *not* refer to the believers' eternal election (cf. Eph. 1:4-5); it only speaks of Jesus choosing these Twelve to be his disciples. Please note, second, that the verse does *not* say that Judas was *chosen* to be a devil. That was entirely his own choice and responsibility. Scripture declared beforehand that the "son of perdition" would be lost (John 17:12), but (a) it does not say that Judas had been *chosen* beforehand to be that "son of perdition," and (b) Scripture *predicting* something is essentially different from God *decreeing* something beforehand.

Proverbs 21:1 says, "The king's heart is a stream of water in the hand of the LORD; he turns it wherever he will." This does not mean that kings do not have their own responsibility because they are like robots or puppets with God pulling the strings. History is full of kings and emperors, warlords and generals, who all had (and have) their own freedom of choice and their own responsibility. At the same time they can move only within the boundaries set by the Lord. I think this is the meaning of the "mountains of bronze" in Zechariah 6:1. The four "chariots," which represent the four world empires known from Daniel 2 and 7, think they can move as they please (Zech. 6:1-8). But in reality their freedom is restricted by the mountains of bronze. The rulers of the four empires did not know the Lord, and certainly did not know his voice. Yet, God speaks to them (v. 7), and they have to do what he commands them to do, even if unconsciously. It even seems likely to me that the drivers of these chariots are in fact the angelic princes of these four empires—and *they* definitely know the voice of the Lord (cf. Job 1-2).

In summary, we might express the mystery mentioned above in the following way: all that happens in human history falls one hundred percent within the boundaries of God's sovereign will, and at the same time all these events—sometimes even, to some extent, natural catastrophes—are one hundred percent Man's responsibility. Evil in itself can never be God's will; but no evil can ever occur apart from God's will. Here we see the paradox again, in full power.

In all the cases I have mentioned, we can see the same pattern: God's *counsel* refers to decisions he himself makes beforehand, sovereignly, that is, entirely of his own free will. God's *ways* refer to the manner in which God realizes his counsel, which also depends on human responsibilities and choices. God attains his goal sovereignly and omnipotently, but in a manner that has *not* been decided beforehand. His goal is definite, but the ways in which he reaches his goal are not; these ways partly depend on human decisions, and these are often wrong (sinful) decisions.

## God's Breath

We now come to another question that is vital for the Christian view of history, namely, *how* does God work in history? It would be very wrong to think that God's working in history consists of the natural course of things, once in a while interrupted by divine supernatural interventions. Basically, there is nothing supernatural about God's presence, God's "hand," in the course of history, just as there is nothing supernatural about his presence, his "hand," in nature. God is involved in nature and history all the time, uninterruptedly, in a way that is fully natural to him.

Let me give a concrete historical example. In 1588, during the Eighty-Years War of the Dutch against the Spanish, the *Armada Invencible*, the "Invincible Fleet" of the (Catholic) Spanish (consisting of one hundred and thirty ships!) was sent against the Protestant countries of England and the Netherlands. The Fleet was tremendously damaged by severe storms; it lost almost half of its ships, plus twenty thousand men, and, heavily discouraged, the survivors sailed back to Spain. In Middelburg, capital of Dutch Zeeland, a coin was made with the inscription: *Deus flavit et dissipati sunt* ("God blew and they were scattered"; cf. Job 4:9a, "By the breath of God they perish"; also cf. Isa. 11:4b). What did the authorities in Middelburg mean by this? Is *every* storm-wind the breath of God? Or were the storms of 1588 in the North Atlantic a special intervention by God, to be distinguished from "normal" (natural) storms?

This is not an easy question. Jonah 1:4 says that "the LORD hurled a great wind upon the sea, and there was a mighty tempest on the sea." But does this mean that *every* tempest is "hurled" by God? About the Red Sea we read: "At the blast of your [i.e., God's] nostrils the waters piled up; the floods stood up in a heap" (Exod. 15:8). Exodus 9:28 speaks of "God's thunder and hail." God sometimes "answers in thunder" (Exod. 19:19), or "thunders from heaven" (1 Sam. 2:10 NKJV; cf. 1 Sam. 7:10; 2 Sam. 22:14; Ps. 18:13), or he "may send thunder and rain" (1 Sam. 12:17). Job speaks of "the thunder of his power" (Job 26:14), and Elihu of "the thunder of his voice" (Job 37:2; cf. v. 4-5; 40:9). Psalm 29 says that David heard in the thunder the voice of the Lord, while Psalm 81:7 speaks of "the secret place of thunder," and Psalm 104:7b says: "[A]t the sound of your thunder they [i.e., the waters] took to flight." Isaiah says, "[Y]ou will be visited by the LORD of hosts with thunder and with earthquake and great noise, with whirlwind and tempest, and the flame of a devouring fire" (Isa. 29:6).

However, does this mean that *all* thunderstorms are the voice or working of God? What about Elijah's experience: "And behold, the LORD passed by, and a great and strong wind tore the mountains and broke in pieces the rocks before the LORD, but the LORD was not in the wind. And after the wind an earthquake, but the LORD was not in the earthquake. And after the earthquake a fire, but the LORD was not in the fire. And after the fire the sound of a low whisper" (1 Kings 19:11-12).

The God of the Bible is not a storm-god of the kind we know from the Sumerian, Semitic, and Indo-European pantheons; he is no Indra, no Enlil, no Zeus, no Thor. He can speak *in* the thunder, but we cannot say that every thunder is by definition his voice. He can act through storms, earthquakes and fires, but he must not be *identified* with any of these natural phenomena as is the case with storm-gods. The God of the Bible sometimes prefers to speak through the "sound of a low whisper," or through a rustle in the tops of the balsam trees (2 Sam. 5:24). However, at the same time we must maintain that there is no storm, no shower and no sunshine apart from God's will. This follows from what the Apostle Paul told the Gentiles: God "did not leave himself without witness, for he did good by giving you rains from heaven and fruitful seasons, satisfying your hearts with food and gladness" (Acts 14:17). And Jesus said that the Father "makes his sun rise on the evil and on the good, and sends rain on the just and on the unjust" (Matt. 5:45).

In conclusion, we may recognize God's hand in some way or another in *every* storm, but some storms stand out, such as the one that destroyed the Armada, or the thunderstorm that changed the life of Martin Luther. In July 1505, when Luther was 21, he was on his way to Erfurt, and got caught in a horrific thunderstorm. When a bolt of lightning struck the ground near him, he screamed in terror, "Help me, Saint Anne [i.e., the mother of the Virgin Mary], and I will become a monk." He was saved, and shortly afterward, he entered the monastery in Erfurt. Without this vow, or (we could even say) without this thunderstorm, the course of history might have been very different.

## Two Ways of Divine Working

There are two ways in which the Bible speaks about God's presence and working in nature or history. First, there is the cosmic order, the law-order that God has instituted for the entire cosmic

## PROBING THE PAST

reality. This is a *creational order*, an orderly system, which must be explained as a product of God's creational power and will. Theologians like to speak of God's "creational ordinances" instituted for nature as well as for history, which must be obeyed by all his creatures. God speaks of the "ordinances of the heavens [or, the skies]" (Job 38:33). Psalm 119 says: "Forever, O Lord, your word is firmly fixed in the heavens [or, the skies]. Your faithfulness [as seen in your ordinances. WJO] endures to all generations; you have established the earth, and it stands fast" (v. 89-90); "he commanded and they [i.e., the celestial bodies] were created. And he established them forever and ever; he gave a decree, and it shall not pass away" (Ps. 148:5-6); "... the LORD, who gives the sun for light by day and the fixed order of the moon and the stars for light by night" (Jer. 31:35).

These ordinances, given once and for all, are never to be understood in a deistic sense, that is, as fixed laws that God instituted at the time of creation and that since then are fixed in place and function, in an automatic way, independently of God (more or less like a government promulgating laws, which henceforth function independently of that government, through police and tribunals). Creation and history are not a kind of gigantic clockwork, robot or automaton, once installed, and forever afterward working by itself.

Therefore, it is important to see that there is a second way in which the Bible speaks of God's providence, namely, as his direct action within nature and history. Let us think of God's "word," which can mean a word given at creation, and since then in force forevermore, but also a "word" that is given each time anew. A beautiful example is Psalm 147:15-18: "He sends out his command to the earth; his word runs swiftly. He gives snow like wool; he scatters frost like ashes. He hurls down his crystals of ice like crumbs; who can stand before his cold? He sends out his word, and melts them; he makes his wind blow and the waters flow."

I repeat that this must not be understood in the sense of supernatural interventions now and then, but as God's *permanent* acting within nature and history. In a general sense, Scripture says not only that God created all things in, through and for Christ but also that in Christ "all things hold together" (Col. 1:16-17), and that God the Son "upholds the universe by the *word* of his power" (Heb. 1:3, italics added), that is, by commanding all things all the time so to speak. More specifically with respect to history, God "gives to all mankind life and breath and everything... In him we live and move and have our being" (Acts 17:25, 28). In Daniel 5:23, the prophet speaks to King Belshazzar about "the God in whose hand is your breath, and whose are all your ways." These "ways" are the king's own responsibility, his own free choices. At the same time, they are entirely in God's hand.

Think again of Proverbs 21:1, where it says that God turns the king's heart "wherever he will." And think of another word of Daniel, addressed this time to King Nebuchadnezzar, who had to learn "that the Most High rules the kingdom of men and gives it to whom he will," and "that Heaven rules" (Dan. 4:25-26). This is the greatest challenge to every ruler in the world, to recognize that he may indeed rule, but that behind and above him "Heaven" (i.e., the Most High God) is the actual ruler. Solomon says: "The heart of man plans his way, but the LORD establishes his steps" (Prov. 16:9). "Many are the plans in the mind of a man, but it is the purpose of the LORD that will stand" (Prov. 19:21). "A man's steps are from the LORD" (Prov. 20:24; cf. Jer. 10:23).

All these verses of Scripture show how Man, in his freedom and responsibility, may consider and decide, but that his pathway can only run between the boundaries of God's purposes. As I said, the great church father Augustine expressed it wonderfully: even that which happens against God's will does not happen apart from his will. Again, this is a mystery, a paradox. God does not force people to act this way or that; no, he guarantees Man's freedom, but always within the limitations prescribed by his plans. "My counsel shall stand, and I will accomplish all my purpose" (Isa. 46:10b). The Apostle Paul speaks of "the purpose of him who works all things according to the counsel of his will" (Eph. 1:11b).

## Further Biblical Examples

Studying some further examples from Scripture will help us to understand the fine but highly complicated balance and interaction between God's sovereignty and Man's responsibility. In Genesis 45:5, Joseph says to his brothers: "And now do not be distressed or angry with yourselves because you sold me here, for God sent me before you to preserve life." And at a later time, he says: "As for you, you meant evil against me, but God meant it for good, to bring it about that many people should be kept alive, as they are today" (Gen. 50:20). Here we see that God can ordain, or at least allow, bad things in order to attain a good goal. But we have to read carefully. Joseph says that *God* sent him to Egypt, and that *God* made something good of the evil that the brothers had devised. But Joseph does *not* say that it was God who enticed the brothers to sell Joseph to Egypt. It is as James 1:13 says: "Let no one say when he is tempted, 'I am being tempted by God,' for God cannot be tempted with evil, and he himself tempts no one."

This is one of many examples that show us that people who do evil things are personally responsible for it, and never God. What would be the material difference between God in his counsel *deciding* that person P will do a certain evil act—after which P *has no other choice* than to do that evil thing—and a God with all his power *enticing* P to do that evil? To my mind, assuming such a difference would be sophistry. No, the brothers' selling of Joseph was *not* part of God's counsel, *nor* was it a thing that he enticed them to do. It was God's *counsel* to send Joseph to Egypt, and in his *ways* he used the brothers who, of themselves, decided to sell Joseph. These are two different things. They are linked, but distinct.

Another example is Exodus 21:12-13: "Whoever strikes a man so that he dies shall be put to death. But if he did not lie in wait for him, but God let him fall into his hand [NIV: God lets it happen], then I will appoint for you a place to which he may flee." This passage does not say that fatal events are sometimes intentional acts of God, but at best that God sometimes allows such events to happen. God hates evil, but he sometimes allows it in order to prevent a greater evil from happening, or to lead a believer back to the good path, or as a means to reach a greater good than would otherwise have been possible.

It is in this light, I feel, that we should view verses like these: "Who has made man's mouth? Who makes him mute, or deaf, or

## THE PROVIDENCE OF GOD

seeing, or blind? Is it not I, the LORD? (Exod. 4:11); "I will put none of the diseases on you that I put on the Egyptians" (Exod. 15:26b). "If he [i.e., Shimei] is cursing because the LORD has said to him, 'Curse David,' who then shall say, 'Why have you done so?'" (2 Sam. 16:10). "And after all this the LORD struck him in his bowels with an incurable disease. In the course of time, at the end of two years, his bowels came out because of the disease, and he died in great agony" (2 Chron. 21:18-19). "I am the LORD, and there is no other. I form light and create darkness, I make well-being and create calamity, I am the LORD, who does all these things" (Isa. 45:6b-7). "The former things I declared of old; they went out from my mouth, and I announced them; then suddenly I did them, and they came to pass" (Isa. 48:3). "Who has spoken and it came to pass, unless the Lord has commanded it? Is it not from the mouth of the Most High that good and bad come?" (Lam. 3:37-38). "Does disaster come to a city, unless the LORD has done it?" (Amos 3:6b). "Immediately an angel of the Lord struck him [i.e., King Herod] down, because he did not give God the glory, and he was eaten by worms and breathed his last" (Acts 12:23).

## God Handling Sin

In summary, we can conclude that, against evil as it occurs in history, God has several options how he may respond. First, he can *prevent* it, as he said to Abimelech: "[I]t was I who kept you from sinning against me," namely, sinning by taking Sarah, Abraham's wife (Gen. 20:6). God kept the enemies of David from "swallowing" him (Ps. 124:1-3). Believers pray to God so that he may keep them from sinning (e.g., Ps. 19:13; 141:3; 1 John 3:6, 9; 5:18). And Jesus, our great Intercessor, prays for *us*: "I have prayed for you that your faith may not fail" (Luke 22:32; cf. Rom. 8:34; Heb. 7:25; 1 John 2:1).

Second, if God does not prevent evil, he can at least *restrict* it: "God is faithful, and he will not let you be tempted beyond your ability" (1 Cor. 10:13). For instance, God limited Satan's power with respect to Job: "Behold, all that he has is in your hand. Only against him do not stretch out your hand" (Job 1:12; cf. 2:6, where God tells Satan to "spare his life"). The imprisoned Apostle Paul said about the visit of his friend Epaphroditus: "Indeed he was ill, near to death. But God had mercy on him, and not only on him but on me also, *lest I should have sorrow upon sorrow*" (Phil. 2:27, italics added).

Third, God can *use* it, employ it, that is, he can make it subservient to his own purposes. The supreme example is, as I said before, Man's Fall into sin, which God uses to reach a far better world than would ever have been possible if it had not happened. Several other examples that I have mentioned so far in this chapter fall into this same category, such as Joseph being sold into Egypt (Gen. 45:5; 50:20), or the rejection of Jesus by his people (Acts 2:23, 36). How beautiful is the way in which God uses Israel's being temporarily put aside by him: "For if their rejection means the reconciliation of the world, what will their acceptance mean but life from the dead?... [A] partial hardening has come upon Israel, until the fullness of the Gentiles has come in. And in this way all Israel will be saved" (Rom. 11:15, 25b, 26). A few chapters earlier, he said, "And we know that for those who love God all things work together for good" (Rom. 8:28).

Fourth, God may *allow* evil to strike unbelievers, to teach them a lesson or lead them to repentance. Paul gave this example: "God gave them [i.e., debauched pagans] up in the lusts of their hearts to impurity, to the dishonoring of their bodies among themselves... God gave them up to dishonorable passions... And since they did not see fit to acknowledge God, God gave them up to a debased mind to do what ought not to be done" (Rom. 1:24-28). Or God may allow evil for the testing or training (education) of his own people in particular: "And you shall remember the whole way that the LORD your God has led you these forty years in the wilderness, that he might humble you, testing you to know what was in your heart, whether you would keep his commandments or not" (Deut. 8:2). "God left him [i.e., King Hezekiah] to himself, in order to test him and to know all that was in his heart" (2 Chron. 32:31).

Sometimes we see how the third and fourth methods are combined. God uses powers that in themselves are evil as instruments to discipline his own people. For instance, Assyria was the "rod" of God's anger, the "axe" and the "saw" that he used to

## THE PROVIDENCE OF GOD

bring judgment on Israel (Isa. 10:5, 15). But because arrogant Assyria itself acted wickedly, the wrath of God turned also against this country: "Shall the axe boast over him who hews with it, or the saw magnify itself against him who wields it? As if a rod should wield him who lifts it, or as if a staff should lift him who is not wood! Therefore the Lord God of hosts will send wasting sickness among his stout warriors, and under his glory a burning will be kindled, like the burning of fire" (Isa. 10:15-16).

In Habakkuk 1, we find a striking example of the same principle. The prophet complained about the wickedness of Judah, and God answered him by telling that he would bring the Chaldeans (Babylonians) against Judah as a judgment. But then Habakkuk complained all the more strongly because in his eyes the Babylonians were even worse than the Judeans. This is one of the great riddles of history. By nature, all people are sinful, but why do sinful people often have to suffer under those who are far more wicked than they are? What was God's answer to Habakkuk? It is basically this: "[T]he righteous shall live by his faith" (2:4b). I read this as follows: "Do not try to understand all my ways; do not complain if these ways seem bizarre. Simply trust me; I know what I am doing. In the end, Judah will be restored, and Babylon will be destroyed. Look at the *end* of things."

This is the same lesson that David's singer and poet Asaph had to learn. He complained that the righteous are suffering, whereas the wicked are doing well. This is the injustice of history. How can it be? How can God allow such an unfair, unequal situation? Then Asaph himself gives the answer: "But when I thought how to understand this, it seemed to me a wearisome task, until I went into the sanctuary of God; then I discerned their end" (Ps. 73:16-17). That is, in the sanctuary, where he began seeing things through the eyes of God, he learned to watch the end of both the righteous and the wicked. The righteous inherit the Kingdom, the wicked go to eternal punishment.

Elsewhere we read: "It is for discipline that you [i.e., God's people] have to endure. God is treating you as sons. For what son is there whom his father does not discipline?... For the moment all discipline seems painful rather than pleasant, but later it yields the peaceful fruit of righteousness to those who have been trained by it" (Heb. 12:7-11). "Later"! Afterwards! Look at the outcome of things! In the end, the righteous will harvest the fruits of his sufferings. "You have heard of the perseverance of Job and seen the end [intended by] the Lord—that the Lord is very compassionate and merciful" (James 5:11 NKJV).

## The Role of Satan

God's "allowing" of evil should not be taken in too passive a sense. If God "allows" something, he *wants* that thing, because if he really had not wanted it, he would have prevented it. Amidst this tension—God wanting evil, God not wanting evil—we bump again into the mystery of God's providence in history which I have mentioned before. God cannot want evil, because evil is an enemy, and God hates his enemies (cf. Ps. 5:5; 11:5). But sometimes he apparently does want a certain evil to happen, because he uses it as an instrument in his service, to reach a higher goal than would have been possible without that evil.

Replace "it" by "him," because evil is often a person: *the* evil one, Satan (Matt. 5:39; 6:13; 13:19, 38; John 17:15; Eph. 6:16; 2 Thess. 3:3; 1 John 2:13-14; 5:18). Sometimes God uses even Satan as an instrument in his service. In such cases, God passively allows evil, or makes it actively subservient to his purposes, but in such a way that Satan is the actual agent. When Proverbs 16:4 says that the Lord has made everything for its purpose, even "the wicked" for the day of trouble, one might, by way of application, specifically think of the devil here. In the "day of trouble" (lit., "day of evil"), even the devil has to play his historic role. Whenever this happens, Satan's own responsibility is fully maintained, as well as the responsibility of the humans whom Satan uses.

We already briefly looked at the example of Job, which illustrates this. Here, (a) God allowed the evil that struck Job, (b) Satan was the active agent of evil, and (c) the Sabeans belonged to the human instruments whom Satan used (Job 1:15). The actions of the three agents are fully intertwined.

Another striking example is 2 Samuel 24:1, "Again the anger of the LORD was kindled against Israel, and he incited David against them, saying, 'Go, number Israel and Judah,'" whereas the parallel passage says, "Then *Satan* stood against Israel and incited David to number Israel" (1 Chron. 21:1, italics added). Here, apparently, Satan's action is subservient to, and embedded in, God's action; God is the initiator, Satan carries it out.

In summary I may quote the *Belgic Confession* here (Art. 13): "We believe that the same God, after he had created all things, did not forsake them, or give them up to fortune or chance, but that he rules and governs them according to his holy will, so that nothing happens in this world without his appointment; nevertheless, God neither is the author of, nor can be charged with, the sins which are committed. For his power and goodness are so great and incomprehensible, that he orders and executes his work in the most excellent and just manner, even then, when devils and wicked men act unjustly... being persuaded, that he so restrains the devil and all our enemies, that without his will and permission, they cannot hurt us."

# Chapter Eight
# THE KINGDOM OF GOD

After having dealt with the general principles of God's dominion in history (see the previous chapter), I now come to a new and very important point. We will never understand the essence of the dominion of God if we do not see that, from the outset, God wanted to put his Kingdom *under the feet of Man*. He did not create humans only to be his obedient subjects, under his dominion, in his Kingdom. On the contrary, he involved and continues to involve Man in his plans, and even in his royal dominion. God makes a partner, a viceroy, a fellow worker of Man (cf. 1 Cor. 3:9, "For we are God's fellow workers").

Of course, this is an unequal partnership. God makes his way through history from beginning to end, always remaining the sovereign God, the God who has to give account to no one, neither to humans nor to angels. Yet, he has sovereignly chosen to involve Man as a partner in his plans. From the very beginning of history, God and Man are inseparable. This is a very impressive truth. On the one hand, there was an eternity in which God was without Man, until the moment when he created Man. On the other hand, there will be an eternity in which God will never be without Man, in everlasting relationship with him, never to be separated again. No matter how shocking or irreverent this may sound, there is no future for God without Man.

## God's Kingdom under Man

How did God involve Man in his plans? After he had created Adam and Eve, one of the remarkable things is that he addressed them directly and gave them a command: "Be fruitful and multiply and fill the earth," but also: *"subdue* it [i.e., the earth], and have *dominion* over the fish of the sea and over the birds of the heavens and over every living thing that moves on the earth" (Gen. 1:28, italics added). God puts everything that he has created under the feet of the first two humans. He does not place it under the feet of Adam alone, Eve having at best an assisting role; no, the Hebrew speaks in the plural: *you both* subdue and have dominion. It was to both of them that he entrusted the rule of the world. And, I may add, when God put Adam and Eve in this ruling position, over their heads he saw, in the distant future, the "last Adam" (1 Cor. 15:44) and, so to speak, the "last Eve," the Bride of Christ, of whom Adam and Eve were only foreshadowings (cf. 2 Cor. 11:2; Eph. 5:25-32; Rev. 19:6-9; 21:9; 22:17).

This double perspective of Genesis 1—the first as well as the last Adam—comes to light in a striking way in Psalm 8: "When I look at your heavens, the work of your fingers, the moon and the stars, which you have set in place, what is man that you are mindful of him, and the son of man that you care for him? Yet [lit., And] you have made him a little lower than the heavenly beings [or, God; Septuagint: angels; Heb., *elohim*] and crowned him with glory and honor. You have given him dominion over the works of your hands; you have put all things under his feet" (Ps. 8:3-6).

If we had known this psalm only, we would have hardly discovered a Messianic meaning in it, and would have connected it solely with Genesis 1. However, under the guidance of the Holy Spirit, Hebrews 2 applies this psalm to *the* Son of Man: "For it was not to angels that God subjected the world to come, of which we are speaking. It has been testified somewhere, 'What is man, that you are mindful of him, or the son of man, that you care for him? You made him for a little while lower than the angels; you have crowned him with glory and honor, putting everything in subjection under his feet.' Now in putting everything in subjection to him, he left nothing outside his control. At present, we do not yet see everything in subjection to him. But we see him who for a little while was made lower than the angels, namely Jesus, crowned with glory and honor because of the suffering of death, so that by the grace of God he might taste death for everyone" (Heb. 2:5-9).

Apparently, there is a depth dimension in Genesis 1 that we might easily overlook. As I said earlier, in the person of the "first Adam" God already saw the figure of the "last Adam" concealed. When he said: "Subdue the earth and have dominion," he thought

## THE KINGDOM OF GOD

of Christ and his Bride. Indeed, the story of the Kingdom of God starts on the first page of the Bible, and it continues up to the very last page, where we receive a wonderful view of a new heaven and a new earth: "[T]he throne of God and of the Lamb will be in it [i.e., in the new Jerusalem], and his servants will worship him. They will see his face, and his name will be on their foreheads… and they will reign [Greek *basileusousin*, "reign as *kings*"] forever and ever" (Rev. 22:3-5). It will be under God's overarching rule, and it will be "in Christ," yet they are called to be kings forever.

The Old Testament types provide us wonderful examples of this. The first one is Joseph (a type of Christ) who became viceroy under the supervision of the Pharaoh (a type of God), with Asenath, the bride (of pagan descent) at his side (a type of the Church) (Gen. 41:37-45). The second example is from the Book of Esther. "Mordecai the Jew was second in rank to King Ahasuerus, and he was great among the Jews and popular with the multitude of his brothers, for he sought the welfare of his people and spoke peace to all his people" (Est. 10:3). According to an authoritative rabbinical tradition, Esther was not only Mordecai's cousin but also his wife.

God never gives up his plan, even though we see on the first pages of the Bible that Adam and Eve, who had received dominion, handed it over to Satan. After the Fall of Man, God did not come up with some Plan B; no, it is still Plan A he is carrying out. This is history, which is always basically salvational history. It is the long route by which God, through endless detours caused by sinful Man, ultimately reaches the goal of his Plan A. This plan is to put everything not only in subjection under the feet of Christ, but also under the feet of those who belong to him. The Apostle Paul told the Roman believers: "The God of peace will soon crush Satan under your feet" (Rom. 16:20). Also compare these other words from Paul: "Or do you not know that the saints will judge the world? … Do you not know that we are to judge angels?" (1 Cor. 6:2-3). When Christ reigns, the glorified believers will reign with him (Rev. 20:4, 6). Just as there is no first Adam without the first Eve, there is also no last Adam without the last Eve.

PROBING THE PAST

# The Kingdom of Satan

Genesis 3 describes the story of Man's fall into sin. There is more to this story than just the matter of Man's disobedience: he not only lost the fellowship with God, he also lost to Satan the Kingdom that God had entrusted to him. The fellowship with God was restored very soon ("the Lord God made for Adam and for his wife garments of skins and clothed them," Gen. 3:21), but the restoration of the Kingdom would still take thousands of years, and will only be complete at the second coming of Christ.

Genesis 3 does not say explicitly that Man handed over the Kingdom entrusted to him to Satan, but we see it in the consequences. From the moment Man falls, Satan is the captain in this world (of course always under the general dominion of God, and within the boundaries that God has established). The "ancient serpent" in the Garden of Eden is none other than the "devil and Satan," as Revelation 12:9 and 20:2 explicitly tell us. The word *devil* comes from the Greek word *diabolos*, which means the one who "mixes up," "scrambles," "confuses." The word *Satan* comes from a Hebrew word that means "adversary." Since the Fall, and because of it, the adversary has received far-reaching authority, such that Man is now forced to comply with this strange power, to which he himself had foolishly handed over world dominion.

Jesus explained that there is indeed something called the kingdom of Satan: "Every kingdom divided against itself is laid waste, and no city or house divided against itself will stand. And if Satan casts out Satan, he is divided against himself. How then will his kingdom stand?" (Matt. 12:25-26). It is no longer the "first Adam" who is (under God) the king of this world, but Satan. There is no kingdom (Greek *basileia*) without a king (*basileus*); since Genesis 3, Satan was the *basileus* of the world. Jesus himself called Satan "the ruler (Greek *archôn*) of this world" (John 12:31; 14:30; 16:11). There is no real distinction between *basileus* and *archôn*. Satan is "the prince (*archôn*) of the power of the air, the spirit that is now at work in the sons of disobedience" (Eph. 2:2). And as the world cannot live without a god, Satan is also called the "god of this world" (2 Cor. 4:4). Satan is *the* "cosmic power of this present darkness," that is, *the* ruler of this present dark cosmos (cf. the plural in Eph. 6:12).

## Satan versus Christ

When Jesus came to establish God's Kingdom again in this world, the very first act of his ministry was to confront Satan. Therefore, after he had been baptized by John the Baptist and anointed with the Holy Spirit (cf. Acts 10:38), Jesus was immediately led by the Spirit into the wilderness (Matt. 4:1; Luke 4:1). Before he was allowed to do any work, to preach any word, to perform any miracle, he had to be confronted by his greatest enemy.

This is the tremendous significance of what happened in that desert; it was a power struggle between the old ruler of the world and the new claimant who had appeared. One could also say it was a power struggle between "the god of this world" (2 Cor. 4:4) and "our great God and Savior Jesus Christ" (Titus 2:13). It was a struggle that had to be continued on the cross of Calvary, and that would ultimately decide the course of world history. It revolved around the question of who was going to triumph in the end: the powers of the three L's—love, life and light—or the powers of the three D's—devil, death and darkness.

During one of the three temptations in the wilderness, the devil took Jesus to a "very high mountain and showed him all the kingdoms of the world and their glory" (Matt. 4:8). Then the devil told him that the authority over these kingdoms "has been delivered to me, and I give it to whom I will" (Luke 4:7). This is a striking statement. Satan did not *create* the kingdoms of the world, nor did he *conquer* them—they were *given* to him. I read this verse in this way: at the fall of Man, God allowed the kingdom of this world to pass from Adam and Eve to Satan. It was their fault. Satan even claimed that since he now had this authority over the world, he could give it to anyone he wished. Please note that Jesus did not contradict this. Satan presented himself as the ruler of the world, and Jesus implicitly recognized this fact.

However, since the first coming of the Messiah, the kingdom of Satan is in permanent conflict with the Kingdom of God, until Messiah's second coming. This is a new way to define the history especially of the last two thousand years; it is the ongoing struggle between two kingdoms and two rulers, between darkness and light, between hatred and love, between death and life, between unrighteousness and justice, between disharmony and peace, between sadness and joy (cf. Acts 27:18; Rom. 14:17; Col. 1:13; 1 Pet. 2:9).

Since Genesis 3, it is no longer Man who is the viceroy under God—Satan is. Since Genesis 3, the entire Old Testament shows us on the one hand the power of evil, and on the other hand the promises of God, the permanent perspective of the future Kingdom of God. This is the leading moral principle of all history: hope. As the Apostle Paul tells us: "For the creation was subjected to futility, not willingly, but because of him who subjected it, in hope that the creation itself will be set free from its bondage to corruption and obtain the freedom of the glory of the children of God. For we know that the whole creation has been groaning together in the pains of childbirth until now. And not only the creation, but we ourselves, who have the firstfruits of the Spirit, groan inwardly as we wait eagerly for adoption as sons, the redemption of our bodies. For in this hope we were saved. Now hope that is seen is not hope. For who hopes for what he sees? But if we hope for what we do not see, we wait for it with patience" (Rom. 8:20-25).

## The Announcement of God's Kingdom

This great hope that dominates history is essentially this: in the "first Adam" everything was lost, but in the "last Adam" everything is going to be restored (1 Cor. 15:45, 47). The certainty of this hope is rooted in the foundation that the Lord Jesus laid on the cross. Already in the Garden of Eden, God told Satan: "I will put enmity between you and the woman, and between your offspring and her offspring; he [i.e., her descendant] shall bruise your head, and you shall bruise his heel" (Gen. 3:15). This is the first prophecy of the Bible, and it has become a ruling principle of history: the ongoing battle between the "children of the devil" (1 John 3:10; cf. John 8:44) and the children of God. Every person in this world basically belongs to either of these two groups.

This continual struggle between darkness and light is immediately illustrated in the birth of Eve's two sons: Cain, a spiritual child of the devil, who slays Abel, a spiritual child of God (Gen.

## THE KINGDOM OF GOD

4:1-16; cf. 1 John 3:12, "We should not be like Cain, who was of the evil one and murdered his brother. And why did he murder him? Because his own deeds were evil and his brother's righteous"). This killing goes on to this very day. The children of the devil will, like true serpents, continually "bruise the heels" of God's children (cf. Gen. 49:17, "Dan shall be a serpent in the way,... that bites the horse's heels"). This means that the wicked will strike the righteous time and again, persecute them, torture them, and murder them (cf. Matt. 23:35, which mentions "all the righteous blood shed on earth, from the blood of righteous Abel to the blood of Zechariah the son of Barachiah"). Ultimately, however, the true "offspring of the woman," that is, the Messiah, God's anointed King, will bruise the head of the serpent.

In Genesis 3, at the very beginning of human history, God announces the eventual defeat of Satan through the hand of a Man, who would be the "second Man," the "last Adam." The latter would destroy the kingdom of Satan, and usher in a new Kingdom, such as God had intended it from the beginning: "The kingdom of the world has become the kingdom of our Lord and of his Christ [or, Messiah], and he shall reign forever and ever" (Rev. 11:15). This is the great hope of both the Old and New Testaments. Jesus did not come only to solve the problem of sin, however important this may be (cf. John 1:29; Heb. 9:26b), but also for this purpose: "The reason the Son of God appeared was to destroy the works of the devil" (1 John 3:8). "Since the children [i.e., God's people] share in flesh and blood, he [i.e., Jesus] himself likewise partook of the same things, that through death he might destroy the one who has the power of death, that is, the devil, and deliver all those who through fear of death were subject to lifelong slavery" (Heb. 2:14-15).

The Apostle Paul says that God through Jesus "disarmed the rulers and authorities and put them to open shame, by triumphing over them," namely, at the cross (Col. 2:15 note). This does not mean that the battle is all over. On the cross, the foundation for the ultimate victory was laid; but the battle itself rages until the very end. We are still wrestling "against the rulers, against the authorities, against the cosmic powers over this present darkness, against the spiritual forces of evil in the heavenly places" (Eph. 6:12).

**PROBING THE PAST**

The German theologian Oscar Cullmann (1902-1999), in his book *Christ and Time*, used a historical picture that has become generally known. He compared the day of Jesus' dying on the cross to D-Day, "Decision Day," that is June 6, 1944, when the Allied forces (made up of British, American, Canadian, and Polish troops) landed in Normandy. From there, the re-conquest of Europe took place, very gradually, to free Europe from its Nazi occupation. Many people thought that now the war would soon be over. In reality, it still lasted eleven months longer, until May 8, 1945. These eleven months were actually the worst part of the Second World War, during which many people starved to death or succumbed in the last desperate attempts of Adolf Hitler to turn the tables. May 8, 1945, the day of the total surrender of the German army, was V-Day, "Victory Day." The decisive day that ultimately led to the victory was June 6, 1944. But the actual victory itself did not come until eleven terrible months later.

With the Kingdom of God it is very similar. D-Day was the day Jesus died on the cross; without this Day of Decision there could never be a future Day of Victory. V-Day will be the day of Jesus' second coming. In between lie many centuries of war, hatred, darkness, violence, and oppression; this is the continually raging battle between the Kingdom of God and the kingdom of Satan. The day Jesus died was D-Day, the decisive day, the turning point in history, which will ultimately lead to V-Day, the day when Jesus will come again to destroy the enemy once and for all. It will be the day of the total triumph over the powers of evil. But the foundation for this was laid two thousand years earlier, on the cross of Calvary. Since D-Day, the ultimate victory has been absolutely certain—nevertheless Jesus' followers will have to struggle against Satan and his powers every day, until V-Day will dawn.

## The Kingdom: Spiritual Aspect

Jesus announced that one day God's Kingdom—or, the Kingdom of heaven (Matt. 8:11; 13:37-43)—would arrive in power and majesty, as the prophets had predicted (see also Matt. 16:27-28; 24:30-31; 25:31; 26:64). When that Kingdom breaks through, that is, when Christ returns, the earth will be filled with peace and righteousness (e.g., Isa. 9:6-7; 32:1-2, 15-18). The earth will be full of the glory of the Lord (Hab. 2:14).

That is an incredible perspective—incredible because even the believing student of history has difficulty imagining that, in this world of war, disharmony, unrighteousness, and sadness, such a kingdom will ever be established. It will be a world in which the Lord Jesus Christ is the center of the Kingdom, as Philippians 2:9-11 says: "God has highly exalted him and bestowed on him the name that is above every name, so that at the name of Jesus every knee should bow, in heaven and on earth and under the earth, and every tongue confess that Jesus Christ is Lord, to the glory of God the Father."

The expectation of the Jews in Jesus' time, including that of the disciples, was that Jesus would deliver them from the Roman occupants, after which he would introduce political peace and righteousness, in the sense of the absence of war and injustice. Many Christian commentators have argued that this was not the thing that mattered; they claimed that God's Kingdom was and is of a purely "spiritual" nature. They found support for this view in Jesus' own words before Pilate: "My kingdom is not of this world. If my kingdom were of this world, my servants would have been fighting, that I might not be delivered over to the Jews. But my kingdom is not from the world" (John 18:36).

However, one chapter earlier we can see that "not of this world" (John 17:14, 16) does not exclude being "in the world" (17:11, 13), and being "sent into the world" (v. 18). God's Kingdom is certainly of a spiritual nature; it is not set up and ruled according to worldly principles. Yet it finds itself in *this* world, and is fully involved in the history of this world.

## A Heavenly Kingdom on Earth

Moreover, the expression "Kingdom of heaven" may be misleading here. We find it in Matthew's Gospel only, and in parallel passages we can see that is exactly the same as the Kingdom of God (for instance, compare Matt. 3:2 with Mark 1:15; Matt. 5:3 with Luke 6:20; Matt. 11:11 with Luke 7:28). It is therefore a great mistake to assume that the Kingdom of heaven is a heavenly Kingdom, that is,

## PROBING THE PAST

a Kingdom *in* heaven. Martin Luther was one of those who made this mistake. This is how the Apostle Peter got his legendary place at the gate of heaven: it was a mistake based on Matthew 16:19, where Peter receives the keys to the Kingdom of heaven. To be sure, the Kingdom of heaven is a heavenly Kingdom, yet it is fully *on earth*. "Heaven" is only a euphemism for God here (cf. Matt. 5:33; Luke 15:18, 21); it expresses the truth of Daniel 4:26, "Heaven rules," that is, "God rules," namely, *over the earth*.

One might say that God rules over "the heavens and the earth," a phrase used throughout the Bible to mean the entire created world. "Heaven" here—basically the sky—is something very different from the place where God dwells, and where the glorified saints will eventually dwell. The term "heaven" can have many meanings, and that is sometimes quite confusing. Here it unequivocally refers to the Kingdom of God which includes the entire empirical world.

If the spiritualizers are right, we must think of a Kingdom being realized today, *within* present-day history, and at the second coming of Christ flowing into the "eternal state" (the new heavens and the new earth). I do not believe that this is the Kingdom which the New Testament anticipates. It is *this* earth that will be full of the knowledge of the Lord (Isa. 11:9). It is on *this* earth that the Branch of David, the King, "shall reign and deal wisely, and shall execute justice and righteousness" (Jer. 23:5; cf. 33:15). And it will be on this same earth where the King once came to Zion, "righteous and having salvation, humble and mounted on a donkey, on a colt, the foal of a donkey," that one day "he shall speak peace to the nations; his rule shall be from sea to sea, and from the River to the ends of the earth" (Zech. 9:9-10; cf. Matt. 21:1-11).

Imagine that we had to believe that the world constantly follows its normal course, with some spiritual Kingdom of God in it, until one day, Jesus Christ unexpectedly interrupts this course in order to introduce a new heaven and a new earth. If this were the case, what meaning would history have? History would not have a *goal* toward which it is working, but one day it would simply be interrupted and *stopped*. What good would it do to develop a Christian view of history if this would really be its end? No, history is "on its way" to the full blossoming of the Kingdom of

God—not on some new earth, but on this very earth. The new earth will come later. To my mind, a Christian view of history makes sense only if we can already point out today the "lines" in history that will flow into the imminent Kingdom of power and majesty, peace and justice, to be established in this world. Some of these lines I have tried to follow in my book *The Ninth King*.

## The Fullness of the Times

Paul speaks in Ephesians 1:10 of the "fullness of the times"; not the "fullness of time," as ESV has it. This is a confusion with Galatians 4:4, where "fullness of the time" (*plèrôma tou chronou*) means that the time (*chronos*) was fulfilled to send God's Son into this world (cf. NIV: "the set time"). In Eph. 1:10, however, the expression is *plèrôma tôn kairôn*, "fullness of the times," where, in my view, *kairos* means "epoch." All the previous epochs of world history will find their ultimate fulfillment in this coming "dispensation" (KJV).

Jewish tradition made a distinction that we also find in the New Testament, namely, between "the present age (or, world)" (Matt. 12:32; 13:40; Luke 16:8; 20:34; 1 Cor. 1:20; 3:18; 2 Cor. 4:4; Gal. 1:4; Eph. 1:21; 2:7; 1 Tim. 6:17; 2 Tim. 4:10; Tit. 2:12) and "the age (or, world) to come" (Matt. 12:32; Luke 18:30; 20:35; Eph. 1:21; Heb. 6:5), that is, the age (or, world) of the Messiah. The present age and the age to come are two epochs within the same history of the same earth.

It may help to point here to Revelation 3:21, where Jesus promises the victorious believers in the church of Laodicea: "The one who conquers, I will grant him to sit with me on my throne, as I also conquered and sat down with my Father on his throne." There is a clear distinction here between two periods and two thrones: in the *present age*, Jesus is sitting with his Father on *his* [i.e. the Father's] throne, and in the *age to come*, the victorious believers will sit with him on *his* [i.e. Jesus'] throne. The latter throne can in fact be none other than the one God had promised to Jesus: "the throne of his father David" (Luke 1:32). In the *present age*, Jesus is sitting on the throne of his Father *in heaven* (Heb. 8:1; 12:2; cf. Matt. 26:64; Rom. 8:34; Eph. 1:20; Col. 3:1; Heb. 1:3; 1 Pet. 3:22). In

## PROBING THE PAST

the *age to come*, that is, the age of the Messiah, Jesus will be sitting on his own throne *on earth* (Matt. 19:28; 25:31; Acts 2:30; Heb. 1:8).

## Yet Spiritual Too

Of course, the "physicalizers" of the Kingdom—those who main-ly underline the physical and political aspects of the future Mes-sianic Kingdom—are just as extreme as the "spiritualizers." The Kingdom of God is much more than a merely physical and politi-cal Kingdom of power and majesty, peace and justice. It is *also* a spiritual Kingdom in the sense that no one will have a share in it without a regeneration of the heart: "[U]nless one is born again he cannot see the kingdom of God... [U]nless one is born of water and the Spirit, he cannot enter the kingdom of God" (John 3:3, 5). If people refuse to change internally—if they do not first receive a peaceful and righteous *heart*—a Kingdom of peace and righteous-ness will be useless, or even impossible.

This was not a new insight. The prophet Ezekiel had already declared that Israel would not be able to enter the Messianic King-dom without such an inner purification: "I will sprinkle clean water on you, and you shall be clean from all your uncleannesses, and from all your idols I will cleanse you. And I will give you a new heart, and a new spirit I will put within you. And I will remove the heart of stone from your flesh and give you a heart of flesh. And I will put my Spirit within you, and cause you to walk in my statutes and be careful to obey my rules" (Ezek. 36:25-27).

A beautiful example of this need for inner change is found in Jesus' parable of the wedding feast (Matt. 22:1-14). After the majority of the Jews had rejected the Kingdom as Jesus had pro-claimed it, the Gentiles were invited to enter it. However, Jesus made clear that, no matter who you are, you cannot enter the Kingdom of Heaven on your own conditions. The king said to one of the guests: "Friend, how did you get in here without a wedding garment?" (v. 12). Apparently, these wedding garments had been handed out at the entrance of the wedding hall, but this man had refused one. He thought he could take part in the feast just the way he was, which was a very serious mistake (cf. v. 13). *Everyone* is invited to the feast; but *if* you come, you need to change first.

The "gospel of the kingdom" (Matt. 24:14) is not in the first place a political program—as some horizontalist Christians seem to believe—which, if carried out, would at best change the outward conditions of people. Granted, such outward changes would not be totally worthless; the world profits when peace and justice reign. But it would not be enough. Outward changes without inner changes of the heart do not really lead to a better world.

The Bible emphasizes this so strongly that one could even get the impression that Jesus' message was quite apolitical. But this was not the case. Let me give just one example. Could Jesus not have done a much better job dealing with, for instance, the problem of slavery which was heinous in his time? No, what Jesus did was not to change slavery politically; instead, he spiritually changed the hearts of the *slaves*, and of the *masters* as well: "Bondservants are to be submissive to their own masters in everything; they are to be well-pleasing, not argumentative, not pilfering, but showing all good faith, *so that in everything they may adorn the doctrine of God our Savior*" (Titus 2:9-10, italics added). The consequence is that, even if it took a few centuries, with all those changed masters and slaves, in the end slavery itself would also disappear from Roman society. This is exactly what happened (although in later centuries, evil minds sometimes introduced slavery again).

## The Kingdom: Political Aspect

As I said, we must avoid two extremes here. The Kingdom of God is not *only* political, but it is not *only* spiritual either. That is the same as saying that it should be neither physicalized nor spiritualized, as I have argued earlier. The Kingdom of God is first peace in the heart (Phil. 4:7), but then it is definitely also peace on earth (Luke 2:14). First there must be new people, but then there must also be new, peaceful relationships. First, the sword of the Spirit is wielded (Eph. 6:17), but eventually, actual swords are beaten into plowshares (Isa. 2:4). First hearts must be harmonious hearts, and then harmonious earthly conditions will follow. First the divine order must be established in our personal lives, and in the lives of our families, and then the divine order will follow in all societal relationship, and all over the earth.

## PROBING THE PAST

This is beautifully shown in the instructions of Jesus. After his resurrection he appeared time and again to his disciples: "He presented himself alive to them after his suffering by many proofs, appearing to them during forty days and speaking about the kingdom of God" (Acts 1:3). If we could hazard a guess, what do we think he would have spoken about for forty days? All the instructions to the apostles he was going to leave behind revolved around this great central theme: the Kingdom of God. Perhaps we would have loved to be present during these lessons of Jesus. But in the first place, the disciples had not yet received the anointing of the Holy Spirit, so that this saying of Jesus was still valid: "What I am doing you do not understand now, but afterward [i.e., after Acts 2] you will understand" (John 13:7; cf. 1 Cor. 2:10-16). In the second place, we may be certain that all the relevant post-resurrection teaching on the Kingdom of God can today be found in the Book of Acts, the Epistles, and the Book of Revelation.

Of course, this teaching of Jesus was not only about the Kingdom in its future form, after his second coming, but also, (and perhaps especially) about the Kingdom in its present form, the Kingdom as it manifests itself in the hearts, lives and societal relationships of Jesus' followers (for more details, see my earlier volume, *Power in Service*). This was the Kingdom that the Apostles also preached (Acts 8:12; 19:8; 20:25; 28:23, 31). Of this forty-day "Kingdom course" of Jesus only one question of the disciples is reported to us, along with Jesus' answer. But this little conversation is worth mentioning. The question was this: "Lord, will you at this time restore the kingdom to Israel?" (Acts 1:6). In other words, now that you are risen from the dead, is this the time when the Kingdom will finally arrive of which all the prophets have spoken, the Kingdom of which Israel will be the center (e.g., Isa. 2:2-4; Dan. 7:13-27), and where the Messiah will sit on the throne of David (Isa. 9:7; Luke 1:32)?

It is amazing how many commentators suggest that this in fact was a foolish question asked by the disciples because Jesus' Kingdom was allegedly a purely spiritual one, and Israel's time was over anyway. However, in cases where the disciples really asked foolish questions, Jesus responded very differently: "O you of little faith… Do you not yet perceive?" (Matt. 16:8-9). "O faith-

## THE KINGDOM OF GOD

less generation, how long am I to be with you? How long am I to bear with you?" (Mark 9:19). "Have I been with you so long, and you still do not know me, Philip?" (John 14:9). This is not the case in Acts 1, however. Apparently, Jesus took the disciples' question seriously, and gave it a very direct answer: "It is not for you to know times or seasons that the Father has fixed by his own authority" (v. 7). In other words, he did not deny the restoration of the Kingdom to Israel; on the contrary, he implicitly confirmed it by saying as it were: The Kingdom will certainly come, but not now; the time of its coming lies in the Father's hands. I think we can safely say that this will be the time when Jesus will come again (cf. Mark 13:32, "But concerning that day or that hour, no one knows, not even the angels in heaven, nor the Son, but only the Father").

Jesus continued: "But you will receive power when the Holy Spirit has come upon you, and you will be my witnesses in Jerusalem and in all Judea and Samaria, and to the end of the earth" (Acts 1:8). That is, you will still have to wait for the restoration of the Kingdom to Israel—we know that so far this period has lasted almost two thousand years already—but in the meantime you will receive something that is at least as great, which is the power of the Holy Spirit. In the Kingdom as it exists already today, Jesus himself is absent; he is hidden with God (cf. Col. 3:3). However, the power of the Holy Spirit is present in it. This is the power of which the Apostle Paul speaks: "For the kingdom of God does not consist in [idle] talk but in power" (1 Cor. 4:20; cf. v. 19).

In the power of the anointing of the Spirit, the Apostles would go out and recruit disciples (pupils, followers, subjects) for the King. Jesus gave them the explicit command to do this; they had to win disciples (pupils, followers, subjects) for the One who had all authority in heaven and on earth (Matt. 28:18-20). New disciples are being recruited, though not yet for the Kingdom in power and glory, not yet for the Kingdom in peace and righteousness filling the earth. On the contrary, the history of the last two thousand years has been full of continual struggle between the Kingdom of light and life and the kingdom of darkness and death. Yet, even today, God's Kingdom in its present form is *internally* a place of "righteousness and peace and joy in the Holy Spirit" (Rom. 14:17).

**PROBING THE PAST**

The subjects of the Kingdom in its present form are living in a world full of unrighteousness, war and sadness, but through the Holy Spirit they have righteousness, peace and joy in their hearts and in their mutual relationships. "The Father... has delivered us from the domain of darkness and transferred us to the kingdom of his beloved Son" (Col. 1:13).

## Christian Rulers?

For a Christian view of the history of the last two thousand years, it is of great importance to understand the two forms of the Kingdom that I have mentioned. First, there is the present Kingdom, which is a spiritual Kingdom, but one which is hastening toward the coming of the Lord and the establishment of his Kingdom in power and glory, which will be both a spiritual and a political Kingdom. In the ideal sense, one could imagine even in the present time a nation state where the majority of the people are Christian, and where there is a Christian government in a truly biblical sense of the word. In such a situation, the Kingdom of God would also manifest itself in the political structure (see again my book *Power in Service*). Perhaps this ideal was approximated during the seventeenth century in the Netherlands, or in the early years of the United States, if we do not pay too much attention to the many shortcomings.

Apart from such approximations of a high ideal, history has seen a number of "Christian" countries, or even empires, where the head of state (a king, an emperor) professed to be a Christian but where very un-Christian principles and practices prevailed. We can think especially of the Christian Western Roman Empire (380-476), the Christian Eastern Roman Empire (380-1453), the Holy Roman Empire of the German Nation (962-1806), and subsequently the first rising nation states (France, England, Spain). At least until the time of the Reformation, these empires and states were only cartoons or parodies of the Kingdom of God, characterized by violence, debauchery, intrigues, and the suppression of dissenters. In a Christian view of history, the negative stories of these so-called Christian empires and states must constantly be viewed—and condemned—against the background of God's ideal of his Kingdom of peace and righteousness.

Of course there were outstanding exceptions. Among my favorite Protestant rulers, I first point to Elizabeth I (1533-1603), who was crowned Queen of England in 1558, and under whom England blossomed. Second, there is William III, Prince of Orange (1650-1702), Stadtholder in the Netherlands, and from 1689 on, King of England and Ireland (as William II King of Scotland)—a man greatly respected, even by Napoleon. Third, I will mention Abraham Lincoln (1809-1865), elected President of the United States in 1861, who abolished slavery and saved the Union.

Among my favorite Eastern Orthodox rulers is Justinian I (c. 482-565), who in 527 was crowned Emperor of the East-Roman Empire (in spite of his suppression of dissenting beliefs). Under him Byzantine culture flourished. He was the great reviser of Roman law in his *Corpus Iuris Civilus*, which still forms the basis for civil law in many modern states. Even the American Lutheran Churches honor him as a saint.

Among my favorite Roman Catholic rulers are Charlemagne (c. 747-814), who in 800 became the first Emperor in Europe after the fall of the Western Roman Empire (476), and was called *pater Europae* ("Father of Europe"). Although he instigated the forced conversion of the Saxons, he also inspired the Carolingian Renaissance. Another Catholic ruler who deserves to be mentioned is Joseph II (1741-1790), who became Holy Roman Emperor in 1765, and from 1780 on was also king of Bohemia, Croatia and Hungary. Although he was an absolute monarch, he has been called one of the most unselfish rulers in history.

## Rulers of Light and Darkness

Aside from these exceptions—and we must remember that even all of these had their great shortcomings—many empires and states that were Christian in name were in practice often nothing but instruments governed by the powers of darkness. Satan often manifests himself as an "angel of light" (2 Cor. 11:14), but especially when the rulers of empires and states are on his side, he can freely reveal himself as the "roaring lion," who "prowls around," "seeking someone to devour" (1 Pet. 5:8).

## PROBING THE PAST

In this context, it is worth our while to pay attention to the relationships between the earthly and celestial rulers. According to Colossians 1:16, God in Christ created all things that are in the heavens and on earth, the visible and the invisible. To the latter category belong the angelic powers, here described as thrones (*thronoi*, i.e., powers on royal thrones), dominions (*kyriotètes*, from *kyrios*, "lord"), principalities (*archai*), and authorities (*exousiai*). In Ephesians 1:20-21, Christ is placed in the heavenly realms above all principality (*archè*), authority (*exousia*), power (*dynamis*), dominion (*kyriotès*), and every name (i.e., and every other great angelic power). Ephesians 3:10 speaks of *archai* and *exousiai*, Romans 8:38 of angels, *archai*, and *dynameis*, and 1 Peter 3:22 of angels, *exousiai*, and *dynameis*.

In summary it says in these passages that God created the celestial powers in and through his Son, and that the glorified Christ was elevated above them. After he had finished his great work of redemption, Jesus could truly say: "All authority in heaven and on earth has been given to me" (Matt. 28:18), that is, all authority, both over the heavenly powers and over the earthly powers. They are all subject, not just to God the Son, but to the glorified *Man* at God's right hand. All things are under the dominion of *Man* again, that is, the "last Adam" (see above).

With the (probable) exception of Titus 3:1, the Apostle Paul always used the word *archai* to mean "principalites" in the sense of angelic powers, both good and evil. The evil powers are at least implied, if not exclusively intended, in Romans 8:38; Ephesians 1:21; 3:20; Colossians 1:16, and certainly intended in Ephesians 6:12. Through Christ's redemptive work on the cross, the *archai* and *exousiai* have been disarmed and denounced (Col. 2:15); he subjected them to himself (Eph. 1:21; 1 Pet. 3:22) and placed himself as Head over them (Col. 2:15), so that they could no longer threaten the believers (Rom. 8:38). Their final destruction is described in 1 Corinthians 15:24, "Then comes the end, when he delivers the kingdom to God the Father after destroying every rule and every authority and power."

Ephesians 6:12 is of special interest here. In this passage, Paul points out that the actual conflict of God's people is not with visible powers of flesh and blood, but with invisible powers in the

# THE KINGDOM OF GOD

heavenly realms: the (evil) *archai*, the *exousiai*, the *kosmokratores* ("world rulers") of this darkness—read, the "angelic princes of this dark world"—and the *pneumatika* ('spiritual powers") of wickedness. The word *kosmokratôr* in particular is fascinating. Originally, it referred to a planet or planetary god, or in a wider sense, to a ruler (cf. *kratos*, "force") of a certain celestial (cosmic) sphere, and then also to the rulers of the universe, who determine the fate of people (as in astrology!). Later, the term was used for the gods in the Greek world. In Ephesians 6:12, it is one of the terms for demonic powers. It is not impossible that something of the notion of (evil) angelic princes is still retained in it in the sense of princes who each have a certain territory of the cosmos under them, allotted to each one of them by their "prince," Satan (cf. Eph. 2:2, "the prince of the power of the air, the spirit that is now at work in the sons of disobedience").

## The Kingdom of God and the Roman Empire

Paul also mentions the "rulers (*archontes*) of this age [*aiôn*]" in 1 Corinthians 2:6 and 8, where we possibly find the same meaning. In agreement with this, Satan is called the "god of this age" (2 Cor. 4:4). He is a "god," an *elohim*, an angelic prince, in the evil sense; he is the greatest prince known in the present "age," that is, the world with its present *zeitgeist*, which is foreign to God. This fits in well with the expression I have already mentioned, "ruler (*archôn*) of this world" (John 12:31; 14:30; 16:11). Satan is the head of all apostate national angelic princes, for he can, to a certain extent accurately, say that he has power over all kingdoms of the world, as he does in Luke 4:5-6.

Actually, we do not find the word *cosmos* in Luke 4, as in Matthew 4:8, but *oikoumenè*, literally the "inhabited [earth]," which in Luke always seems to refer to the Roman Empire. In Luke 2:1, the "world" is not *cosmos* but again *oikoumenè*; Caesar Augustus gave out a decree that all the *oikoumenè*, that is, the whole Roman Empire, was to be registered. In Acts 11:28, a prophet foretold that there would be a great famine over all the *oikoumenè*, which indeed happened in the days of the Roman Emperor Claudius. In Acts 17:6-7, Paul and his co-workers are accused of having "turned

171

the *oikoumenè* upside down," and of "acting against the decrees of Caesar [i.e., the Roman Emperor], saying that there is another king, Jesus."

Notice what is happening here. The Apostle Paul came to Europe not just to preach a message of sin and forgiveness. If he had limited himself to that, he would probably have had little trouble, since such messages were quite common. But he did more. He proclaimed the Kingdom of God (cf. Acts 20:25). This did not involve presenting Jesus as a King who wished to rule only over the hearts of his followers. No, it implied a direct confrontation with the powers of that time, and apparently Paul's audience understood this very well. The people already acknowledged a "king"; this was the powerful emperor in Rome (in the East, the emperor was called *basileus*, "king"). Now Paul came and preached a "different king," a *basileus* who was even more powerful than the Emperor in Rome.

In fact, Jesus himself had already expressed similar thoughts. In Luke 4, he did not refuse the kingship over the kingdoms of the *oikoumenè* as such—he only refused to receive it from the hands of Satan. One day, he will be king over the *oikoumenè*, but at that time Satan will be subject to him as well.

Another interesting confrontation was the one between Pilate and Jesus. The Roman governor, as a representative of the mighty Roman Empire, asked Jesus: "Do you not know that I have authority to release you and authority to crucify you?" Jesus answered him, "You would have no authority over me at all unless it had been given you from above" (John 19:10-11). In other words, the Roman Empire may be mighty, but it can only operate within the boundaries set by God. Jesus is on the side of God, he is even the Son of God (cf. John 19:7), and therefore he is mightier than the Roman Empire. This is the tremendous significance of the following verses: Pilate had to choose between Caesar, the *basileus* in Rome, and this Man, whom he himself called *basileus* of the Jews (John 19:14-15, 19-22). The people cried: "If you release this man, you are not Caesar's friend. Everyone who makes himself a king opposes Caesar" (v. 12). Exactly! It was a choice between *basileus* Caesar or *basileus* Jesus. In the end, not only Pilate but also the mob preferred the *basileus* in Rome to the *basileus* of the Jews: "We have no king but Caesar" (v. 15).

## THE KINGDOM OF GOD

Since that time, every person in the domain of the ancient Roman Empire, from England to Greece, as well as all their heirs, from North America to New Zealand, have had to choose, consciously or unconsciously, between the *basileus* in mighty Rome and the *basileus* of inconspicuous Israel. Actually, I should express this more precisely. Even the Emperor of Rome was not the real adversary of Jesus; it was in fact the angelic prince of Rome. In the Book of Revelation this is the "dragon," that is the devil and Satan (Rev. 12:9; 20:2). It is this dragon that gives the "beast" (the eschatological Roman *basileus*) its strength, its throne and great power (13:2). When the dragon itself is described, this monster turns out to exhibit the features of the beast, that is, of the Roman Empire or its head, namely, the seven heads and the ten horns, and on the heads seven crowns (cf. 12:3 with 13:1-2). The dragon is the invisible personification, or the angelic prince, the "god," of the Roman Empire, just as, conversely, the beast (the head of that empire) is the "incorporation" of the dragon.

Please note this crucial point: since the fourth century, the Roman Empire has been called a "Christian" Empire, both in the East and in the West, but its real angelic prince is Satan, the "dragon," the invisible celestial power behind "the Beast," that is both the Roman Empire and the head of it. I have to restrain myself on this fascinating subject because I have worked it out in great detail in my book *The Ninth King*. For now, let me limit myself to the following statement: effectively, the choice for every citizen of the world is not only between the beast and the Lamb, but between the dragon and the Lamb. The whole of world history, at least since the first century, could be summarized as the great conflict between the dragon and the Lamb.

Try to imagine this in a graphic way: a Lamb is brought into the world arena to fight a dragon (a kind of Tyrannosaurus rex)! It will not be the fire-breathing dragon that gains the victory in the end (cf. Leviathan: "Out of his mouth go flaming torches; sparks of fire leap forth," Job 41:19), but the fire-breathing Lamb (so to speak): "[W]ith the breath of his lips he shall kill the wicked" (Isa. 11:4b). "And then the lawless one [i.e., Antichrist] will be revealed, whom the Lord Jesus will kill with the breath of his mouth and bring to nothing by the appearance of his coming" (2 Thess. 2:8).

## Chapter Nine
# A CHRISTIAN VIEW OF PREHISTORY AND EARLY HISTORY

In the two remaining chapters, I will limit myself to a few historical subjects that I have not yet touched upon, where a Christian approach seems to be of special interest. I am referring to the Neolithic Revolution (First Great Turn) and the Axial Age (Third Great Turn).

The era before the beginning of the great ancient civilizations, that is, before the rise of the Sumerian and Egyptian civilizations (the time of what is generally known as the Neolithic Revolution), is referred to as *prehistory*. This term is rooted in a certain definition of *history* (see chapter 1). History is not just a mere series of *events*, but also an *awakened human awareness* of what is happening, and the urge to record this awareness of what has happened in a written form. As the German psychiatrist and philosopher Karl Jaspers (1883-1969) expressed it in his *Vom Ursprung und Ziel der Geschichte* (English translation, *The Origin and Goal of History*, 1953), history is only history if there is also an awareness of history. (The term "Neolithic Revolution" was coined by Australian archeologist V. Gordon Childe [1892-1957].)

## Development of Awareness

The consequence of Jaspers' statement is quite striking. The invention of writing is important for the historian because, in this way, an epoch began for which he can consult written documents. But the origin of writing also implies that, in the ancient civilizations, we are dealing with a new kind of Man. This was Man not just as an existing being, but as thinking about the fact that he lives, and how he lives, and putting this down in writing. In due time, this writing became *independent* with respect to the writing person, that is, it remained as a historical testimony standing on its own, in contrast to oral tradition, which changes along with changing Man.

The Neolithic Revolution, which occurred about fifty-five hundred years ago, deserves our special attention, just like another epoch of great significance, called by Karl Jaspers the *Achsenzeit* (the *Axial Age*) which occurred in the sixth century BC (see chapter 10). As Jaspers described it, from the Neolithic Revolution onwards, Man was *aware* of what happened, and recorded it; in the Axial Age, Man became aware of this awareness and reflected upon it, with all possible philosophical and religious consequences. Before the Axial Age, Man reflected upon what happened to him; *during* the Axial Age, Man began to reflect upon reflection as such. This went very deep, and as a result, philosophy was born. The preceding thinking had gone much less deep. As a consequence, the religions of the ancient civilizations have disappeared almost entirely, except for the general belief in the divine; but those of the Axial Age are still as vital as ever. Here we see a historical *development*, or, if you like, a further *unfolding* (awakening, unfurling) of Man's potential.

With the Neolithic Revolution, the clear self-awareness of Man did not necessarily *begin* but, for the first time since Noah's Flood (Gen. 6-9), it became clearly *visible*. Or perhaps we should say that it became visible *again*? Was true reflection before the Fall of Man (Gen. 3) not possible? One could say that reflection presupposes *problems*. In a sense, the world became *problematic* only after the fall into sin. It is questionable whether Man had time enough to learn to focus upon this problematic character of the world after the Fall. At any rate, it is only during the Axial Age that deep philosophical and religious reflection emerged; by this we mean thinking about Man's self-awareness in the light of the transcendent (divine) world.

Before the Neolithic Revolution, which was the *First Great Turn* in post-flood human history, there was history because Man was aware of himself. During the Neolithic Revolution, this awareness became clearly visible; Man began to think about himself and about what was happening.

## A CHRISTIAN VIEW OF PREHISTORY

When (after Adam, Enoch and Noah) the true God revealed himself to Abraham around the nineteenth century BC, and later at Mount Sinai to Israel through Moses about the fifteenth century BC, Man became aware of the true God, and thus received a new awareness of himself; this was the *Second Great Turn*. From that time onward, an entire Chosen Nation began to think about God, and thus it also saw itself, as well as the rest of the world, in a different light.

During the Axial Age, which was the *Third Great Turn*, the awareness of Man's self-awareness became visible. Gentile Man began to think about thinking itself—the start of philosophy—but yet without knowledge of the true God.

The coming of Christ, which was the *Fourth Great Turn*, marked the beginning of the Christian Church, which was the crucial moment in this process of becoming aware. A few Jews and millions of Gentiles began to think in the light of God, as revealed in Christ, and thus arrived at the deepest thinking, which was the profoundest self-knowledge possible. For where God revealed himself in Christ, Man too was revealed to himself in the deepest possible way. Jaspers said that the Church was presumably the greatest and highest organization form of the human mind that had ever been.

With the *Fifth Great Turn* that we can distinguish, the rise of Islam, the greatest religious adversary of the Church began its development. The nations began to think in the twilight of the anti-god (empires arose east and south of the Mediterranean, the earliest being the Rashidun Caliphate founded after the death of the prophet Muhammad, the latest being the Ottoman Sultanate which lasted until 1922).

The *Sixth Great Turn* was the beginning of the Modern Era in the sixteenth century, specifically the Scientific Revolution concomitant with it. Man learned not only to *know* his environment better but in particular to *control* it. In this way, he not only changed the world, but he also changed himself (again) in his very being: the "Enlightened" Man of the eighteenth century began to think in order to control nature without God, which led—and still leads—to a false notion of emancipation, and actually to self-estrangement.

PROBING THE PAST

## Two Kinds of Prehistory

Coming back to the First Great Turn, we can easily grasp the necessity of distinguishing between *absolute* and *relative* prehistory. Absolute prehistory refers to the age preceding the Neolithic Revolution, say, 3500 BC. Relative prehistory refers to those nations that remained outside the scope of the great ancient civilizations even after 3500 BC, and persisted in their old condition. These nations began to develop their culture at a later stage—e.g., the Chinese, the Western, Northern and Eastern Europeans, the Mayas, the Incas—but for some other nations, the prehistory lasted until our own time (e.g., the Amazon Indians, the Papuans).

With respect to the evolutionary view of prehistory, let me make two remarks. First, from an evolutionist viewpoint, the absolute prehistory necessarily took a very long time. The Pleistocene Age supposedly started about 2.6 million years ago, coinciding with the Paleolithic Age, that is, the Old Stone Age, and ended about 11,700 years ago. This is a tremendous and incomprehensible contrast: the Old Stone Age allegedly starting 2.6 million years ago, and human "history" starting at best only 5,500 years ago. Some place the beginning of the Neolithic Era or New Stone Age, at about seven or eight thousand years ago, but still the enormous discrepancy between 2.6 million and 8,000 remains. The time of the Neolithic is that of the great ancient civilizations in three great river basins: that of the Nile in Egypt, that of the Euphrates and the Tigris in Mesopotamia, and that of the Indus in Northern India and Pakistan. Later, there is also a fourth one: that of the Huang Ho in China.

Where the evolutionist standpoint is rejected and the validity of the Bible's account of early history is taken seriously, the necessity to postulate a very ancient humanity vanishes. Apart from the period between creation and Noah's flood (about which we cannot say anything more than the very few things the Bible communicates to us), in biblical terms absolute prehistory is nothing but the time between the Flood and the origin of the great ancient civilizations. We must be careful here, but perhaps this whole period did not last longer than a few thousand years.

## Development?

My second remark is this. On the one hand, prehistory is distinct from history in that prehistoric Man did not yet know the regulation of water, which is so important for protection, irrigation, and drinking water. Nor did he know the idea of "nation," nor the use of horses, nor, in particular, writing. Without any historical awareness, he still lived in the mere "present," and was still vitally bound to nature, and thus to the natural spirits (Jaspers).

On the other hand, in evolutionary terms, prehistory is differentiated from the preceding evolutionary development of mankind through the following characteristics. Prehistoric Man did know how to make fire, as well as tools on which his existence depended. He knew the formation of groups and communities, with the striking characteristic of the regulation of sexuality ("marriage"), and masculine solidarity in hunting and war. Men (or probably women) knew agriculture. They wore clothes. They were still bound to nature, but, in contrast with the apes, Man differentiated himself from nature through his taboos, his myths, and his artistic capacities. There seems to be no single tribe, no matter how primitive, which did not have some religious awareness (whether it be hunting magic, a fertility goddess, or tombs with grave goods) as well as some artistic awareness. And in particular, prehistoric Man knew *language*—which is perhaps the most conspicuous and striking difference from animals.

Again, when we view the situation from a biblical perspective, it looks very different in the sense that a pre-prehistoric "primordial Man" does not exist. Virtually from the outset, Man is described as someone who has language (Gen. 2-3), and knows the use of fire, musical instruments, and tools (Gen. 4). Marriage was a divine institution even before the Fall (Gen. 1-2). Man was sharply distinguished from the animals in that he had been created in God's image, and after God's likeness (1:26). There was no biotic development preceding prehistory. From the outset, Man displayed a cultural, historical and religious discontinuity with respect to the animal kingdom. "Primordial Man" from before the Neolithic Era is unknown in the Bible. People whom we still call "primitive" because they still live in the Stone Age can be brought to full development within one generation, and turn out to have the same intellectual and other capacities as the "civilized" nations.

Something that is even more striking in Genesis is that even before the Flood, Man already seems to have known writing. Genesis 5:1 refers to "the book of the generations of Adam"; "book" in Hebrew is *sefer*, which means something written (from *s-f-r*, "to write"). This "book"—a list of Adam's progeny—might be much older than the Five Books of Moses, and might even be older than the flood. One may wonder how people after the Flood would have known this genealogy otherwise, unless such a written document were available.

## Does Prehistory Exist?

In conclusion we can say that, in the strictly biblical sense, there is no question of an *absolute* prehistory. With the sons of Noah and their offspring in Genesis 10, we are on perfectly recognizable historical ground. Most of the seventy nations mentioned in that chapter can be easily identified. Some of the names even carry us directly to the domain of the ancient civilizations. One of the sons of Ham is Mitzrayim, which is the common Hebrew name for Egypt (some translations even translate "Egypt" in Gen. 10:6). Mitzrayim's (great-) nephew Nimrod founded Babel, Erech (i.e., Uruk), Akkad, and Calneh in the land of Shinar, which historians know under the name Sumer.

Genesis 10 has no room whatsoever for any "prehistory." How could it have been otherwise? As soon as the new mankind, in the centuries after the Flood, found places where cultural formation was possible, this is precisely what happened. At first it took place in the caves where people hid during the severe circumstances right after the flood: "They had to live in the clefts of the valleys, in caves of the earth and the rocks" (cf. Job's probably very ancient memories in Job 30:6), later in the fertile river basins that Man encountered. It would give a wrong impression to call these centuries between the Flood and the first ancient civilizations "prehistory."

If, for practical reasons, people still prefer the term "prehisto-

## A CHRISTIAN VIEW OF PREHISTORY

ry," then it must *not* be understood in the sense of some necessary "developmental stage," gradually leading up to historical Man. It is highly questionable whether people who left us only their hand-axes were really less intelligent than we are. Were they perhaps more courageous and inventive than we are, because they killed cave bears and mammoths with hand-axes instead of machine guns? Tribes who, until recently, lived under "Stone Age" circumstances exhibit unequivocal evidence that their mental capacities are no less than ours, as I mentioned before. The Pleistocene people who made the wonderful cave paintings were no less artistic than present-day artists. Moreover, they possessed kinds of paint that did not fade, that we have not been able to imitate. Who would dare to call them more "primitive" than we are?

Not in the remotest sense could we honestly assert that the more ancient cultures in the Middle East gradually developed from the Stone and Bronze Ages, in the course of hundreds of thousands, or even millions, of years. In the very oldest tombs of the Sumerian culture, those of the kings of Ur, golden instruments have been found, ornamented in the most splendid way. Jewelry and many other objects made of gold, silver and bronze have been brought to light. Civilization as we know it did not develop gradually but appeared relatively suddenly, about five and a half thousand years ago. In a historical model that starts with the biblical data of Noah's flood and the aftermath, this is far more easily understandable than a gradual development over a very long period, because apparently there never *was* such a "development."

One would expect people to have found more and more primitive forms of culture the deeper the excavations were. However, this has not been the case, neither in Sumer, nor in Egypt, although these are the regions that have known the most ancient cultures of the world. The English archeologist Leonard W. King (1869-1919) wrote in 1910 that, although the earliest Sumerian settlements in South Babylonia must be dated to a relatively remote past, it turns out that their founders had already reached a high level of civilization. The English Egyptologist and historian Henry R.H. Hall (1873-1930) wrote in 1913 that, when civilization arose, it was already full-grown, and that the Sumerian civilization at its appearance was already fully finished. I am not aware of significant new archeological developments that would fundamentally alter this picture.

A similar situation has been described for other regions that developed an astonishingly high level of civilization already at an early stage, such as the river basins of the Indus and of the Huang Ho. If we follow the theory of human evolution, we would expect that culture evolved as gradually as Man allegedly did himself. Instead of this, we observe a real miracle. After hundreds of millennia have supposedly passed in which Man has little more than hand-axes, suddenly there is a fully flourishing civilization, in which the various visual arts as well as the architecture—for example, the pyramids and the ziggurats—have apparently reached the highest levels of development. In a sense one could claim that there simply never was a developmental history of civilization. Some 5,500 years ago it was "suddenly" there, and since then there has been no development to ever higher levels of civilization (apart from modern technology).

## The Three Lines of History

As far as the main lines are concerned, I follow here the view of the British-Canadian archeologist and anthropologist Arthur C. Custance (1910-1985). This remarkable man distinguished three lines in world history, which apparently correspond with Noah's three sons:

1. *Shem* is characterized by true *religion*, that is, religion in the phenomenological (immanent) sense of the word, but based on true divine revelation. Shem therefore represents what we call Religions of the Book, all founded by Semites. They are Judaism, then Christianity which grows out of Judaism, then Islam which grows out of both Judaism and Christianity, though forming a distorted variety of both. In terms of Christian philosophy we can say that in Shem's inheritance it is the *pistical* modality that dominates the others.

2. *Ham* is characterized by *culture, art* and *technology*, albeit without the *Japhethite* intellectualism that has brought forth science in the modern sense of the word. Because of this feature,

## A CHRISTIAN VIEW OF PREHISTORY

most ancient civilizations were Hamitic. They were the culture of the Sumerians in Mesopotamia (the later Babylonians were Semites), that of the Egyptians in the Nile Valley, that of the oldest inhabitants of the Indus Valley, and of the East-Asiatic (in my view, that is Hamitic) Chinese people in the Huang Ho valley. Only the black nations of Africa have never founded a comparable civilization. In my terminology, in Ham's inheritance it is the *formative* (and to a lesser extent the *aesthetic*) modality that dominates the others.

3. *Japheth*, exemplified by the Greeks, the Romans, and later the Europeans in the wider sense, is characterized by *intellectualism*, which finds expression in traditional philosophical thinking. This thinking started with the Japhethite Greeks in the sixth century BC, during the Axial Age (see chapter 10), and extended over the entire Indo-European (especially Western) world. During the last five centuries the typical Japhethite form of science and technology came forth from this. This priority of Japheth became visible as early as the Second Great Turn, the Axial Age; Greek philosophy and Persian Zoroastrianism were Japhethite. Also developing Hinduism, and its offshoot Buddhism, besides having the much older Hamitic roots, had especially (younger) Japhethite roots (the Aryans). The exception during the Axial Age was the Chinese "philosophy," which had nothing to do with Western intellectualism but was typically Oriental wisdom; this was rather of a Hamitic nature. In my terminology, we can say that in Japheth's inheritance it is the *logical* modality that dominates the others.

## Comments

Arthur Custance claimed that these three lines, corresponding with Noah's three sons and their descendants, also represented the triple nature of Man's basic needs: the spiritual (Shem), the intellectual-metaphysical (Japheth) and the physical-practical (Ham). In my terms, Shem is the praying line, Japheth the probing line, and Ham the practical line. Custance associated these lines with spirit, soul and body respectively (with reference to 1 Thess. 5:23). Those who are already familiar with my book *Search-*

## PROBING THE PAST

*ing the Soul* will understand why I cannot be overly happy with this tripartite division. I would rather suggest three of what I call the *spiritive* modalities—three different aspects of the human mind—as characteristic of Noah's three sons: the pistical, logical, and formative (as well as the aesthetic) modalities, corresponding respectively with believing, thinking and willing (doing).

In all these respects, Shem, Ham and Japheth have been subservient to God as well as to all mankind. But Ham has been the most subservient to the other two, as is understandable from the story in Genesis 9:20-27. It was the Hamites who, after the confusion of tongues at the Tower of Babel (Gen. 11:1-9), were the first to live in almost all parts of the world, and who explored and cultivated these regions. It was the Hamites who developed agriculture (potatoes, maize, beans, and cereals). They developed weapons, utensils, means of transport, sewn and woven clothes, medicines, medical instruments and methods, trading methods, means of writing and other forms of communication. At the same time, it is striking that, in most cases, at a later stage both Semites and Japhethites began to occupy Hamitic territories and to adopt Hamitic inventions, and have made these inventions subservient to their own religious and intellectual enterprises, respectively.

These facts may help us to develop a somewhat more nuanced view of the alleged superiority of the Indo-European nations (which many of them believe to be an established fact). One could definitely say that everything that the Indo-Europeans have achieved—and their accomplishments are many—would have been inconceivable without Hamitic technology or Semitic faith. The radically new element that the Japhethites developed was entirely within the intellectual domain. Rationalism, as it dominated Western thought for twenty-five centuries, was an Indo-European "invention." With the help of their deep thinking, the Indo-Europeans reshaped both Semitic religion and Hamitic technology in a way that was both positive and negative. (It is good to keep this in mind when we call the Chinese and Japanese of today the great imitators of Western technology.)

This reshaping had a double consequence. First, during the Middle Ages, religion was "captured" in a theoretical-analytical-rationalistic (especially Scholastic) theology. Shem was conquered

## A CHRISTIAN VIEW OF PREHISTORY

by Japheth. Japheth began to dwell in the tents of Shem (cf. Gen. 9:27), but with his own furniture and utensils. Second, the foundations that Hamites had laid for our civilization, including their great mathematics, astronomy and medicine, combined with Indo-European philosophical-scientific thinking, ultimately led to the modern scientific-technological breakthrough, beginning in the sixteenth century (the Sixth Great Turn).

## Exceptions

Of course, the three lines described here must not be separated too forcefully. First, there were zalways a-religious as well as technical or philosophical Semites, especially when they were heavily influenced by Japheth. We need think only of the great—and largely secular—Jewish philosophers such as Baruch de Spinoza (1632-1677), Moses Mendelssohn (1729-1786), Karl Marx (1818-1883), Edmund Husserl (1859-1938), Henri Bergson (1859-1941), Martin Buber (1878-1965), Ludwig Wittgenstein (1889-1951), Karl Popper (1902-1994), Emmanuel Levinas (1906-1995), Thomas Kuhn (1922-1996), and Jacques Derrida (1930-2004). Also when we look at technological developments, many recent Western inventions have been attributed to Japhethites, whereas in reality Jews were first: the zeppelin (David Schwarz), the airplane (Otto Lilienthal), the record player (Emile Berliner), the telephone (Johann Philipp Reis), and the radio (Heinrich R. Hertz).

Similarly, there were also always a-technical as well as religious or philosophical Hamites. We can think of Confucius and Lao-Tze in the sixth century BC) who have a place in the Axial Age as great inspiring thinkers and moralists (see chapter 10).

There were also always non-rationalist as well as technical or religious Japhethites. Think of the great (non-Jewish) Western inventors, engineers and Christian leaders, from the church fathers and the Reformers up to the present (although I must admit that rationalism was a constant threat to them). The Sixth Great Turn (the Modern Era, the Industrial Revolution) was also a Japhethite matter. After Copernicus and Vesalius (see chapter 5), James Watt, Nicholas-Joseph Cugnot (inventor of the lorry), Robert Street (who designed the first internal combustion engine), Alessandro Volta (builder of the first battery), Daniel Bushnell (inventor of the first submarine), and Samuel Crompton (inventor of the first spinning machine), were all Japhethites. What is amazing is that these six men all devised their inventions within the same very short period of time, namely, the 1770s! Here again, we are struck by the synchronicity of the events (cf. chapter 5).

In spite of these exceptions, all in all, the idea that Noah's three sons represented three trends that have characterized the whole of human history is worth considering.

## Division

Genesis 10 supplies us with a survey of the descendants of Shem, Ham and Japheth, divided into exactly seventy nations (not counting the individual Nimrod). It is worth pointing out that Semites, Hamites and Japhethites (Indo-Europeans) do *not* represent three *races*, such as the white (Caucasian), yellow (East-Asiatic) and the Black race. On the contrary, one could almost say that, within the three family branches, just about all human races are represented. Therefore it was so foolish to identify the Hamites with the Black race, and to find in this even a justification for black slavery, or for South African *apartheid*. This implies a great ignorance of what the great Hamitic civilizations have been, and the fact that it was not Ham himself but his son Canaan who was called "servant of servants" (Gen. 9:25).

Another point to consider is that, in modern linguistics, expressions such as Semitic and Hamitic refer to linguistic families, not *biological* families. Therefore, we cannot assume that people who speak a Semitic, Hamitic or Indo-European *language* today belonged to the original Semitic, Hamitic and Japhethite *nations* respectively. For instance, the Phoenicians and the original Egyptians were Hamites, but the former spoke an Indo-European language, and the latter still today speak a Semitic language (Arabic). And even though the Central- and East-Asian nations were also Hamitic, no modern linguist would call their *languages* Hamitic.

According to Genesis 10, the Japhethites divided into two different currents, one of which migrated toward the north-west (Europe), while the other moved east: these were the ancestors of the Medes (and partly of the Persians) as well as of the (Aryan) Indians. The Hamites arrived in Africa, in the Middle East and in the Far East, and from there (across the Bering Strait?) they crossed to the Americas ("Native Americans") and to Oceania. Of the three main currents, the Hamites have occupied by far the largest territory. The Semites settled mainly in the Middle East, and received the smallest territory. Perhaps the final division between the three currents took place in the days of Peleg: "To [Shem's descendent] Eber were born two sons: the name of the one was Peleg [= division], for in his days the earth was divided" (Gen. 10:25).

## The National Angels

The division of the earth was in God's own providential hand. Historians have all kinds of theories about the distribution of the nations, but Deuteronomy 32:8-9 has this to say: "When the Most High gave to the nations their inheritance, when he divided mankind, he fixed the borders of the peoples according to the number of the sons of God [this is very probably the correct reading! WJO]. But the LORD's portion is his people, Jacob his allotted heritage." These verses imply that, when the world was divided into a number of nations, each with their own territory or "inheritance," each of them was placed under a "son of God," that is, an angel (cf. Job 1:6; 2:1; 38:7), to take care of the respective nations. The Lord received for himself his chosen people of Israel as an inheritance.

Because Genesis 10 speaks of precisely seventy nations, Jewish tradition speaks of seventy "national angels" who were divinely placed over these nations. These angels came to be revered as "gods" by the respective nations, which was the basis for their idolatry. Thus, one could say that God assigned the territories of the seventy nations to the seventy "gods." Conversely, Deuteronomy 4:19 ("the sun and the moon and the stars,... that the LORD your God has *allotted* to all the peoples under the whole heaven") and 29:26 (Israel "went and served other gods and worshiped them, gods... whom he had not *allotted* to them," italics added) teach us that God *allotted* these "gods" (angelic princes, associated

## PROBING THE PAST

with celestial bodies) to these nations. In Deuteronomy 4:19-20 we find the same thought as in 32:8-9, namely, that God allotted to the other nations the "gods" but chose for himself Israel as an "inheritance." The "gods" (sun gods, moon gods, star gods) each received their own nation, but the Lord received Israel.

On this whole subject of "national angels," see my book *The Ninth King* for many more details. Here I will point only to one important passage, Psalm 82, where God pronounces judgment on these "gods" insofar as they have not sufficiently cared for the nations that had been entrusted to them: "God has taken his place in the divine council; in the midst of the gods he holds judgment: 'How long will you judge unjustly and show partiality to the wicked?... I said, 'You are gods, sons of the Most High, all of you; nevertheless, like men you shall die, and fall like any prince'" (Ps. 82:1-2, 6-7). In these last verses, God refers to the eternal judgment on these angelic "gods" (cf. Rev. 20:10). For further comments and analyses, I refer to the book I have just mentioned.

The three Noahic lines do not have a geographical meaning only, but also a historical significance. First Ham was predominant, then Shem, then Japheth. This is the order in which Noah's sons are mentioned in his prophecy (Gen. 9:25-27). The first empires, in the four great river basins (Nile, Euphrates/Tigris, Indus, Huang Ho), were Hamitic. The last Hamitic empire in the West was that of the Phoenician settlement of Carthage (c. 650 BC–146 BC), which was destroyed by the Japhethite Romans. After the victory of the brilliant warlord Hannibal (247-c. 182 BC), it seemed that Japheth was being forced to make room for Ham again. But Japheth triumphed in 146 BC due to the great victory of Publius Cornelius Scipio (185-129 BC). In this way, the power of the Hamites in the Western world was finally brought to an end. Also the thirteenth century Mongol storm in Eastern Europe, with Genghis Khan (c. 1162-1227) as its first warlord, could no longer alter this fact. Hamitic world power started with Nimrod (Gen. 10:8-12), and it finished with the Third Punic War (149-146 BC).

The Semites have known their own great empires too. A very early Semitic empire was ancient Babylonia, with Hammurabi as its greatest king (1729-1686 BC). A Semitic empire in much later time was the great Arab empire that in the seventh century AD

## A CHRISTIAN VIEW OF PREHISTORY

extended from Spain to Persia, and which ended in Spain only in the fifteenth century. Not all Muslim empires were Semitic, though. According to Jewish as well as Muslim tradition, the Turks descended from Togarmah, a descendant of Japheth (Gen. 10:3). Thus, the Ottoman Empire (1517-1917) would basically have been a Japhethite empire. The world empires of the Macedonians and Greeks (ruled by Alexander the Great), and later of the Romans (led by their great emperors)—the third and the fourth empires of Daniel 2 and 7 (see for many more details my work *The Ninth King*)—were also Japhethite empires.

And what is the situation today? There are strong Semitic countries, especially the wealthy Arabic oil states (all Islamic). There are strong Hamitic countries of various religious and ideological backgrounds, such as China (Communist and Buddhist), India (Hindu), Japan (Shinto), and Indonesia (Muslim). And there are strong Japhethite countries, most of them (nominally) Christian (the United States, the European Union, Russia, Brazil, Australia), and a few of them Muslim (Turkey). Please note that in all three groups—Semitic, Hamitic, and Japhethite—there are mighty Muslim countries.

## The Neolithic Revolution

As I said, if there ever was an "absolute prehistory," it was nothing but the period between Noah's Flood and what has been called the Neolithic Revolution. It is worthwhile to look at the characteristics of this Revolution—the First Great Turn that I distinguish in human history after Noah's Flood—because they tell us something about the foundations of the ancient civilizations:

(a) *River basins*: According to the usual chronology, climatic changes during the Late Paleozoic or the Mesozoic Era led to a large desert girdle from the Sahara to the Kirgiz Steppe. From these arid territories, people moved to the basins of the great rivers I have mentioned before. This was not only because of the abundance of drinking water, but also because these rivers regularly flooded the land and made it fertile in this way; the application of other manures to the soil was not yet known. In this way, permanent settlements and regular agriculture could be developed.

## PROBING THE PAST

*Biblical aspects*: Presumably, the formation of deserts was a remote consequence of Noah's Flood. The former hunters and food collectors were not more primitive than the agrarians but lived under far more difficult circumstances. Long *before* the Flood, already during the second generation, Cain was a "worker of the ground" (Gen. 4:2-3). That is, agriculture goes back to the beginnings of human history.

(b) *Economics and technique*: In the river basins I have listed, a food producing economy developed in which part of the people was involved, leaving another part free for all kinds of handicrafts and techniques. In Sumer, these were especially metalworking (the melting of metals from ores), the manufacturing of jewels, the application of the wheel (for chariots and potters' wheels), the baking of bricks, the hewing of square rocks, the building of multi-angular walls, stone polishing, the baking of refined (thin-walled) pottery, and the making of great plastics.

*Biblical aspects*: These handicrafts and techniques did not develop only during the Neolithic Revolution. Some of them are mentioned already before the Flood, such as playing the lyre and pipe, and the forging of instruments of bronze and iron (Gen. 4:19-22). Other elements are mentioned after the Flood: the bricks (Gen. 11:3), the wheel (Exod. 14:25), etc., but this does not mean that they did not exist before the Flood.

(c) *The horse*: The domestication of the horse deserves particular mention because through the use of horses the whole world was opened up. Riders and chariots drawn by horses could travel large distances [longer] at a much higher speed than people on foot could. Man was "freed" from the soil, and henceforth could move more easily to other territories. The use of the horse also led to new battle techniques, such as the battle chariot, and a new elite, characterized by the taming of wild horses and by the courage of the rider and conqueror.

*Biblical aspects*: In the Bible, the chariot (implying the use of horses) is mentioned first in Genesis 41:43, the horse is specifically mentioned in Genesis 47:17 (the time of Joseph), and the battle chariot appears in Joshua 11:4 (at the time of the conquest of Canaan).

(d) *Writing*: One of the most important characteristics of these rising cultures was the development of writing. At first this in-

## A CHRISTIAN VIEW OF PREHISTORY

volved a simpler pictorial writing, and subsequently cuneiform writing; in Egypt the hieroglyphs were used. As early as the second millennium BC, an alphabetic writing system was developed. Through writing, commercial, political and other kinds of correspondence became possible. Moreover, in these cultures, annals and chronicles (i.e. historiography) originated, as well as literary works, such as the famous Epic of Gilgamesh, king of Uruk (c. 2,500 BC?). These people not only lived and worked but became aware of this, and accounted for it in a written form. In Egypt in particular, time calculation (a *calendar*) was added to this; such a calendar presupposed a certain measure of astronomical and mathematical knowledge. (The Mesopotamians and the Egyptians already knew a decimal system, but the former sometimes also used a heximal (or senary) system. As a consequence, we still divide the day into 4 x 6 hours, the hour in 10 x 6 minutes, and the minute in 10 x 6 seconds.) Without writing or a calendar, no sense of "history" is possible, and even less a registration of it.

*Biblical aspects*: The Hebrew verb s-f-r, "to write," occurs for the first time in Exodus 17:14, but the root occurs even earlier in Genesis 5:1 ("book," Heb. *sefer*). This may suggest that writing was known already before the Flood.

(e) *The city*: Another revolutionary and important characteristic was the origin of fortified urban settlements near rivers. The oldest city—after the Flood!—which is one of the oldest cities as far as we know, was Jericho in Canaan (standard chronology gives the date of its founding as 9,000 BC). Another ancient, and by now famous, example outside Mesopotamia and Egypt is Çatal Hüyük in Turkey (7,500 BC). Cities, with their monumental buildings, became the centers of the productions and trading of goods, of commerce and government. Each city set itself three aims in particular: first, offering security to a part of the community, second, the development of commercial relationships with other cities and regions, and third the regulation of the river water in order both to defend itself against the river, and to get water from it to irrigate the soil.

*Biblical aspects*: Jericho is mentioned first in Numbers 22:1. But long before Noah's Flood, mention is already made of a city: "When [Cain] built a city, he called the name of the city after the name of his son, Enoch" (Gen. 4:17). Possibly he built this city—a fortified settlement—to secure himself from being killed by other men. We will have to assume that this city was destroyed by the Flood.

(f) *Religion*: In the newly built cities, and the territories around them, government was in the hands of the king, who was also the religious leader. In Mesopotamia, this was the priest-king, who was viewed as the representative of the god to whom the city belonged. In Egypt, the Pharaoh was even considered to be the embodiment of the god himself. Religious thought was further dominated by polytheism (the worship of many gods) and magic (faith in the mysterious powers of nature, hidden to ordinary people, and the ability of certain humans to manipulate them for good or evil purposes).

Biblical aspects: Although he belongs to a much later time, Melchizedek is a striking example of such a priest-king (Gen. 14:18-20). As for magic, we may consider the magicians at Pharaoh's court (Exod. 7–8), and the prohibition of magic in Israel (Exod. 22:18; Lev. 19:26; Deut. 18:10).

(g) *Territorial enlargement*: Typical for urban settlements was the natural urge to enlarge their territories. Once the idea of the *nation* had emerged, the first to arise were the city-states and soon the first nation-states or even empires developed, each with its own worldview, determined by its own language, culture and religion. On the one hand, "world empires" included nations who either saw themselves as associated or were forced into such an arrangement. On the other hand, the rulers used this concentration of power to defend themselves against the surrounding nomadic tribes or nation-states.

*Biblical aspects*: Nimrod was the first and most important example of this tendency (again, after the Flood). He built an empire around the city states of Babel, Uruk, Akkad and Calneh. In Asshur, he built an empire around Nineveh, Rehoboth-Ir, Calah, and Resen (Gen. 10:10-12).

## Philosophical Aspects

As I mentioned before, the oldest era after the First Great Turn (the Neolithic Revolution) was in fact the Hamitic Era. In a cer-

## A CHRISTIAN VIEW OF PREHISTORY

tain sense, it can also be called the Mythical Era (Karl Jaspers). The myth here is an uncritical belief concerning the supernatural powers of nature, or concerning the gods, a story about their struggles, and especially about the origin and the history of the world as seen from a supernatural perspective (cf. chapter 4). This Mythical Era ended with what Jaspers called the Axial Age (see chapter 10). He describes the characteristics of the Axial Age as follows: Man became aware of "Being" as a whole, of himself, and of his limitations.

Jaspers said that, during the Neolithic Revolution, Man left behind the state of *Ungeschichtlichkeit* ("un-historicity") and entered into history; Jaspers wondered what internal change occurred within Man so as to lead him to what we call history. He suggested a few points that characterized this leap from the prehistorical to the historical, to which I add some brief comments:

1. *Memory*: Awareness, memory and transfer of spiritual acquirements. In this way, Man freed himself of the naked present.

*Comment*: According to some, the Hebrew word *olâm* (normally rendered "age, eternity," sometimes "world") in Ecclesiastes 3:11 could alternatively be rendered as follows: God has put an "awareness of time" (cf. the Expanded Bible) or a "sense of history" in Man's heart. See the beautiful definition of the Amplified Bible: "A divinely implanted sense of a purpose working through the ages which nothing under the sun but God alone can satisfy." The Contemporary English Bible explains it this way: "He puts questions in our minds about the past and the future." It is a sense of the flow of the ages, from the distant past to the future.

2. *Technique*: The rationalization of some alleged meaning and relevance of existence, plus the concomitant technical possibilities implied in this reasoning. Thus, Man freed himself from being vitally bound to whatever happens in the surrounding natural world, and began to take precautions and safety measures (think again of the regulation of river water which is both necessary and threatening).

*Comment*: This kind of control which Man has over his environment is a typical difference from the animals (beaver dams are exceptional). If we adopt the evolutionary approach, we might say that during a certain period the genus *Homo* made this elementary step from an ape-like ancestor to Man. But according to the biblical approach, there never was such a step; Man distinguished himself from the animals right from the beginning.

3. *Heroes*: The exemplary influence of certain people—both rulers and wise people—whose deeds, achievements and trials functioned as objectives for subsequent generations. Thus, Man freed himself in principle from the fuzziness of self-awareness, and from the fear of the evil powers of nature.

*Comment*: The great, though negative example of this was Nimrod, whom I have mentioned before: "He was a great hunter before the LORD. At first Nimrod's kingdom covered Babylon, Erech, Akkad, and Calneh in the land of Babylonia. From there he went to Assyria, where he built the cities of Nineveh, Rehoboth-Ir, and Calah. He also built Resen, the great city between Nineveh and Calah" (Gen. 10:9-12).

## Culture, Good and Bad

As a further comment on Jaspers' deliberations, I would suggest that, since the fall of Genesis 3, civilization is both "decline" and "delight," both self-destruction and blessing. There is always both the demonic and the divine in it. This is the paradox of history: it is *sinful* but still highly gifted Man who creates culture. On the one hand, there is what has been called the "cultural mandate" (see the famous *Stone Lectures on Calvinism* by the Dutch theologian and statesman Abraham Kuyper [1837-1920]). This is the calling to cultural formation, that is, the active unfolding of the potential given in creation, even after the Fall (Gen. 1:26-28; 2:8, 15; 3:17-19, 23).

The remarkable point, however, is that this task seems to have been taken up primarily by Cain (Gen. 4:2), rather than by Abel; but Cain did so, not for the service and honor of God, but for the service of himself and his own honor. It was also Cain who founded the first urban community, and it was his descendants who practiced animal husbandry, music and metalworking, not the descendants of Seth (Gen. 4:17, 20-22).

Thus, the cultural mandate remains valid, but a curse rests on it, at least if it is carried out in a "Cainite" way—and this is

## A CHRISTIAN VIEW OF PREHISTORY

usually the case (cf. on this subject the German theologian Erich Sauer [1898-1959]). Man *cannot* do otherwise than to form culture, for this is how God made him. Without culture, Man would be swallowed up by the powers of nature; culture is bringing nature under control. Therefore, culture is never wrong as such, on the contrary. No one can get around these things in life. Thus we see that the priest-king Melchizedek reigned over a city (Gen. 14:18-20), and when we consider Abraham and his descendants we hear of herds and flocks (they were even "shepherd princes"; Gen. 12:16 etc.), of music (Gen. 31:27), and of metalworking (Gen. 13:2; 24:22, 35, 53).

However, already in Genesis 13:7 there was strife between the herdsmen of Abraham and those of Lot. In Judges 5:16 when the tribe of Reuben played the flutes, this was a way to cover up their laziness and cowardice. And metalworking led to advanced weapons, which could cause much damage (Gen. 22:6, 10; 27:40 etc.). On the one hand, sinful Man cannot do without culture; on the other hand, he cannot deal properly with culture either. This is the curse of cultural history.

Indeed, it seems to be an iron historical law that each cultural leap forward that Man makes in history leads to both new cultural blessing and new curses. This has always been the case, from the invention of the wheel and the discovery of how to make fire up to the invention of the computer and the Internet. With all four of these, and so many other cultural acquirements, one can do a lot of good or create a lot of havoc. Before the Messiah finally establishes his Kingdom of peace and justice, we will have to live with this cultural-historical tension between blessing and curse. Within this Messianic Kingdom, on the one hand, the nations will bring their cultural treasures to the city of God (Isa. 60:5-11; cf. Rev. 21:24, 26). On the other hand, all the weaponry will be burnt (Ezek. 39:9-10), or beaten into useful utensils (Isa. 2:4; Micah 4:3).

# Chapter Ten
# THE AXIAL AGE

Besides the Neolithic Revolution (around 3500 BC) and the Scientific Revolution of the Modern Era, probably one of the most important, mysterious and fascinating turns in world history in the common historical handbooks is the Axial Age which occurred in the sixth century BC. German philosopher Karl Jaspers gave it this name (*Achsenzeit*) because during this period time turned like a wheel around its axis. The great turns took place in four regions: China, India, the Middle East, and the Greek speaking world. These are the same as the original four great river basins, with one significant exception: Egypt has been replaced by Greece. Thus, we have two Hamitic, one Semitic, and one Japhethite region.

One reason why it is useful to discuss this subject is that the effects of the Axial Age have spread over the entire world, and have lasted to this very day. Another reason is that this extraordinary subject gives us an opportunity to show what specific light a Judeo-Christian approach to the subject might throw upon it. The subject is a case study of how a Judeo-Christian philosophy of history might work. I could have chosen several other such case studies. But I am sure this is one of the most striking ones.

## Significance of the Axial Age

In his list of the characteristics of the Axial Age, Jaspers states that Man became aware of "Being" as a whole, aware of himself, and aware of his limitations. This awareness led to asking the most radical questions, and to the most thorough reflection. For the first time, awareness became aware of itself, thinking began to think about itself. It is true that people reflected a lot even before that era; how else would the many inventions of the Mythical Era, including ones in the spiritual domain, have been conceivable?

## PROBING THE PAST

But we have to assume that people still did not reflect much on thinking itself. This has been one of the greatest "inventions" in the history of thought: thinking about thinking itself. It is taking one step back as it were, and observing oneself as a thinking person: do I think well, correctly, logically? It implies the birth of what we call philosophy, which means "love of wisdom." Thinking about thinking is basically an attempt to acquire wisdom, that is, "good" thinking in the broadest sense.

During the Mythical Era, life and the world were generally accepted as self-evident, just as little children still do today. Perhaps this is a good parallel: the Neolithic Revolution was the birth of post-Flood mankind, and the Mythical Era was its infancy. Children, too, can be very intelligent and refined, but their reflection on life is still very limited. The Axial Age was the puberty of alluvial mankind; the maturing young person becomes a problem, not only to his environment but to himself. After the Axial Age, the subsequent Metaphysical Age was like adolescence, which led to full adulthood only with the coming of Christ (cf. Gal. 4:1-6, where the imagery of childhood and adulthood is worked out). As Jaspers explains, the Greek, Indian and Chinese philosophers, as well as the Buddha, with all their decisive insights, and the Israelite prophets with their idea of God, were non-mythical. It was the newly rising *logos* against outdated *mythos*.

The consequences of all this were enormous. Apart from the general belief in the divine, all the acquirements of the ancient civilizations were lost, *except* those that were adopted during the Axial Age, and were worked into the new insights. Conversely, the acquirements of the Axial Age themselves were never lost. They have retained their spiritual and intellectual power to this very day, as we will see. Man still lives on the insights that were developed during that period. The Asian world religions are still flourishing, while Christian civilization lives out of both its Jewish and its Greco-Roman roots. Through memory and return— "renaissances"!— these insights have been refreshed time and again.

The Axial Age started within limited areas (Israel, India, China, Iran, Greece), but gradually it grew to include the entire world. A nation that does not share in its acquirements remains

# THE AXIAL AGE

a "primitive" nation bound to nature. Insofar as the previously highly civilized nations (Egypt and Babylonia) no longer shared in it, they got further behind. New nations that later shared in it are, in the West, the Macedonians, the Romans, the Celtic, Germanic, Slavic and Hungarian nations, and in the East the Japanese, the Malays, and the Thais. *Within* the region mentioned, the Axial Age apparently originated completely independently in three worlds (China, India, and the Mediterranean region); yet there was a deep mutual understanding between the three views. Thinkers were occupied with the same fundamental questions and, in important respects, even the answers share more similarities than a superficial study might suggest.

## Synchronicity

As early as 1856, the German philologist Ernst von Lasaulx (1805-1861) wrote in his philosophy of history that it cannot be a coincidence that, more or less at the same time, shortly after 600 BC, several reformers of popular religion were active: in Persia there was Zoroaster, in India the Buddha, in China Confucius and Lao-Tze, in Israel some of the greatest prophets (Jeremiah, Ezekiel, Daniel), and in Greece the first philosophers (Thales, Anaximander). In his famous commentary on the Chinese thinker Lao-Tze, German historian Viktor von Strauss (1809-1899) pointed to the same remarkable spiritual movement that went through all cultural nations of that time: China, Israel, Greece, Persia and India.

Indeed, there is something mysterious about this Axial Age. Many attempts (biological, historical, and sociological) have been made to explain how it came that, in very different regions on earth, which as far as we know were hardly in contact with one another, if at all, such a Great Turn could occur. No one has really succeeded in providing a satisfactory explanation; at least, many thinkers have refused to speak of a mere coincidence. The German philosopher Hans Joachim Störig (1915-2012), in his short world history of philosophy, described the essence of the Axial Age as follows: "The human mind made a gigantic step forward, and in the aforementioned persons [see above] it discovered itself as it were." And then he called it both miraculous and inexplicable.

**PROBING THE PAST**

I am fully convinced that a biblical metaphysical explanation is possible here, which perhaps forms the only possible explanation. Again, I am tying it in with the three lines corresponding to Noah's three sons. The Jewish prophets were Semites, the Chinese thinkers were Hamites (in my broad definition of the term!), and the (Aryan) Indians, Persians and Greeks were Japhethites. The Chinese were a bit different from the others. In fact, Confucius (551-479 BC) was not a philosopher in the theoretical-analytical sense as were the Greek thinkers. Nor was he the founder of a religion, as was the Buddha. Confucius was a practical sage, a moral preacher, who never mentioned the name of God, nor was he concerned with the Beyond but only with leading the right life here on earth.

With the Indians and the Greeks, it was very different. Both groups offered a true *metaphysics*, that is, a doctrine about what is behind, or beyond (Greek *meta*) the physical world. Each group did it in quite a different way—the Indians more practically, the Greeks more theoretically—yet both thought systems were forms of metaphysics. Both nations were *Japhethites* (*Indo-Europeans*). It is worth noticing that it was *not* the original (Hamite) inhabitants of the Indus basin who designed Hindu metaphysics as we know it today, but the Aryans, an Indo-European nation that penetrated the region around 1500 BC.

## Shem *versus* Japheth

As far as the Jewish prophets are concerned, they can in no way be grouped with the Aryan Indians, the Persians and the Greeks. On the contrary, in many essential points they were completely *opposite*. Whereas the Indo-European nations were searching for (theoretical) *insight*, the Jewish prophets were searching for (practical) *righteousness* (Custance). The former strove for intellectual light, the latter for moral light. In several studies, Jewish-American sociologist Jessie Bernard (1903-1996) has pointed out that the continual search for intellectual insight was never a Jewish matter, and that some great philosophers who, although Jewish, were secularized (e.g., Marx, Husserl, Bergson, Derrida; see chapter 9) had become unfaithful to their true Jewish inheritance. Perhaps we should add

## THE AXIAL AGE

that Jewish thinkers such as Maimonides (1135-1204), and much more recently, Martin Buber (1878-1965) and Emmanuel Levinas (1906-1995), did search for a synthesis between Western philosophy and the wisdom of Torah and Talmud.

The tremendous contrast between the Jewish prophets and the Greek philosophers has often been described. Thus, the British cultural critic Matthew Arnold (1822-1888) wrote in his *Culture and Anarchy* about two forces dominating Western Man: the *energy* that drives to practical action (servitude, self-control, labor), and the *intellect*, which is the basis for proper action. To Arnold, these two forces, although complementary, were competitors. He called them the forces of Hebraism and Hellenism, which he reduced to their respective Semitic and Indo-European roots.

The American philosopher William C. Barrett (1913-1992) described them as the difference between *doing* and *knowing* or, to use the technical terms, between *praxis* and *theoria*. The Jew was focused on the right acting, the Greek on right thinking. The former asked: What should I *do*? The latter asked: What can I *know*? The Jews exalted the moral virtues of life, and did not want to go against his conscience. The Greek exalted the intellectual virtues of life, and did not want to go against his understanding. Of course, we should not make this contrast too absolute; the Greeks were also occupied with questions such as evil and suffering, and the Jews also strove for knowledge of an existential nature.

The Scottish philosopher and historian Thomas Carlyle (1795-1981) once said that "Socrates is terribly at ease in Zion." Matthew Arnold retorted that the Jews themselves were always deeply convinced of the *impossibility* of ever being "at ease" in Zion. The reason is the Jewish—and later Christian—awareness of sin, imperfection, weakness, and finiteness (Barrett) in opposition to God's Word (the *Torah* and the Prophets, later the *New Testament* and the *Talmud*). The Greeks gave us philosophy and science, while the Jews gave us the Tanakh (i.e., the Old Testament). Think of the biblical Book of Job, in which Man does not reason about God in a logical-critical way but stands in opposition to God in his full humanity, with all his indignation, demanding that God account for what he is doing. This is not a rational-theoretical-distanced relationship, but a practical-existential relationship of immediate

## PROBING THE PAST

(and passionate) concern. In the Psalms, we find this same relationship time and again (cf. for more details my previous volumes, *Wisdom for Thinkers* and *What Then Is Theology?*). Israel's prophets argued *with* God—complained to him, or even about him—but they never argued *about* God. They analyzed their plight, but they never ventured even to think of analyzing *God*.

In Greece, the Axial Age began with the Greek thinkers disentangling themselves from the visionary (cf. the earlier Greek poets Homer and Hesiod), the religious, and the mythical. As a consequence, they began asking specific questions that to this very day occupy the minds of philosophers and scientists. The English mathematician and philosopher Alfred N. Whitehead (1861-1947) once claimed that the "safest general characterization of the European philosophical tradition is that it consists of a series of footnotes to Plato." In other words, Plato has already defined all the philosophical problems we are still wrestling with (except the problem of modern technology), and even gave the first tentative but intelligent answers to them. The biblical prophets and apostles defined our ideas of morality and virtue, but the Greeks defined our thought problems.

As long as Man was still caught up in mythical thinking, it never occurred to him to ask such questions as the Greek philosophers did. And *if* by chance he did, he answered them in an uncritical way, naïvely appealing to the world of the gods and magic. The Greek thinkers broke away from this mental attitude and began to give all the priority to reason. In doing so, they gave us what we call today *science* (lit., "knowledge," that is, theoretical knowledge). No one can doubt that this has brought great *gain* to mankind. However, the great *danger* inherent in this was losing the link with divine revelation and practical wisdom, that is, insight into what to do and what not to do, so much so that people began to believe that science could even solve our moral questions.

Wisdom is also a form of knowing. However, it is not the intellectual knowledge of the world but the existential knowledge of God and his commands, the love towards God, in service and obedience: "Teach me good judgment and knowledge, for I believe in your commandments (Ps. 119:66). "I am your servant; give me understanding, that I may know your testimonies" (v. 125).

## THE AXIAL AGE

"Concerning Your testimonies, I have known of old that You have founded them forever" (v. 152 NKJV).

During the Axial Age, the way of science and the way of wisdom separated—although, thank God, there have always been people in whom they met.

## The Eclipse of God

I now wish to point to two historic events in ancient Israel that are of importance to all of mankind. To the Romans, Judea was just an inconspicuous "corner" of the vast Roman Empire. To the prophets, however, Jerusalem was the very center of the world. Ezekiel called it the "navel of the earth" (Ezek. 38:12 NIV note). Seen from God's perspective, Jerusalem was the capital of the world: "Thus says the Lord GOD: 'This is Jerusalem. I have set her in the center of the nations, with countries all around her'" (5:5).

The first historic event took place in the mid-tenth century BC; it was the descent of the *Shekinah*, the "cloud" of God's glory on the newly-built temple of King Solomon in Jerusalem (1 Kings 8:10-13; 2 Chron. 5:13-14). Solomon was well aware that the Most High was too great to dwell in an earthly home; even the "highest heaven" could not "contain" him (1 Kings 8:27; 2 Chron. 6:18). In itself, this was perfectly true, of course. Yet, it was of the greatest meta-historic significance that God chose for himself a very concrete "address," a dwelling-place on earth, namely, Solomon's Temple in Jerusalem. It did not matter whether the Gentile nations recognized this, and it is irrelevant whether present-day historians acknowledge this. The Lord caused his name to dwell in Jerusalem, and from there this name was glorious in all the earth (cf. Ps. 8:1, 9). From Jerusalem, he ruled over all the earth (Ps. 47:2, 7; cf. 48:1). The LORD is "the Lord of all the earth" (Ps. 97:5). Even Solomon's throne is called the "throne of the LORD" (1 Chron. 29:23).

But less than four hundred years later, in 586 BC, both the city and the temple were destroyed by the Babylonian king Nebuchadnezzar (c. 630-c. 561 BC). Shortly before this dramatic event, the *Shekinah* withdrew from the temple. Because of the great seriousness of this withdrawal, it is described in great detail in Ezekiel 9-11. This was the second great event that I wanted to mention. It is my impression that this withdrawal had tremendous meta-historic significance. Through it, God obtained a new name; he was no longer primarily "the LORD of all the earth" (cf. Josh. 3:11, 13; Ps. 97:5) but "the God of heaven" (Ezra 1:2 etc.; Neh. 1:4 etc.). In Daniel 2, this meant very concretely that God's throne was no longer in Jerusalem but that his sovereign rule of the earth was henceforth associated with the head of the nations, Nebuchadnezzar to begin with.

In a certain sense, God had become a *deus remotus*, a "removed God." It is my thesis that this was reflected in the religions and philosophies that originated in that very period. Through the withdrawal of the *Shekinah*, not only did God's relationship to Israel change but also his relationship to the world as a whole. If God left the capital of the world, he left the world. This withdrawal involved a real "eclipse of God," to use an expression introduced by the Jewish thinker Martin Buber (see above); compare God's own words: "Then my anger will be kindled against them in that day, and I will forsake them and hide my face from them" (Deut. 31:17; cf. 32:19-20). It is God's voluntary "exile." If people do not want God anymore, he withdraws himself, just as the sun hides behind the moon during an eclipse. Or to mention an example concerning Jesus: "Then all the people of the surrounding country of the Gerasenes asked him to depart from them, for they were seized with great fear. So he got into the boat and returned" (Luke 8:37). If people did not want him, he did not force anyone but left. God hid himself in order that people would seek him again.

## The Wonder of Simultaneity

Let us now see what great thinkers were involved in the Axial Age, and how great the chronological coincidence was. Here are the thinkers according to their chronological order (of course, with all due reservation):

Jeremiah: c. 647 (or 627?)–after 586.
Zoroaster: c. 628–551 (but often dated much earlier!).
Thales: c. 624-545.
Buddha: c. 624/23–544/43 (others: c. 560–480).

## THE AXIAL AGE

Ezekiel: c. 623–after 570.
Daniel: c. 620?–after 537.
Anaximander: c. 611–549.
Lao-Tze: c. 604–517.
Mahavira: c. 599–527 (others: c. 540–468).
Anaximenes: c. 585–525.
Pythagoras: c. 580-500.
Xenophanes: c. 565–470.
Confucius: 551-479.

September 586 was the crucial month in which the *Shekinah* withdrew from Jerusalem, and the city and its temple were destroyed. In 586, Jeremiah was about 61 (or 41?), Zoroaster 42, Thales 38, Buddha 38 or 37, Ezekiel 37, Daniel 34, Anaximenes 25, Lao-tze 18, and Mahavira 13. Anaximenes was born about one year after 586, Pythagoras six, Xenophanes nineteen, and Confucius thirty-five years. When we consider the life-spans of all these individuals, the time they existed was altogether not more than one long human life! No matter how imprecise the dates may be here and there, they are really incredibly close.

What makes all this even more exciting is the story Herodotus told of the very first Greek philosopher, Thales (c. 624–546 BC), in which he astonished his contemporaries to the utmost by predicting the eclipse of the sun on May 28, 585. Because of this prediction, some have pointed to this date as the start of Greek philosophy, and thus of Western thinking. Of course, this is a bit arbitrary. But it *is* quite remarkable that this predicted solar eclipse in May 585 was only eight months after September 586, the month of the "eclipse of God." This is more than mere word play: with the philosophy of Thales, the "eclipse of God" in Western thinking began very concretely, as we will see. Moreover, it is equally striking that the Buddha presumably attained his "enlightenment" between 589 and 586, which marked the start of Buddhism (at least according to some chronologies).

The four events I have just mentioned are so close that it reminds us of the work of the Dutch psychologist and cultural philosopher Jan Hendrik van den Berg who, as I said earlier, assigned great significance to the synchronicity of historic events (see chapter 5). He pointed out that at certain crucial moments in cultural history simultaneous changes occur within science, the arts and religious experience. In the present case, this means that the changes in thinking in Greece, India, China and Iran during the Axial Age were related to a change in the world itself, namely, the withdrawal of the Divine Presence from earthly reality. (This is my own conclusion, not van den Berg's.)

If it is indeed true that events coincide more or less, the principle of simultaneity always applies, according to van den Berg. The coincidences are virtually always significant. In other words, the developments in Israel, Greece, India, China and Iran may have taken place "independently," but meta-historically they are necessarily related because they are both exceptionally meaningful and simultaneous. The more important and far-reaching the events concerned are, the more certain the meta-historic relationship between them is. In my Dutch book, *De Zesde Kanteling* ("The Sixth Great Turn"), I have worked this out in great detail for all the religions and philosophies involved.

## Secularization in Greece

Perhaps the most basic feature that all the thinkers and prophets during the Axial Age had in common was what I would call *secularization*. There are two important phases in this secularization: the Axial Age in the sixth century BC and the Scientific Revolution which began in the sixteenth century, resulting in the eighteenth-century Enlightenment. The term comes from Latin *saeculum*, which here means "world" (although in other cases it means "age, century"). The more God withdraws from the world, or is pushed out of the world, the more "worldly" (secular) the world becomes. Worldliness is not just doing certain wrong things, but thinking, speaking and acting without taking God into account (cf. Rom. 12:2; 2 Cor. 7:10; Titus 2:12; 1 John 2:15-17; Jude v. 19).

Secularization involves actively pushing God to the edges of society and civilization—removing God from public life—and, passively, God withdrawing from public life because Man no longer has a place for him. *All* new religions and philosophies of the Axial Age are attempts, in a world that has become dark and cold after the withdrawal of God, to think of very new ways—ways in which Man

## THE AXIAL AGE

can create some light and warmth without God. The well-known title of a book by the American theologian and philosopher Francis A. Schaeffer (1912-1984), called *How Should We Then Live?* (cf. Ezek. 33:10 KJV), which he applied to the decline of modern Western culture, can be perfectly applied to the Axial Age as well. In all the developments I have mentioned we find this same element; they are *ways of survival* in a world that has grown dark and cold.

Before the "invention" of Greek philosophy, that is, of theoretical thinking, the Greek "seer," who was able to look into the higher world of gods and spirits (e.g., Orpheus, Homer, Hesiod), was viewed as the possessor of divine wisdom, as the true "scientist" (knowledgeable person), so to speak. Therefore, the rise of theoretical thinking involved a kind of "secularization": true knowledge was no longer knowledge of the "higher" (divine) things but, where the higher dimension was falling away, knowledge was more and more based on the lower dimension of logical arguments. The "seer" was replaced by the "thinker"; the eyes of the heart were replaced by the eyes of the mind. (On the difference between "seeing" and "thinking," see the detailed discussion in my book *Wisdom for Thinkers*.) This was a form of the eclipse of God: cosmic reality was no longer explained in terms of *divine knowledge*, but in terms of *human thinking*. The one deity, or the gods, were not denied, on the contrary; but they were "darkened," driven to the edge of thinking. Their relevance was diminished. In order to explain our world, and afterwards also, to control our world by thought, the deity played a subordinate role, or none at all.

This can also be expressed as follows: theoretical thought as it developed during the Axial Age, was a *secular* attempt to return to Paradise Lost. The Greeks too knew about evil, and about the instability that is given with it. Theoretical thought, and the science which resulted from it, was a means to restore order and stability. The Greeks supposed that the perfect order of Paradise was the order of *reason*, even more specifically, a mathematical order (cf. Pythagoras' idea that "everything is number"). For Plato (c. 428–c. 424 BC), the longing for Paradise was still a form of "escapism"; he tried to escape from evil and instability by fleeing into the transcendent world of the Ideas. But his pupil Aristotle (384–322 BC) exhibited in particular the desire to restore Paradise within our material reality by learning to *control* the instability.

The enormous *advantage* of the new approach, which no sensible person would ever wish to give up, is the critical striving after the how and the why, where earlier generations had simply referred uncritically to the world of the gods and magic. Viewed in this way, theoretical thought is nothing but a special expression of the critical mind that the Creator himself had bestowed on Man, although I must add that it was never the Creator's intention that Man would use it *independently* of him.

Here we see the *disadvantage* of the new approach, namely, the danger that the divine world would become altogether superfluous, the danger of an absolute "here-and-now" mentality. Or even more strongly, we could say that it is the danger of not wanting to combat the disorder only, but to bring the order instituted by God under one's own control. That is actually, the wish to correct this order, to improve on God, to have dominion over reality *like* God. *This* is the sin, originally suggested by Satan, of wanting to be *like* God (Gen. 3:5); that is, not to be viceroy but king. Never before had the danger of taking God's place been so great as during the eclipse of God.

It is striking that, in spite of these negative aspects, some of the early church fathers were very impressed by the Greek philosophers. Or at least they gave the impression of being so in order to win the sympathy of the pagans. Thus, Justin Martyr (c. 100-165), an early Christian apologist (defender of the Christian faith), was convinced that divine Reason (*Logos*, cf. John 1:1-3) had even illuminated the Greek philosophers Socrates (469-399 BC) and his pupil Plato (see above), so that they had become aware of the grossest errors of paganism. However, argued Justin, full truth had been revealed only in the "new Socrates," the "Teacher" Christ, the incarnated *Logos* of God (John 1:14). We find similar ideas in the writings of the early Christian thinker Clement of Alexandria (c. 150-c. 215). In the Middle Ages, Thomas Aquinas (1225-1274) and many others considered Aristotle (see above) to be the forerunner of Christ *in naturabilis* ("in natural things"), just as John the Baptist had been the forerunner of Christ *in spirituabilis* ("in spiritual things").

## Architecture

Let me point out here a remarkable synchronicity during the Axial Age that concerns the development of secularization in ancient Greece. From Acts 19, every reader of the Bible knows about the great veneration of the Ephesians for Artemis, the ancient mother-goddess. It is striking that the building of the world-famous temple of Artemis in Ephesus began around 590 BC. Not only is this is the time when Thales, the first Greek philosopher philosophized, and when the Buddha and Zoroaster preached, but it is also the time when the *Shekinah* withdrew from the temple in Jerusalem, and the eclipse of God began. In the very time when the newly "invented" philosophy began to push the traditional gods to the background, this gigantic building for the Mother-goddess was erected.

In other places, we find similar architectural wonders. During the life of the first of the three Attic philosophers, Socrates (see above), the construction of the famous Parthenon was begun (c. 448) in Athens; it was consecrated to the "virgin" (Greek: *parthenos*) Pallas Athena, the guardian goddess of the city.

What do these grandiose religious buildings tell us? Did the worship of the ancient gods simply continue after all, in spite of the new philosophy, which around 440 was already a hundred and fifty years old? In my view, the temple of Artemis, the Parthenon and similar expressions of art were rather symbols of the greatness of Greece itself. Greece was not great because its gods were, but by now, their gods were great because Greece was. The same spiritual freedom that started philosophy in the Greek colonies in Asia Minor also caused a free, *secularized* art to flourish. The fact that this art depicted religious themes says just as little as, for instance, the many masses that were composed by nineteenth-century Romantic composers but that, because of their "secular" character, were perfectly unsuitable for the liturgy. This kind of art glorifies the "free artist" rather than God or the gods—with the exception of the truly religious artists.

## Secularization in India: the Upanishads

In India, the Axial Age was in the first place the time of the Upanishads. These writings formed the last part of the Vedas, the wisdom literature of ancient Hinduism. The Upanishads have been called the "Himalayas of the Soul"; they belong to the most influential religious writings in the world, and have fascinated important thinkers up to our own time. The German philosopher Arthur Schopenhauer (1788-1860) called the Upanishads "the most rewarding and elevating literature that is possible in the world. This has been the consolation of my life, and will also be that of my death." About the philosophies of this period—the Upanishads, as well as Jain and Buddhist writings—the Indian scholar Kshitimohan Sen (1880-1960) wrote that in them "it is Man who stands in the center of interest, whereas the gods are subordinate... In general, we see that during this period the sacrifices make place for human ethics, monotheism replaces polytheism, and instead of the Vedic moral there is a growing inclination to knowledge and devotion."

It is certainly striking that we found the same transition from ritual to moral, and from polytheism to monotheism, in the writings of various Greek philosophers of the Axial Age. Moreover, God as Transcendence gives way to God as Immanence; that is, God is pantheistically demoted to an aspect of the cosmos, or even of the human Ego. That too is a form of secularization: God is reduced to some aspect of ourselves. This is basically the same as saying that Man is upgraded to the level of the gods (see again Gen. 3:5).

Compared with the optimistic joy of life of the earlier Aryans, the Upanishads exude a strikingly resigned atmosphere; the gloominess and transience of earthly existence are predominant. In the center is the question of what Man must do to find true happiness, to be freed from earthly suffering, and acquire spiritual freedom. In spite of all the differences, there are striking similarities here with the teachings of the early Greek philosophers. Both the Greeks and the anonymous writers of the Upanishads desired to understand the world, to understand its deeper unity and coherence in the midst of all diversity. In India, too, existential knowledge became more important than sacrifices and other rituals, that is, knowledge that leads to enlightenment, to a deeper understanding of the Self (cf. the Greek saying *Gnôthi seauton*, "Know yourself," inscribed in the temple at Delphi).

# THE AXIAL AGE

This too is secularization. True knowledge, true understanding, is not sought in the (transcendent) god or gods but within oneself. It is of secondary importance whether it is more reason that is emphasized (Greek), or feeling, intuition (Indian). Basically, God becomes nothing but "me." In the most famous conversation of the Upanishads, between Uddalaka Aruni and his son Shvetaketu, the conclusion is always the same: true, divine reality (Sat) is nothing but the Atman (that is, the impersonal, transcendent Ego), "that's you, Shvetaketu!" This is the deepest insight, which leads to self-redemption: the divine is you. Self-redemption through knowledge is the basic principle of all later religions of India, such as late Hinduism, Buddhism and Jainism (and, much later, also of the Gnostic mutations of Judaism and Christianity). Self-redemption in its deepest sense means that Man is henceforth going to take his destiny into his own hands. This is secularization; for God is no longer necessary to fulfill Man's deepest need, redemption. Man has to satisfy this need himself, and he is considered capable of doing this.

## Buddhism

Besides the Abrahamic religions, Buddhism is the most influential religion in the world. It originated in the Axial Age, and involved the most successful and consistent continuation of the spiritual course set out by the Upanishads. Whereas the Upanishads looked for the divine within Man himself, other thinkers began to deny the divine as such. Gautama Siddhartha, better known as the Buddha, (a title which means "awakened" or "enlightened") allegedly found the true knowledge that leads to self-redemption within himself, without any need of gods.

Gautama attained his enlightenment sitting under a tree, just like Mahavira ("great hero"; see before), that other Indian who founded a new religion at the same time, though it is not nearly as well known as Buddhism. This other religion was Jainism. Both Mahavira and the Buddha received a new, esoteric knowledge under a tree—so different from that other man sitting under a tree, Nathanael (whose name means "God gives"), a Jewish *tzaddiq* ("an Israelite indeed, in whom there is no deceit!"), who would "see heaven opened, and the angels of God ascending and descending on the Son of Man" (John 1:47-51). The first two believed they had found new *insight* within themselves, which would change the world; the third would receive ("God gives"!) a spectacular *sight* outside himself: the Son of Man in his glory. Greeks and Indians alike cried: Look within! Jesus cried: Look up!

In my Dutch book *De zesde kanteling*, I have argued that the Buddha attained his "awakening" between 589 and 586 BC, which is strikingly close to the withdrawal of the *Shekinah* in 587 or 586 BC. While the true light withdrew from Jerusalem, the "navel" of the earth, somewhere at the "end" of the world (cf. India in Esther 1:1!) a false light appeared which would mislead many millions of people, and does so to this very day. If the dates are correct, the synchronicity is too great to be coincidental, the more so if we realize that Buddhism—and not Islam—is the greatest religious rival of Judeo-Christian religion. Both religions are classless, both are international, both preach compassion, and both preach a strikingly similar moral. However, Judaism and Christianity aim to lead Man to God—even after the withdrawal of the *Shekinah*, which only returned to Jerusalem in the person of Jesus Christ, the Son of God (see below)—whereas Jainism and Buddhism are rooted in the very denial of God.

The purpose of the Abrahamic religions is to lead Man to God, whereas the purpose of the newer Indian religions is to lead Man to his own inner self. The former religions lead (or at least pretend to lead) to God, whereas the latter lead away from God. Of course, atheism does the same, but it does not pretend to offer any form of self-redemption; it does not use this kind of language, and is not even interested in it. On the meta-historical level, first, the newer Indian religions were invented to supply some form of light and warmth in a world that had been abandoned left by the glory of God. Second, after this glory had reappeared in the person of Jesus Christ, Islam was invented to offer an alternative to the God of Jesus by degrading Jesus to the status of a mere prophet and by substituting Muhammad for him. Third, atheism was invented to rob Man once again of his God but also of the surrogate light and warmth that the Eastern religions at least tried to offer.

In many respects, the Buddha agreed with the authors of the

Upanishads. In both forms of secular wisdom, ignorance was the source of all misery. Both emphasized the finiteness, transience, and relativity of earthly life. Both sought Truth beyond empirical reality, namely, in an esoteric world, the world of Self. However, the Buddha was much more practical than the Upanishads, and placed much more emphasis on human suffering, the intense compassion with those suffering, and a concrete way out, namely, the "de-identification" of one's own Ego. Buddhism was a typical product of the eclipse of God during the Axial Age in that it constituted a religion of self-redemption without the need of any God. Buddhism has been called the religion of compassion, but this is the compassion that the Buddhist (allegedly) has for others. In his thinking, there is no room for the idea that one could be redeemed by the compassion that God has for *us*.

## Emancipation

Both Jainism and Buddhism, as well as Greek thought, believed in a world order of both cosmological and ethical meaning. All three wished not only to understand the world, but to influence it, or at least to influence and change Man and his destiny. For this purpose, none of the three needed God any longer. God had withdrawn from Jerusalem, from the world, into heaven. Exactly at the same moment, the spiritual powers began offering to thinking Man in both Greece and India a way to make life tolerable without God or the gods. There may have been enormous differences between a Pythagorean, a Jain, or a Buddhist commune, but here is where we can find the similarity. During the Axial Age, Man took his life into his own hand. He was like a little child from whom a toy is taken away, and who cries: "I do not *need* (or *want*) that toy anymore." It reminds me of a parable of Jesus (although its original purpose is rather different): "A nobleman went into a far country to receive for himself a kingdom and then return... But his citizens hated him and sent a delegation after him, saying, 'We do not want this man to reign over us'" (Luke 19:12-14).

Secularization, both during the Axial Age and two thousand years later during the Scientific Revolution, is a powerful tool used to "emancipate" modern Man, that is, to make him "grown up," independent of God, like the prodigal son in the well-known parable of Jesus (Luke 15:11-13). Emancipation occurs when the heavenly Father sadly watches his sons and daughters depart, like the father in this parable. As the adolescent grows up, emancipation is a natural development. But this is not so in the relationship between the heavenly Father and his spiritual children. Here, emancipation means that Man wants to stand on his own feet, to control his own destiny, and therefore wants to get away from the Father. However, like the younger son in the parable, he is only capable of such a life—and seemingly so at that—only as long as his "substance" allows him such "riotous living" (Luke 15:13 KJV).

The question is how long this will last. After the Axial Age, it took almost six centuries until the coming of the Son of God. Since the beginning of the Modern Era, five centuries have gone by. The parable tells us that, at the moment of despair, the prodigal son discovered that not even pig feed was available to him. At that moment, he "began to be in need" (v. 14), and "came to himself" (v. 17). At the first coming of Christ, millions of people within the Roman Empire (including Greece, but also in India, and in so many other countries) began to see their need and "came to themselves"—a vital condition for coming back to God. I believe we are not far removed from the second coming of Christ. Will millions again discover their need, come to themselves, and then return to God?

Interestingly, the Dutch philosopher Cornelis A. van Peursen (1920-1996) spoke already in 1988 of the *Post-Secular Era*. Indeed, this may be the time that millions will learn to say: "I will arise and go to my father" (v. 18). Or should we say that this is a time during which there will be room again for the Deity in Western culture—not for the God of the Bible, but for many strange new gods? Remember what I have said about the *translatio imperii*, the "transference of the empire," namely, from the Middle East to Europe, from Europe to the America's, and now, from the America's to the Far East? The English commentator Hamish McRae (b. 1943) called the nineteenth century the Century of Europe, the twentieth century the Century of North America, and the twenty-first century the Century of Asia. It is expected that, within a few de-

# THE AXIAL AGE

cades (or even less), China will be more powerful than the United States, both in terms of its military and economical strength. But it is also expected that, by that time, there will be more committed Christians living in China than in the United States. Will the wise men come from the east again? We will have to wait and see what will be the consequences of these facts for our Western world.

## The *Shekinah* Again

There is one thread in this chapter that I would like to pick up again, and briefly complete. What happened to the *Shekinah* once it had withdrawn from the temple in Jerusalem into heaven? Many commentators, both Jewish and Christian, have noticed that, when a new temple was built and dedicated after the return from the Babylonian Exile, we never hear of fire coming down from heaven upon the altar, nor of a descent of the *Shekinah*, as had happened earlier at the dedication of the tabernacle (Exod. 40:34) and of the first temple (2 Chron. 7:1-2). The Second Temple was an empty shell, so to speak; because the Ark of the Covenant had never returned from Babylon (cf. 2 Chron. 36:18; Jer. 3:16), it was no longer there, nor was the *Shekinah*, nor the fire of God.

Because the *Shekinah* did not dwell in the Second Temple, it is better to translate Ezra 1:3c, not as "... the house of the LORD, the God of Israel—he is the God who is in Jerusalem" (ESV) but as "... the house of the LORD God of Israel, (He is God), which is in Jerusalem" (NKJV). If the Shekinah did not dwell in the Second Temple, strictly speaking it is doubtful if one could say that "God was in Jerusalem." He was still the "God of heaven" (v. 2; 5:12; 6:9-10; 7:12; 21, 23), but there was not the slightest sign of his returning. (Please note that God's omnipresence has nothing to do with this.)

The first time we find a clear reference to the *Shekinah* again is at the transfiguration on the Mount, where the "cloud" is mentioned (Matt. 17:5 and parallel passages). 2 Peter 1:17 identifies the cloud, from which God's voice was heard, as the Majestic Glory, that is, the *Shekinah*. Luke 9:34 says that the "cloud overshadowed" Jesus and his companions. "Overshadow" (Greek *episkiazô*) is the same word that we find at the dedication of the tabernacle, when

**PROBING THE PAST**

the cloud "overshadowed" it (Exod. 40:35 Septuagint). When Jesus was on earth, the *Shekinah* rested upon him, or, dwelt in him. Therefore, he could say of his own body: "Destroy this temple, and in three days I will raise it up" (John 2:19); the temple in which the *Shekinah* dwelt at that time was not the one built by Herod but Jesus' body. John tells us that Jesus "tabernacled" here on earth (*eskènôsen*, John 1:14; from *skènè*, "tent, tabernacle"), that is, his human flesh was a tabernacle in which the *Shekinah* dwelt, as it had dwelt before above the ark in the tabernacle and the temple (cf. Num. 7:89; Ps. 80:1).

When the Kingdom of the Messiah has been established in glory and majesty, after Jesus' second coming, we hear again of the descent of the *Shekinah* after the construction of the Third Temple. In the words of the prophet Ezekiel: "And behold, the glory of the God of Israel was coming from the east. And the sound of his coming was like the sound of many waters, and the earth shone with his glory... And I fell on my face. As the glory of the LORD entered the temple by the gate facing east, the Spirit lifted me up and brought me into the inner court; and behold, the glory of the LORD filled the temple... I heard one [i.e., God] speaking to me out of the temple, and he said to me, 'Son of man, this is the place of my throne and the place of the soles of my feet, where I will dwell in the midst of the people of Israel forever" (Ezek. 43:2-7).

This will be the grand finale of world history:

"It shall come to pass in the latter days
    that the mountain of the house of the LORD
shall be established as the highest of the mountains,
    and it shall be lifted up above the hills;
and peoples shall flow to it,
    and many nations shall come, and say:
'Come, let us go up to the mountain of the LORD,
    to the house of the God of Jacob,
that he may teach us his ways
    and that we may walk in his paths.'
For out of Zion shall go forth the law,
    and the word of the LORD from Jerusalem.
He shall judge between many peoples,

and shall decide for strong nations far away;
and they shall beat their swords into plowshares,
    and their spears into pruning hooks;
nation shall not lift up sword against nation,
    neither shall they learn war anymore;
but they shall sit every man under his vine and under his fig tree,
    and no one shall make them afraid,
    for the mouth of the Lord of hosts has spoken.
For all the peoples walk
    each in the name of its god,
but we will walk in the name of the LORD our God
    forever and ever."

(Micah 4:1-5)

www.ingramcontent.com/pod-product-compliance
Lightning Source LLC
Chambersburg PA
CBHW071907290426
44110CB00013B/1312